JOURNAL FOR THE STUDY OF THE NEW TESTAMENT
SUPPLEMENT SERIES
13

Executive Editor, Supplement Series
David Hill

Publishing Editor
David J.A. Clines

Department of Biblical Studies
The University of Sheffield
Sheffield S10 2TN
England

JESUS AND THE LAWS OF PURITY

Tradition History and Legal History
in Mark 7

Roger P. Booth

Journal for the Study of the New Testament
Supplement Series 13

To my wife Lisa, to my mother Alice
and to the memory of my father Noel

Published by
JSOT Press
Department of Biblical Studies
The University of Sheffield
Sheffield S10 2TN
England

Printed in Great Britain
by Redwood Burn Ltd.,
Trowbridge, Wiltshire.

British Library Cataloguing in Publication Data

Booth, Roger P.
    Jesus and the laws of purity : tradition
    history and legal history in Mark 7.—
    (Journal for the study of the New Testament
    supplement series, ISSN 0143-5108; 13)
    1. Bible. N.T. Mark VII—Commentaries
    I. Title   II. Series
    226'.306   BS2545

    ISBN 1-85075-023-8
    ISBN 1-85075-022-X Pbk

CONTENTS

PART I
Traditio-historical Criticism

PART II
Historico-legal Criticism

PREFACE

In this book we aim to discover what evidence the passage Mark 7.1-23 furnishes regarding the attitudes of Jesus and of the early Christians towards the law of Israel.

In Part I we use the tools of traditio-historical criticism in seeking to isolate the constituent pericopae and trace their history. We thus attempt to discover whether the various pericopae were created by the early church, or actually originated with Jesus and the Pharisees.

In Part II we attempt to check the results obtained in Part I, by applying to them the yardstick of historico-legal criticism. Before doing so, we study the difficulties involved in dating the Rabbinic material, and adopt a method of treating that evidence.

Our main conclusions are that (1) the evidence in the passage indicates that Jesus did not deny the concept of cultic purity absolutely, but only relatively in comparison with ethical purity, and (2) historico-legal criticism, while not free from difficulty, has a supportive rôle to the conventional disciplines of New Testament criticism, and may usefully be applied to other Gospel passages with a legal content.

The book is a revised version of a doctoral thesis accepted by London University in 1983, and my heartfelt thanks are due to my Supervisor, Professor Graham N. Stanton, for the encouragement and advice unstintingly given to me; to Hyam Maccoby of Leo Baeck College, London, who, through his expertise in Pharisaic law and Christian origins, was able to give me invaluable advice regarding Part II of the thesis, and who read the final draft of that Part; to Bernard Berkovits of the then University College at Buckingham who guided my early steps towards an understanding of Jewish purity law; and, not least, to my wife, Lisa, for her tolerant acceptance of a husband who has spent much spare time immersed in 'Biblical things'.

PREFATORY NOTES

1. *Texts and Translations*

The text of the New Testament which is adopted, except where a variant reading is expressly preferred, is that published in Nestle–Aland, *Novum Testamentum Graece*, Deutsche Bibelstiftung Stuttgart, 1979. The text used of the Hebrew Bible is that of *Biblia Hebraica Stuttgartensia*, and that of the Septuagint is the edition by A. Rahlfs, Stuttgart, 1935. The translation used of the Old and New Testaments is the Revised Standard Version.

The Hebrew text of the Mishnah used is that published by Philip Blackman in *Mishnayoth*, Second Edition, Gateshead, 1977, and the English translation used is that by Herbert Danby in *The Mishnah*, Oxford, 1933. The English translation of the *Babylonian Talmud* used is that edited by I. Epstein, The Soncino Press, London, 1938. The English translation of the Tosephta used is that by Jacob Neusner found passim in his works mentioned below. The English translation of the Dead Sea Scrolls used generally is that by Geza Vermes in *The Dead Sea Scrolls in English*, London, 1962.

2. *References*

Literary works mentioned in the text are briefly described in the notes at the end of the Chapters, and page numbers are given there. The works are fully described in the Bibliography. The following works are not described in the notes, but the author's name in the text is followed by the relevant page number in his work:

K. Berger, *Die Gesetzesauslegung Jesu. Ihr historischer Hintergrund im Judentum und im Alten Testament. Teil I: Markus und Parallelen* (Hamburg, 1972).

H. Hübner, *Das Gesetz in der synoptischen Tradition* (Witten, 1973).

J. Lambrecht, 'Jesus and the Law. An Investigation of Mk 7.1-23', *Ephemerides Theologicae Lovanienses* 53 (1977), pp. 24-79.

W. Paschen, *Rein und Unrein* (Munich, 1970).

E.J. Pryke, *Redactional Style in the Markan Gospel* (Cambridge, 1978).

V. Taylor, *The Gospel according to St. Mark* (London, 1952).

The following works by J. Neusner are also not described in the notes, but his name in the text is followed by Traditions or Purities respectively and the volume number and the page:

The Rabbinic Traditions about the Pharisees before 70, 3 vols. (Leiden, 1971).

A History of the Mishnaic Law of Purities, 22 vols. (Leiden, 1974-77).

3. *Abbreviations*

The following abbreviations are used:

Aland	Nestle–Aland *Novum Testamentum Graece* (as above)
Ant.	*Jewish Antiquities* (*Antiquitates*) by Josephus, with ET by R. Marcus (Loeb edition, 1943)
ARN	*The Fathers according to Rabbi Nathan*, ET by J. Goldin (Yale, 1955)
Bauer	*A Greek-English Lexicon of the NT and Other Early Christian Literature*, ET and edited by W.F. Arndt and F.W. Gingrich (Chicago, 1957)
B-D	*A Greek Grammar of the NT and Other Early Christian Literature* by F. Blass and A. Debrunner, 9th-10th edition, ET by R.W. Funk (Chicago, 1961)
BDB	*A Hebrew and English Lexicon of the Old Testament*, edited by F. Brown, S.R. Driver and C.A. Briggs (Oxford, 1966)
BT	Babylonian Talmud
Danby	*The Mishnah* (Oxford, 1933)
Danby's Appendix	Appendix (III) of Rabbinical Teachers in the Mishnah, to Danby's above translation
ET	English translation
ExpT	*Expository Times*
GK	*Gesenius' Hebrew Grammar*, as edited and enlarged by E. Kautzsch (Oxford, 1910)
JBL	*Journal of Biblical Literature*
JJS	*Journal of Jewish Studies*
JSJ	*Journal for the Study of Judaism*
JSNT	*Journal for the Study of the New Testament*
LXX	The Septuagint
MT	Masoretic text of the Hebrew Bible
NTS	*New Testament Studies*
PT	Palestinian Talmud
RSV	The Revised Standard Version
Soncino Rabbinical Index	The Index of Rabbis mentioned in the Babylonian Talmud, which is contained in the Index volume of the English translation mentioned above
TDNT	*Theological Dictionary of the New Testament* (Grand Rapids, 1964-76)

INTRODUCTION

A. *General*

The object of the present study is to discover what evidence the passage Mark 7.1-23 furnishes towards an assessment of the attitudes of Jesus of Nazareth and of early Christian communities towards the written and traditional law[1] of Israel.

We choose to treat this particular passage since it is generally considered to be an essential one for the interpretation of those attitudes. Certainly, at first sight, the logion of Jesus at v. 15 shows him as denying the possibility of defilement by external sources, and as thereby abrogating the whole dietary and cultic Torah. The passage thus possesses interest for anthropology, which has for long examined the nature of the connection between religion and material uncleanness;[2] the passage also expresses some contrasting views of the first century AD on the meaning of 'defile' in a religious context, and on the true cause of defilement.

We will seek to obtain evidence of the attitudes evinced in our passage towards the Jewish law by applying in the first place the tools of traditio-historical criticism. We will accept the predominant view of source critics that Mark is the earliest Gospel record of the episode, and we will seek, by redaction criticism, to remove editorial additions or amendments; by use of form criticism, we then hope to isolate the constituent pericopae and trace their history. In tracing their history, and by the use of authenticating criteria, we hope to discover whether the various pericopae in the passage were created by the early church[3] or actually originated with Jesus and the Pharisees.

These disciplines have already been effectively applied to our passage with varying conclusions. That conclusions differ is not surprising, since in the use of these critical tools the workman is exercising his subjective judgment. What is needed is a plumb-line or

yardstick by which the individual judgment on tradition history may
be tested. We intend to supply this standard by subjecting the results
reached by the use of critical tools to the test of legal compatibility.
For example, having determined by the application of traditio-
historical tools that a pericope originated with Jesus and the Pharisees,
we will then ask whether the Jewish law expressed or implied in the
pericope accords with the state of Jewish law in the time of Jesus. If
the words of Jesus do not accord with Jewish law, the discrepancy
may deny their claim to authenticity—but not necessarily so: it may
only indicate, depending on the context, that Jesus believed the true
law of God to differ from current Jewish law,[4] or simply that Jesus
was mistaken.[5] Conversely, if the legal content of a saying of Jesus
does conform with Jewish law of the day (which means, for our
purpose, Pharisaic),[6] that does not conclusively prove the saying to
be Jesus-material, although it is evidence in favour of authenticity.
The position is more straightforward in the case of a saying of the
Pharisees, for if that does not accord with their law, then either the
saying is inauthentic, or we are mistaken in our assessment of their
law. Since the Pharisees were intensely interested in the law, it is
likely that their statements about it, if correctly reported, would
either be correct, or if concerning a doubtful or disputed point, have
some support in the law. If a Pharisaic act or word does accord with
what we otherwise know of the relevant Jewish law, then an
authenticity claimed on traditio-historical grounds is supported.
Caution is required in this area for the argument could become
circular: Margoliouth[7] has pointed out that the Gospels themselves
are equally good evidence as the Talmud for the customs prevailing
in the first seventy years of the first century.

Where those critical tools assign a pericope to the early church
then the testing of its legal content will support that assignment if the
law express or implicit in it is shown to belong to an early post-Jesus
era, but will cast doubt upon the assignment if its legal content
prevailed only at an earlier or later stage of legal history. Such legal
incompatibility will not, however, disprove creation by the early
church, for the inaccuracy may be due merely to the church's
mistaken view of the law.

Let us admit immediately that the test of legal compatibility is
difficult to apply because our knowledge of the state of Jewish law in
the time of Jesus is limited. We know the state of the law in the fifth
century BC when the Priestly Code was written, and we have a fair

knowledge of its state at c. 200 AD when the Mishnah reached final form, but between these two poles we have to plot an uncertain course of development. Jacob Neusner has pioneered the method of charting this development, and while we shall have cause to disagree with him, we are indebted to his pointing of the way. He has, indeed, applied the critical tools of NT scholars to the extraction of the history of Jewish law from the Talmudic[8] text which speaks in the language of a timeless present. However, although he probes successfully behind the Talmudic text, he treats Synoptic Gospel passages at their face value in just the same way as NT scholars until recently treated the Talmud.[9] There remains, therefore, a need for the simultaneous application of the disciplines of both traditio-historical and historico-legal criticism to the legal pericopae in the NT. We think that the present book is the first essay towards the satisfaction of that need. Our passage seems a fit object for such bifurcated analysis since it raises an acute conflict of evidence between the NT and the Talmud on at least one point of Jewish legal history. For it is stated in v. 3 of our passage that all the Jews wash their hands before they eat. The Talmudic evidence as interpreted by Büchler[10] indicates that only priests had cause so to wash, and only before eating holy food. Is, then, the statement in Mark inauthentic or inaccurate, or is the conclusion of Büchler, founded on Talmudic research, defective?

Because of the difficulty of asserting confidently the state of Jewish law in the time of Jesus or Mark, we doubt whether the application of the plumb-line of legal history to the conclusions suggested by traditio-historical tools will lead to assured results: but we are sure that the imposition of a second test, from an independent discipline, will help to correct imbalances produced by the application of the first, and usually the only, test.[11]

Lastly, we must consider how much weight as evidence we are prepared to allow to Mark's statements in his Gospel. Writers of earlier times approached the Gospels with a prima facie assumption that they were historically reliable, and only needed correct harmonization. This presumption of accuracy could only be displaced by inexplicable internal conflict. But today, with the advent of traditio-historical criticism, as Käsemann avers, ' . . . our questioning has sharpened and widened until the obligation now laid upon us is to investigate and make credible not the possible unauthenticity of the individual unit of material but, on the contrary, its genuineness'.[12] It is submitted that such a presumption of inauthenticity is too sceptical, and that an approach to the Gospels which is analogous to the forensic treatment of evidence would be more appropriate.[13] The Gospel text, no matter who wrote or amended it, represents assertions by some one or more persons that Jesus or the Pharisees or others, said or did various things. Those assertions constitute evidence that those things were said and done. They may not be strong evidence, owing to their ancient nature and possible distortion in transmission or translation, but they are evidence, and those who deny its accuracy must bring stronger evidence to that effect. Critics have alleged the creativity of the early Christians, but they have not excluded the possibility that original sayings of Jesus were only adapted to the polemical and other needs of the early church. Thus, although the refuter's burden of proof is more easily discharged now, through the demonstrated activity of the church, it still has to be discharged.

Nevertheless, McArthur[14] states that there is sufficient dubious material in the Gospels to justify the conviction that the burden of proof rests with those who allege the authenticity of specific events or motifs. As illustrations, he cites the statements that Pilate publicly declared his belief in Jesus' complete innocence, and that, as a result of an earthquake during the crucifixion, the dead came back to life. In considering whether examples, like these, of 'dubious material' justify a prima facie presumption of inauthenticity in the case of *all* Gospel material, we must take into account that (a) there is much more Gospel material which is internally consistent, and which is intrinsically probable, than the contrary, and (b) it is very rare, judging by our experience of ordinary life, that a person so persistently tells untruths that we presume *all* his statements prima facie to be untrue.[15]

As suggested above, it appears to us more reasonable to view the Gospel evidence in a manner analogous to the position under English law. In that system, any statement of any person if given to a Court in proper form (under oath in Court, if oral, or by affidavit, if written) constitutes evidence of the truth of the content of the statement. That evidence, if unopposed by contrary evidence, will normally be accepted in a civil case as proof of its content. The weight to be given to that evidence, however, if it is opposed by other evidence, will depend on the inherent probability of the facts alleged in it, and the demeanour (if oral evidence) and character of the witness. The burden of proof will normally lie on the party alleging a fact, but in a civil case he will normally discharge that burden by his own uncorroborated evidence if it is not intrinsically improbable and there is no opposing evidence; if there is opposing evidence, he will discharge the burden of proof if his evidence is more likely to be true on a balance of probabilities, and therefore the nature and amount of the opposing evidence are very relevant.

We think that this English forensic approach, by analogy and mutatis mutandis,[16] may be fruitful for NT methodology. Thus, the burden of proof of the authenticity of the statements in the Gospels should lie on the maker of the statements, the Evangelist. But, if a Gospel statement is unopposed by other evidence, then the evidence constituted by that statement discharges the burden, and should be accepted unless its content is intrinsically improbable. In the case of Jesus-material in the Gospels, we should count as opposing evidence any factor which indicates unlikelihood that Jesus spoke the words or did the thing alleged by the Evangelist. Such factors would include (a) a directly conflicting Gospel statement,[17] (b) an established trend of the thought or behaviour of Jesus which is inconsistent with the Gospel statement, (c) a physical phenomenon alleged in the Gospel statement which is contrary to the natural laws, (d) a likelihood that the early church has written back into the life of Jesus later polemic, knowledge or experience, as in the case of Mark 8.34,[18] and (e) acknowledged editorial practices of the Evangelist, such as Mark's summarizing sentences.[19] However, we do not generally treat acknowledged vocabulary of the Evangelist as weighty opposing evidence, since he may merely be re-phrasing traditional material in his own words.

If a Gospel statement is opposed by other evidence admissible as above (or on similar principles in the case of material affecting persons other than Jesus), then the acceptability of that statement will depend upon a balance of probabilities, as in the civil forensic model. By admitting those factors as opposing evidence, we reluctantly introduce subjective elements. For example, scholars will naturally differ over whether a repeated feature of the speech or behaviour of Jesus is sufficiently prominent to constitute a trend, and over whether that trend conflicts with the Gospel statment. As the subjective element is a gateway to error in Gospel criticism, we would reduce its operation as far as possible. Thus, our subjective view that Pilate would not declare his belief in Jesus' innocence, we would not admit as opposing evidence, but the objective natural law that the dead do not come back to life we would admit.

In short, we do not presume authenticity of Gospel statements, but consider them as evidence to be weighed with other supporting and opposing evidence before judgment on historicity is reached.

The contrary presumption of the inauthenticity of the text is closely connected with Bultmann's[20] claim that a piece of tradition is a primary source for the historical situation out of which it arose, but only a secondary source for the historical assertions which it makes. We agree that in considering the original form of a saying of Jesus (and Bultmann's claim related to the logia) we may have to adjust the Gospel form by allowing for elaboration in the course of transmission and, in some cases, for the polemical or other use to which the church or Evangelist has put a saying. But Bultmann's expression of this 'principle which must govern research' assumes that the early church *always* altered the saying. It raises the question of what *would* constitute primary evidence of the spoken words of a person who died before the invention of electrical recording. Even the eye-witness or auditor is liable to error in recounting what he has seen or heard, but is he not a primary source?

Bultmann[21] cites Wellhausen's declaration that the spirit of Jesus breathes in the utterances of the community, but that we do not derive an historical picture of Jesus himself from them. It is surely just because the Christian community is, ipso facto, influenced by Jesus, and therefore models its behaviour on him, that we can expect to receive from the community a reasonably historical picture of its exemplar.[22] Bultmann appears to allow the dog to wag the tail: the adjustments which we must admittedly make to reach the purer form of a saying of Jesus are being allowed to impugn the substantial historicity of the saying itself.

B. *The Programme*

In attempting to discover what light our passage sheds on the attitude of Jesus and of the early Christians towards the Jewish law, we intend to pursue the following programme:

Part I—Traditio-historical Criticism. We will, first, isolate the traditional material in the Marcan version of the passage. At this stage, by redactional critical methods, we aim to remove from that version the links and additions made by the Evangelist or earlier compilers.

The next step will be to identify the separate units of tradition which compose that traditional material. This will be a form-critical and historical enquiry attempting to show the origin of each unit in the life of Jesus or the life of the church. Alleged words of Jesus and the Pharisees which on other traditio-historical grounds appear to originate in the life of Jesus will then be subjected to the authenticating criteria for genuine words of Jesus. However, we aspire to recover only the substantial meaning of the speech of Jesus for, even allowing for Jewish mnemonics, it seems most unlikely that his exact words have been remembered, or if they were, that their particular nuances have been passed from mouth to mouth, and translated from Aramaic into Greek, without any distortion. The variation of meaning which can result from translation has been illustrated by Jeremias[23] in respect of the translation of the parables from Aramaic into Greek, and regarding Paschen's attempt (pp. 162-63) to recover the Aramaic of Mark's purity logion (7.15), Lambrecht comments, 'Both the reconstruction of the Greek "Urfassung" . . . and its re-translation into Aramaic are so uncertain that it seems better not to try to define the original wording and form of the saying in detail' (p. 59).[24]

Part II—Historico-legal Criticism. We will here apply the test of legal history to the units which our examination in Part I indicates to be authentic speech of Jesus and the Pharisees. We will study whether the legal lemmas expressed or implied in those units prevailed in the time of Jesus, either as law applying to all Jews, or as law applying to a sect or group of Jews. Having by this second test either confirmed or modified the attribution of units in Part I to the life of Jesus or the early churches, we finally consider what the evidence thus gleaned shows of the attitudes towards the law possessed by Jesus, the churches and the Evangelists.

PART I

Traditio-Historical Criticism

Chapter 1

THE PRE-MARCAN TRADITION

In Mark 7.1-23 the subjects of Jewish washings, the tradition of the elders, Pharisaic hypocrisy, the release of vows depriving parents, and the source of impurity are treated. The same subjects are treated in Matthew 15.1-20, although in a different order and with an additional element about the blindness of the Pharisaic leaders who will be rooted out (vv. 12-14). The content of the two passages is thus so similar, and, moreover, the wording is so alike, that we must review their literary connection in order to confirm which of the two versions was written first. If there were no variation of meaning or difference of emphasis in the handling of the same topics, then it would not matter which of the two versions we were to take as our starting-point for the discovery of the traditional material. But as there are different nuances and emphases in the two versions, then one version may be closer to the original tradition than the other. To consider whether one version is prior to the other is our initial task.

We must consider first, however, a Lucan parallel. At Luke 11.38 a Pharisee is surprised that Jesus has not immersed himself before dining with him. Both v. 38 itself and the words of Jesus at vv. 39-41 which are framed as replies indicate that the Pharisee uttered his surprise, and thus provoked the replies of Jesus on purity, in the same way as the Pharisaic question at our v. 5. Moreover, lustration before eating is the subject of both the Pharisaic surprise in the Lucan pericope and of the Pharisaic question in the pericopae in Mark and Matthew. But there is an important difference in the purificatory remedy expected by the Pharisees. In Mark, κοιναῖς having been defined in v. 2 as ἀνίπτοις, the Pharisees ask why the disciples eat κοιναῖς χερσίν, while in Matthew the complaint is that they do not νίπτονται τὰς χεῖρας when they eat. In each case, conflict with the tradition through eating without washing *the hands* is in issue. But in Luke, the Pharisee is surprised that before the meal Jesus οὐ πρῶτον ἐβαπτίσθη. The aorist passive ἐβαπτίσθη literally means 'was dipped (or immersed)', which implies *the whole body*.

We think Luke means immersion of the whole body since he uses the verb βαπτίζω in describing John's baptizing in his ch. 3, and John had adapted the Jewish ritual *tebilah* in which the body was immersed.[1] This verb is an intensive or iterative form of the verb βάπτω both of which mean to dip or immerse (Bauer, *s.v.*). Thus at 2 Kings 5.14 (LXX) Naaman ἐβαπτίσατο ἐν τῷ Ἰορδάνῃ. At Luke 11.38 the verb implies the body and not the hands, since in the NT the verb νίπτω is used for the washing of the hands (e.g. Mark 7.3; Mt. 15.2) and the face (Mt. 6.17), but not the body. The evidence at Chapter 4.d. indicates that both before and after Jesus' time the hands were not dipped, but rinsed, for ritual purposes. Mark contrasts the two actions at 7.3-4 where he explains that while the Jews wash their hands before eating, they immerse (βαπτίσωνται) before eating on return from market. As the verb has thus rather a precise meaning, we doubt that Luke would have used it in a more general sense of 'wash himself'. It is, of course, possible that Luke's tradition was simply erroneous in recording that the Pharisee's surprise related to Jesus' failure to *immerse*. We consider the accuracy of this verb according to legal history at Chapter 5.e. As the practice in the *miqveh* was to immerse oneself rather than be dipped by another, the reading in p[45] and miniscule 700 of the middle voice ἐβαπτίσατο is probably correct, with the normal reflexive sense.[2] Other differences are that in the Lucan pericope the invitation to dine and the reclining of Jesus (v. 37) indicate a formal meal, whereas it is not clear in Mark and Matthew whether a meal indoors or in the open air is witnessed; also, the replies of Jesus are formally different in Luke. The reply at v. 39 contrasting the outside and inside of the cup is 'Q' material (par. Mt. 23.25), while the reply at vv. 40-41 concerning the same creator of inside and outside, and the cleansing sufficiency of alms, is from Luke's special source.[3]

These differences in content and source persuade us that the Lucan pericope at least contains tradition nurtured in a different community from those which preserved the traditions in the Marcan and Matthean passages, and may relate a separate incident. The similarities, however, between our passage and the Lucan pericope are striking. In each, (a) there is Pharisaic complaint at the neglect to wash before eating, (b) Jesus defends the neglect on the ground that internal purity is more important than external, and (c) reference is made to the cleansing of cups. Consequently, although we will concentrate our attention on the material in Mark and Matthew, we will have cause to refer to the Lucan pericope in various contexts.[4]

The fact that both the Marcan and Matthean versions of our passage largely deal with the same topics does not show a literary reliance one on the other: each Evangelist could be expressing in his own words the same oral tradition, or expressing in his own words or the words of the traditions, oral traditions formulated in different communities. But the incidents and debate recounted are so similar that it is unlikely that the two versions are records of separate incidents. What persuades us that literary reliance exists, is that, although there are differences of order in the two versions, and an additional pericope in Matthew (vv. 12-14), the scenic structure, the syntax and the vocabulary in the two versions have close similarities.

Accepting, therefore, a literary connection between Mark and Matthew, we need to establish which version of our passage is dependent on the other, for this will demonstrate which version contains the earlier form of the tradition. However, this priority of version is part of the larger question concerning which of the two Gospels was written first. On this issue we are persuaded by the Two Document Hypothesis that where Mark and Matthew have parallel passages, Matthew has copied from Mark and we will accordingly treat Mark 7.1-23 as containing the earlier form of the tradition in our passage.

We will try to identify the amendments and additions made by Mark and earlier (even, perhaps, later) editors to the tradition in the oral or written form in which they received it. The discovery of redaction in Mark is much more difficult than in Matthew and Luke, since in those Gospels we can detect with reasonable confidence where they have departed from their Marcan source and, with rather less confidence, where they have departed from their 'Q' source.

a. *Methodology*

But, first, a problem of method has to be resolved. Should the tool of redaction criticism be applied to our passage before that of form criticism, or vice versa? Should we strip away first the editorial alterations and additions, or identify first the pericopae or units of tradition which originally travelled separately, and were later joined together by Mark? Both tools are being employed to the same end— to isolate the pre-Marcan units: redaction criticism removes what Mark has added, and leaves behind the tradition,[5] while form criticism, by revealing the tradition, places in relief the editorial additions. Thus, if we find that Mark has added something, then it cannot be part of the tradition, but conversely, if we find that something is part of the tradition, then Mark cannot have added it. So, are we to separate the oranges in the basket from the apples there by removing the apples, or the oranges?

This question is much debated. Conzelmann,[6] followed by several other modern scholars, has argued that form-critical investigation must come first, while Farrer[7] and Johnson[8] agree with Johannes Weiss[9] in averring the contrary, and Marxsen[10] claims that the two tools must be applied simultaneously. Stein thinks that these scholars ignore the overlap of the two disciplines. He points out that the first step of each is the same, 'Both must first isolate the redaction of the evangelists. After this is done each discipline concentrates upon its own interests. Form criticism "sets aside" the redaction and concentrates its attention upon the tradition, whereas Redaktionsgeschichte "sets aside" the tradition and concentrates its investigation upon the redaction'.[11] We acknowledge that the two disciplines have a 'common path' until this point, in that they both seek to isolate the two elements of the material, but this statement of Stein ignores the problem of method, namely, with which tool do we cut the two apart? While searching for what Mark has added, the scholar will inevitably find himself pondering whether an apparently Marcan comment or slant in his text could not have been produced or developed in the community, and vice versa, but as a matter of method it is surely necessary consciously to be wielding one tool rather than juggling with two. Marxsen's simultaneous approach hardly constitutes a practical working method.[12]

We think that the discipline to be employed first must depend upon the nature and content of the passage, and particularly upon whether, at first sight, the Evangelist's revision appears to be intertwined closely with the tradition, or to slide away easily. In the case of our passage, portions of it, to our ears, so loudly declare themselves to be editorial that we think recognition of the traditional units will be much assisted by a prior excision of Mark's work. We acknowledge, however, that, as Schmidt[13] first showed, much editorial work is perceived in the 'joins' between the units of tradition, so that if we do not first identify the units, we must endure an increased difficulty in seeing the 'joins'!

b. *Mark as Theologian*

In the nineteenth century, very little room was allowed for theological motivation on the part of Mark: he was merely a collector and editor of traditions, a scissors and paste man. At the beginning of this century, the dominating work was that of C.H. Weisse[14] as built on by Holtzmann.[15] They established the Marcan Hypothesis, namely that Mark's Gospel was, as opposed to Matthew's and Luke's, the Gospel which contained unembroidered historical fact concerning the life of Jesus. This attribution of historicity precluded influence by Mark upon his material except for placing the units of tradition in the correct order, and verbally joining them.[16] Burkitt wrote, 'The other Gospels, even the Gospels according to Matthew and Luke, give us an interpretation of Jesus Christ's life . . . The thing that actually occurred was the life which Jesus Christ lived, and the chief authority for the facts of that life is the Gospel according to Mark.'[17]

But later, Mark's own creativity and theological motivation came to be recognized. Wrede[18] sought to show that Mark's Gospel also was an interpretation of the life of Jesus, and he used for this purpose Mark's insistence on the Messianic secret. He listed several occasions when Jesus enjoined silence about what he had done, or who he was. But, said Wrede, Jesus commanded silence when there was no prospect of silence, for example, at a synagogue meeting (1.25), and in the press of a crowd (3.12). Wrede argued that the injunctions to silence were a device used by Mark to excuse the fact that faith in Jesus as Messiah only arose after the resurrection, and did not exist during his lifetime.

Thus, while it had always been realized that, in putting together the units of tradition, Mark had created the connecting links, it came to be appreciated also that, in arranging the order of the units, Mark was not following an historical sequence or an itinerary, but was making theological statements. Albert Schweitzer pointed out that in order to extract from Mark a coherent life of Jesus, historians had to 'read between the lines' all signs of progressive development. 'Modern theology', he wrote, 'is determined to find evidence in Mark of a development of Jesus, a development of the disciples, and a development of the outer circumstances; and professes in so doing to be only reproducing the views and indications of the Evangelist ... '[19] Modern scholars have stressed that Mark was not interested from the viewpoint of a biographer in the temporal order in which Jesus did things or the geographical locations in which he acted. Lohmeyer wrote, 'the second Gospel scarcely notes one biographical detail which does not have theological significance'.[20] And Marxsen[21] argues convincingly that the geographical data of the tradition are of no interest to Mark: where he finds them, he includes them, but he does not add any. Apart, that is, from Galilee, with which Mark's concern, according to Marxsen, is not 'historical-geographical' but 'eschatological-geographical'. Marxsen believes that the placing of the passion and resurrection prophecy at 9.34 in Galilee, and the placing of the parousia there at 14.27 and 16.7, were the work of Mark. To Mark, Galilee is the Jesus-place where he was nurtured, and was successful, and to which he will return at the Parousia. In contrast to Galilee stands Jerusalem, the place of crucifixion, the site of Satan.

c. *Marcan Schemes involving 7.1-23*

Redaction critics have perceived other Marcan motifs of a comprehensive nature. On a smaller canvas, Quesnell[22] sees an overarching theological purpose on the part of Mark in the section stretching from 6.34 to 7.30. The incidents in this section are grouped together by Mark, as they constitute his answer to the difficulties in the early Christian communities over Jews and Gentiles taking community meals together and, in particular, sharing the eucharistic meal. Under this arch, Quesnell sees the difficult plural τοὺς ἄρτους at 7.2 as referring to the Feeding story of 6.34f., and he detects another subject-link in the section at 7.27 where Jesus' concern that the children first be fed (χορτασθῆναι) relates back to the feeding of them at 6.42 (ἐχορτάσθησαν). Two theological motifs of Mark, according to Quesnell, co-exist in the same material: in our passage and the story of the Phoenician woman (7.1-30), the teaching, like that in Acts 10, is that Jews should eat with Christians, and not treat man or food as unclean, while in the whole section, the offer of the bread of salvation to the Jews at the Feeding at 6.34-44 precedes the abolition of divisive Jewish law in our passage, which is followed by the offer of salvation to the Gentiles in the blessing of the Phoenician at 7.24-30.

Our first reaction is to doubt this analysis on the grounds that (1) even the discerning reader may fail to recognize such interwoven themes, so Mark would not attempt so 'tight' a literary plan, and (2) the realism of the over-arching form is broken by the apparently disconnected walking-on-the-water story and healing report at 6.45-56. On reflection, however, our doubt largely resolves itself because (1) of the interwoven themes, one is a corollary of the other, for if salvation is offered to all, Jewish dietary and other exclusivity must drop away, and (2) Mark is shown to be conscious of the need to maintain the 'bread of salvation' theme by his comment at 6.51-52 that the disciples were astounded at the walking of the water and the ceasing of the wind because 'they did not understand about the loaves, but their hearts were hardened'.[23]

Paschen (pp. 151f.), too, sees Mark's editorial planning as operating over large tracts of his Gospel, and as not confined to the organization of individual pericopae within a passage. He notes that in two cases, 7.14 and 8.34, where Jesus addresses his summons to the people, each summons follows, after intervening pericopae, a feeding narrative at the end of which the people are dismissed. Paschen suggests that by the uses of this dismissal-and-summons device Mark wishes to construct an over-arching narrative stretching from the first feeding story (6.34f.) to the series of logia at 8.34f. which follows the first pronouncement of the passion. Perhaps, however, the ingenuity of the critic here is greater than that of the author. A literary arch must have main pillars at each end, and the first summons and final dismissal are not readily apparent. When Jesus landed at 6.34, the crowd was already there, and remained until late (6.35). Admittedly, in response to the disciples' request that he send the people away, Jesus replies, 'Give them something to eat', which could be interpreted as a constructive summons, being a refusal of a dismissal; but surely an editor intending to arrange his material according to a particular pattern does not risk the reader noticing the design only by implication, but expressly marks it! And at the far end of the arch there is no pillar at all, not even an implicit dismissal, for at 9.2 there is a lapse of six days before Jesus departs. Paschen cites the summons to the crowd at 7.14a as a pillar in the editorial arch, but the corresponding pillar of dismissal is not apparent, or, at most, is again implicit, for at 7.17 Jesus simply leaves the crowd. At 6.45 there is an express dismissal of the crowd, but at 6.54 the people arrive without summons, as they also do at 8.1.

Paschen's perception of a literary arch thus appears defective, for the arch is not continuous, being broken at several points. He does not state explicitly the theological message of this structural motif. It could be the predestinatory nature of entry into the kingdom of God in the sense of 'many are called but few are chosen', but the crowd's permanency as an undivided whole, and the breaks in the continuity, make that message sound forced.

To summarize, we believe that caution must be exercised in the perception of editorial welding together of passages into large sections for either structural or theological reasons. While Mark did, of course, undertake 'macro-redaction' in that he put into consecutive order the many passages of the Gospel, we think he made his theological impact on it by his ordering of the units of tradition within a small passage, and by his revision of those units. Mark certainly possessed theological motivation, and may personally have been both subtle and ingenious, but the first concern of the writer of Good News would be that the News should be understood. We have no reason to think that Mark's readership was intellectually superior to those Corinthians of whom Paul wrote (1 Cor. 1.26) that not many were wise according to worldly standards.[24] Consequently, any sustained theme or over-arching structure would, to be discernible, need to be plain and explicit, not tortuous or allusive. The more would this be necessary in order to over-ride the deep theological impact of the individual pericopae: for example, the long, integrated section identified by Paschen, we may well wonder whether the non-scholarly reader would discern the structure of summons and dismissal, while simultaneously digesting the miracles of the Feedings (with their broad theological implications) and the walking on the water, the teaching on the tradition and purity, the meaning of leaven, and the passion pronouncement, to mention only some of the phenomena in the section.[25] The scholar quietly meditating in his study may disinter vestigial thematic links which Mark never intended, and which his readers were insufficiently sophisticated to apprehend.

Straightforward redactional reasons for the location of our passage in the Gospel are more likely to be correct. Thus Grundmann,[26] like Schmidt,[27] notes that its position in the Gospel produces a climax in the arguments with the opponents of Jesus, and prepares for his immediate crossing into heathen territory. Having studied Mark's editorial activity on the large scale, we now look at his influence on the material immediately preceding our passage.

Schmidt considers that the dispute about handwashing did not follow chronologically after the healings in Gennesaret, as Jesus would naturally have continued from there the interrupted journey to Bethsaida mentioned at 6.45.[28] He believes our passage to be an historical record of a dispute, however, for he writes, 'Precisely such disputes between Jesus and his opponents which were obviously very alive in the first Christian community, receive their form after some loss of time and place',[29] and he compares in this connection 2.18-22, 2.23-28 and 3.1-6. It is surely a mistake, though, to weigh Mark's chronology or geography for historicity, since, as Marxsen has pointed out, Mark was not interested in these things.

We are convinced that Mark's placement of our passage is motivated by theological reasons. Its position before Jesus' departure to the Gentiles has just been mentioned, and we accept Quesnell's reasons for the propinquity of the first feeding story and the story of the Pheoenician woman.

Immediately before our passage, at 6.54-56, a general notice of healing activity is inserted. These verses describe with rising intensity Jesus' famed healing ability, and reach a climax in the healing even by the touch of the κράσπεδον. This is probably the tassel[30] (ציצת) with a cord of blue which, at Numbers 15.38, Yahweh commanded the Israelites to wear on the corners of their garments, for ציצת is translated κράσπεδα in the LXX of this text. The juxtaposition of this pericope to our passage may be intended to show that, notwithstanding the radicality of the purity logion and the railing at the scribes in our passage, Jesus did observe the written law; the healing of the sick by the touch of the tassel may be intended to cast a holy and purifying aura over the Pentateuchal commands. Certainly, the written law is honoured in the Korban incident (τὸν λόγον τοῦ θεοῦ, v. 13), and the command of God is contrasted with the tradition of men throughout vv. 6-13, but at first sight, at least, the purity logion appears to rescind the dietary laws of Moses. On the other hand, it is possible that the healing pericope was found by Mark already joined to our passage in his source, or that he placed it next to our passage, unconscious of any implication from the reference to the tassel. On balance, however, we prefer the view that it was Mark who intention-

ally placed the healing pericope and our passage together: we think
he arranged his material according to theological criteria, and a
general notice as to healing fame would be theologically negative,
were it not for the climax in the power of the tassel.

In concluding our review of Mark's redactional activity *external* to
our passage, we must note that such activity does not directly assist
the recognition of Mark's work *within* the passage, but the discovery
that he settled the order of pericopae by reference to theological
interests rather than historical or geographical actuality will illuminate
the tendencies of his redaction within our passage.

d. *Mark's arrangement of material within 7.1-23*

Turning now to Marcan redaction within our passage, we look first at
his ordering of the various units in the passage. We do not wish to
anticipate the results of our form-critical enquiry below, but it is
generally agreed that our passage is composite in that Mark has
brought together several units of tradition linked by a common
theme or themes. Lambrecht notes (p. 25) the view of several
exegetes that the passage can be divided into two parts, vv. 1-13 and
vv. 14-23, which have separate themes (tradition and defilement),
different addressees (the Pharisee-scribes and the people-disciples),
and even a theological contrast on Jesus' part: in the first part he
appeals to the authority of Moses, while the purity logion, the kernel
of the second part, drastically conflicts with Moses and the law.

Lambrecht himself, however, stresses the binding elements in the
two parts. He instances the domination of the pericope by words
from the root κοιν-. This seems justified, as witness κοιναῖς in vv. 2
and 5, and κοινῶσαι and similar in vv. 15-23. He considers that v. 15
in the second part of the passage gives the real answer to the question
in v. 5 of the first part. He further notes the 'you also' of v. 18, which
equates the disciples with the Pharisee-scribes of vv. 1-13. We think
he presses unity too far, however, when he claims the contrast
'outside-inside' which appears in vv. 14-23, to be present in the
Isaianic contrast of 'lips-heart' in v. 6. There is a formal connection
in that the heart is one of the organs contrasted in each case, but the
essential nature of the dichotomy is different. In the Isaianic quotation
the 'lips-heart' contrast exemplifies hypocrisy, contrasting what 'this
people' protests in worship, with its actual disloyalty to God. The
'outside-inside' dichotomy in the second part is between the sinful
thoughts proceeding out of man which defile him, and food going

into man which does not; there is no suggestion of hypocrisy either in the man eating unclean food or the man uttering unclean thoughts. If the two contrasts are respectively labelled 'lips-heart' and 'stomach-heart', it becomes evident how slight the connection is.

Nor can we accept Lambrecht's suggestion that the first half of the list of 'evil things' in vv. 21-22 may refer to the Decalogue, and thus create an intended link with the Decalogue command to honour parents in v. 10, and that, as the truly defiling way of life, the 'evil things' contrast with the cultic purity supported in the v. 5 question. For, in Mark's list of sins only four are prohibited by the Decalogue, and Matthew can be contrasted in this respect. The reader cannot be expected mentally to isolate half of Mark's integrated list, and relate it back; and even the first half of the list, while mentioning theft, murder, adultery and coveting, starts with fornication, a non-Decalogue sin. And the list is expressed to demonstrate the true causes of defilement, rather than a contrasting way of life.

Lambrecht comments, 'In the editor's mind the whole of these twenty-two verses form a thematic unity'. We grant that Mark has brought together in our passage previously separate units, but the conceptual links which Lambrecht identifies in the two halves appear to us rather nebulous, and we wonder whether they would have crossed the redactor's mind. We see Mark as undertaking a logical thematic progression: an exhortation to wash the hands, which is a practice of the tradition, leads to criticism of that tradition; the emphasis of that tradition is on cultic purity which leads to criticism of that basis of purity, and to teaching on what is true purity. We acknowledge, with Lambrecht, the link between vv. 5 and 15, between handwashing and general purity, which causes the prevalence of the root κοιν- in both halves of the passage, but we doubt whether Mark was influenced by Lambrecht's other unifying features. Our understanding of Mark's over-all internal redactional progression will assist us in the identification of his more detailed editorial activity.

e. *Marcan redaction within the units*

In studying the detailed redaction by Mark within the passage, we must attend to the different ways in which the redactor may affect his material. As Lambrecht (pp. 31-32) has summarized, he can introduce new elements of his own creation into his traditional text, he can arrange in his own order the units of tradition, and he can re-shape and re-write those units.

Pryke explains (p. 28) that he judges by literary, syntactical and vocabulary tests whether words are redactional. But, as we have indicated above, the identification of Marcan redaction is difficult, and more so than in Matthew or Luke. For example, the redaction of a traditional unit may only involve the amendment of a few words; how are we to identify those words? Pryke acknowledges the difficulty, and after commenting that it is at the seams of pericopae where redaction is mainly to be found, adds, 'Nevertheless, unless his work was simply the assembling of sources already in Greek, his own hand may also be present in his sources, in so far as he was himself responsible for the translation or paraphrase of already existing Aramaic oral or written tradition. Further, his own redaction may not have been uninfluenced by linguistic usages already belonging to the tradition. One would expect to find in such a writing as a "Gospel" sometimes redaction in the source, and traditional sayings or expressions preserved, or repeated and used in editorial links. If this is the correct estimate of Mark's situation as a writer, any neat and tidy solution to the problem of redaction and linguistics in Mark must be ruled out of court' (p. 31).

When the redactor may operate in so many ways, and may use not his own preferred language, but the language of the tradition, the recognition of his work is hazardous, as the differing views of Mark's activity in our passage will show us.

Verse 1

We think Mark has inserted the initial καί in this verse. As theological association rather than historicity causes Mark to place pericopae together, it seems unlikely that 7.1 was already attached to 6.56 in Mark's source. But Pryke (p. 161) classifies the whole of v. 1 as redactional, and points to γραμματεῖς, Ἱεροσόλυμα, συνάγειν and Φαρισαῖος as words frequently used by Mark in his redaction. Some critics[31] have seen an artificiality in the reference to 'some of the scribes who had come from Jerusalem'. They may, however, have had general inspectorial duties in Galilee,[32] and not have come solely to see the disciples eating. Although the Greek is not unambiguous, we think, following Grundmann[33] and others, that it was only the scribes (and not the Pharisees) who had come from Jerusalem. Since (1) three of the said four words of Marcan frequency are nouns (two being proper-names) for which alternatives are limited, (2) no Marcan syntactical feature is quoted by Pryke, and (3) although at a seam, the content of the verse is not intrinsically improbable, we find, following the forensic approach described in the Introduction, that Mark has discharged the burden of proof of the authenticity of this verse, apart from the initial καί, there being insufficient opposing evidence.

Verse 2

Pryke (p. 161) does not consider this verse to be redactional, apart from the phrase τοῦτ' ἔστιν ἀνίπτοις explaining κοιναῖς. Most critics regard this phrase as a clarification for Mark's Gentile readers. It would be strange to find vocabulary assistance in the oral tradition, for the more intelligible word would be directly substituted. Moreover, during the earlier transmission of the tradition in Palestine, explanation would be unnecessary.

The fact that κοιναῖς is explained in v. 2 supports the presence in Mark's source of the participial clause starting καὶ ἰδόντες; for if Mark had been writing this part of the passage without a fixed wording in his source, he would probably have directly substituted ἀνίπτοις for κοιναῖς. Treatment of τοὺς ἄρτους as referring to the loaves in the Feeding story would explain its use here, and its inconsistency with the correctly expressed τὸν ἄρτον at v. 5.[34] If this treatment is incorrect, then the inconsistency is best reconciled by the supposition that Mark found both nouns in his tradition, and preserved them; this solution would further support the traditional nature of this verse, apart from the explanation.

Verses 3 and 4

Pryke (p. 161) considers these verses to be redactional, and again, most critics see these verses as a Marcan explanation of Jewish practices for the benefit of his Gentile readers. Lohmeyer,[35] however, accords a more important rôle to these verses in that, through this parenthesis, Mark places the basis of the dispute in a wider context: he here introduces the key-word παράδοσις, and mentions purity customs which do not concern the question at v. 5. Lohmeyer believes that Mark drafts his parenthesis in this way in order to increase the relevance of Jesus' reply which does not directly answer the question, but counter-charges against the customs and tradition of the Pharisees. In similar vein, Suhl[36] stresses that the Isaiah quotation which speaks of the plural ἐντάλματα ἀνθρώπων would very abruptly extend the scope of the dispute, if vv. 3-4 had not prepared the way by amplifying the traditional practices. He cites the question at v. 5 which concerns a single regulation (handwashing), and v. 8 which refers in the singular to τὴν ἐντολήν and τὴν παράδοσιν. Yet v. 5 does mention the general παράδοσιν in its first limb, and, regarding v. 8, παράδοσιν is surely a collective noun, and τὴν ἐντολήν is being used in a collective sense; moreover these v. 8 singulars come after the Isaiah quotation in vv. 6 and 7 which pluralizes the allegations. On the general point, however, we agree with Suhl and Lohmeyer that the preliminary mention of the manifold purificatory practices does prepare the reader for the broader argument, and thus supports the redactional nature of vv. 3 and 4.

Grundmann,[37] however, while seeing the function of vv. 3 and 4 similarly, namely to facilitate the collection in one passage of various words of Jesus on purity and the tradition, considers that the verses may be attributable to tradents. That the editorial work of drafting these verses and inserting them into the tradition should be effected during the course of the oral tradition, we find hard to accept.

We understand Mark to be explaining in advance to his readers in these verses that the reason why the Pharisees will ask the disciples about handwashing is that the Pharisees wash many kinds of things and, in particular, do not eat without first washing their hands πυγμῇ. Mark's explanation, however, is wider than the v. 5 question necessitates, for, to make it intelligible, he need not mention immersion on return from market, or the washing of pots and pans. These other practices prepare the reader for the general subject of the tradition, on which the argument later centres. We accordingly remove these verses from the passage, as redactional.

Verse 5

Pryke (p. 161) treats the words from the first καί in this verse to γραμματεῖς as redactional, but this leaves him with a question at διὰ τί without a prior verb of 'asking', and is thus too drastic a suggestion. We can certainly delete, as secondary, words which are present in v. 5 only because of the need to resume the narrative after the dislocation caused by the parenthesis. καί and οἱ Φαρισαῖοι καὶ οἱ γραμματεῖς can be removed on this ground, but we must retain ἐπερωτῶσιν αὐτόν as a main verb and object after the participial clause commencing ἰδόντες in v. 2.

Lambrecht (p. 48) in his analysis of vv. 1-5 stresses Mark's 'daring editorial activity', and sees him as the formulator of the double question in v. 5, using 'his favourite οὐ . . . ἀλλά phrase'. He thinks that Mark found in his sources an incident about eating with unclean hands, and also the 'Q' saying (Mt. 23.25-26 par.) about the Pharisaic washing of cups and pots. Seeing both washing of hands and of cups as but two rules of the tradition, he has broadened the question in this verse from handwashing to the whole tradition.

Certainly, Mark uses the οὐ . . . ἀλλά construction frequently, but this is the only instance where Mark uses the construction in a question, and in no other case is there marked descent from the general to the particular, as in the two limbs here.[38] ἀλλά, when used by Mark following οὐ, often has a parallel adversative effect of a specific nature, e.g. 'those who are well have no need of a doctor, but those who are sick', and, 'so they are no longer two, but one' (2.17 and 10.7). Moreover, frequency of use of a construction by a redactor does not mean that he is responsible for its presence in the text on every occasion.

Even if we assume that Mark is responsible for the οὐ . . . ἀλλά construction in this verse, this does not show that he created the substance of the double question. If a tradent or the writer of a Gospel is passing on a story, he may, especially if it is in oral form, use some of his own vocabulary in re-telling it; our own experience in telling a joke teaches that! But the use by the tradent or Evangelist of his own words or verbal constructions does not mean that he has invented the story. Thus, from the frequency of Mark's use of this construction, we cannot safely judge here whether Mark was creating new material, or using synonyms for the words in his source, if Greek, or making a correct translation of them, if Aramaic. A different verbal construction may have lain in Mark's source, asking basically the same double question.

Admittedly, syntax is not Lambrecht's only argument for deeming redactional the first limb of the v. 5 question, for he considers that limb to be part of the generalizing tendency of the redactor evinced in πάντες οἱ Ἰουδαῖοι in v. 3, the ἄλλα πολλά clause in v. 4b, and a similar clause at v. 13b. Nevertheless, we feel that Mark's evidence that the Pharisees asked a question in this form, is, at this stage, stronger than the opposing redactional evidence, and that the question should accordingly be retained in its entirety, for examination by form criticism.

Verses 6 and 7
Pryke (p. 161) does not include these verses in his redactional text of
Mark. The extent to which the adapted text of Isaiah so suits Mark's
polemic in vv. 6-8 is so coincidental as to indicate, at first sight, an
intentional alteration by Mark. In vv. 6-8 two different themes are
compressed; the charge of hypocrisy, and the charge of abandoning
the command of God in order to observe the tradition. The charges
are not co-extensive: a man can observe the tradition in preference to
the written law, and frankly express his preference. He is not then a
hypocrite. To assist our study, we set out below the different versions
of Isaiah 29.13 in the Masoretic text, the Targum of Jonathan, the
LXX, and Mark:

Isaiah 29.13

MT

ויאמר אדני יען כי נגש העם הזה בפיו
ובשפתיו כבדוני ולבו רחק ממני
ותהי יראתם אתי מצות אנשים מלמדה

Targum of Jonathan[39]
And the Lord said, Because this people draweth nigh with their
mouth, and with their lips do they honour me (lit. *before* me) but
their heart is far removed from the fear of me; and their fear of (lit.
before) me is become as a precept of those that teach.

LXX
Καὶ εἶπεν κύριος Ἐγγίζει μοι ὁ λαὸς οὗτος [ἐν τῷ στόματι αὐτοῦ
καὶ ἐν][40] τοις χείλεσιν αὐτῶν τιμῶσίν με, ἡ δὲ καρδία αὐτῶν πόρρω
ἀπέχει ἀπ' ἐμοῦ, μάτην δὲ σέβονταί με διδάσκοντες ἐντάλματα
ἀνθρώπων καὶ διδασκαλίας.

Mark
οὗτος ὁ λαὸς τοῖς χείλεσίν με τιμᾶ
ἡ δὲ καρδία αὐτῶν πόρρω ἀπέχει ἀπ' ἐμοῦ
μάτην δὲ σέβονταί με
διδάσκοντες διδασκαλίας ἐντάλματα ἀνθρώπων.

The LXX has a meaning which differs from the Masoretic text
principally through reading a Hebrew ותהו (and the void, cf. Gen. 1.2)
in the place of the MT ותהי (and is); hence the LXX's μάτην δέ.
Moreover, מלמדה was translated in the LXX by both διδάσκοντες and

διδασκαλίας. Thus, while in the MT the complaint of God is that the Israelites only worship him because they have been commanded by men so to do, and have learned the instructions by rote, the LXX states that the Israelites' worship of God is pointless because they teach the commandments (implicitly, not of God but) of men. The MT thrust is against the mechanical recitation of forms of worship learned by heart, whereas the LXX stresses the impossibility of true worship if based on the teaching of man-made laws. The Targum translation is close in meaning to the MT in that their fear of God is said to be like a rule learned in the school-house.

Why the LXX translates מצות אנשים מלמדה so differently is unclear, but perhaps a different Hebrew text was in front of the Greek translators. The change in meaning effected by the LXX certainly makes it a more useful weapon for Mark's polemic, even though he adapts the phrase still further. Indeed, Mark could have left the LXX text of the participial phrase as it stood, for the whole sentence from διδάσκοντες suits his argument that the commandments of men (the tradition of the elders) are contrary to the will of God. Berger (pp. 485-86) considers the changes from the LXX in the διδάσκοντες clause, i.e. the omission of καί and the placing of διδασκαλίας immediately before ἐντάλματα to be the work of Mark on the ground that it is 'nicht denkbar' that Jesus should use the LXX. Lindars,[41] too, writes that the quotation cannot be part of the genuine Gospel tradition since the argument turns on the LXX version. Admittedly, it is almost certain that Jesus would not quote from the LXX, but the LXX may be a correct translation of a non-Masoretic Hebrew version which Jesus may have quoted.

It can hardly be denied, however, that the re-positioning of διδασκαλίας as an appositional accusative in Mark's διδάσκοντες clause, which to many readers would imply a following τοῦ θεοῦ, accentuates the charge that they teach the commands of men *as the doctrines (of God)*.

Suhl[42] believes that Mark was responsible for the insertion of the whole Isaianic quotation. As mentioned above, he stresses that the v. 5 question concerns the breaking of a single regulation, and that v. 8 speaks in the singular of the command of God and the tradition of men, whereas vv. 3f. refer to sundry washing customs, and v. 7 mentions plural commands of men. He continues, 'Once we disregard vv. 3f. and the reference to the prophetic word, it gives the section a completely different sense: then the "Christians" are attacked in a stylistic dispute on a wholly concrete point, and Jesus wards off this attack through a counter-question . . . Do you abandon the ἐντολή of God and observe the regulations of men?' Although we agree that vv. 3 and 4 are redactional, to treat the quotation as redactional largely because of its inclusion of teachings and commands in the plural seems unduly drastic. And while there is no grammatical objection to v. 8 being interrogatory, we think that if it had lain in the tradition next to the v. 5 question, as claimed by Suhl, then Mark would have left it as Jesus' opening counter—where Matthew places his similar question (15.3).

Dodd[43] suggests that Isaiah 29.13 was collected with other prophecies of the disobedience of Israel, which were used especially in the argument about the extension of the Gospel from the Jews to the Gentiles. If J. Rendel Harris's theory,[44] that testimony-books were prepared and used by the early Christians, were correct, then it would be feasible that the διδάσκοντες clause was handed on in Mark's form by the early church, having been adapted in those books for more pointed rebuke than in the LXX form. But Dodd[45] has shown it to be more likely that isolated texts were quoted as pointers to longer passages, for which recourse to a Greek Bible would be necessary. We are persuaded by the above considerations that the conspicuous alteration of the διδάσκοντες clause has been made by Mark, and not by the early Christians (who would more probably repeat the LXX version).

Mark's first sentence in the quotation, οὗτος ὁ λαὸς τοῖς χείλεσίν με τιμᾷ, apart from minor verbal differences, omits ἐγγίζει μοι and ἐν τῷ στόματι αὐτοῦ from the LXX. This could simply be for brevity, or could indicate unwillingness on either Mark's or the church's part to admit that the Israelites did come near to God with their supplications (mouths). The opposing evidence here, however, is so ambiguous as not to challenge Mark's evidence of Jesus' words.

We preserve ὁ δὲ εἶπεν αὐτοῖς for we have no cause to think that Mark did not receive this from his tradition. We similarly preserve καλῶς ἐπροφήτευσεν Ἡσαΐας περὶ ὑμῶν τῶν ὑποκριτῶν for we believe, following Dodd,[46] that the charge of hypocrisy was the original use of the quotation in church/synagogue controversy.[47]

Verses 8 and 9
Pryke (p. 161) considers v. 8 to be redactional, and cites (p. 143) κρατεῖν and παράδοσις as typically Marcan words. Lambrecht

(p. 51) notes that in his redactional vv. 3 and 4 Mark has used κρατοῦντες and τὴν παράδοσιν in v. 3 and κρατεῖν in v. 4. Lambrecht thinks that Mark 'distilled' his favourite term παράδοσις (which he uses five times in ch. 7) out of the ἐντάλματα ἀνθρώπων of the Isaianic quotation. This, we think, places too high a premium on frequent usage. Παράδοσις was a technical term to translate the Jewish קבלת הזקנים. In a passage describing a dispute about its validity, is it surprising that the subject of the dispute is mentioned five times? And regarding the frequency of κρατεῖν, are there many synonyms for 'observance' beyond κρατεῖν and τηρεῖν?

Of the v. 9 wording Pryke (p. 161) lists only καὶ ἔλεγεν αὐτοῖς as redactional. But even if the tradition did not contain these words, it probably contained their equivalent, since this verse appears to be the start of a new pericope, or at least topic, and some note of Jesus speaking would be necessary.

We acknowledge that vv. 8 and 9 are in a redaction-prone area, for they are probably at 'the seam' between two separate units of tradition. Sundwall[48] emphasizes the use by the Evangelist of the 'catchword' principle in linking not only the units from his sources but also his own redactional verses. He suggests that the repetition of words and phrases at the redactional end of a pericope and at the opening of the following pericope show the hand of Mark, the redactor, and also the influence of his sources upon his own style. Berger (p. 487) who attributes the whole of vv. 6-13 to a redactor, notes the intensification of the anti-Pharisaic theme in vv. 7b-9, and this involves repetition of key-words: he cites ἐντάλματα ἀνθρώπων in 7b, which becomes τὴν παράδοσιν τῶν ἀνθρώπων in 8, and scathingly, τὴν παράδοσιν ὑμῶν in 9. Another repetition is the inclusion of τὴν ἐντολὴν τοῦ θεοῦ in both vv. 8 and 9.

We are impressed by these indicators of redaction in these verses, but wonder whether the two verses are sufficiently dissimilar for both to be redaction, since even successive redactors are unlikely to write the same content in consecutive verses. For, omitting the καὶ ἔλεγεν αὐτοῖς in v. 9, we are left with two sentences which run almost parallel in content. Both contrast, on the one hand, τὴν ἐντολὴν τοῦ θεοῦ and on the other, τὴν παράδοσιν τῶν ἀνθρώπων in v. 8 and τὴν παράδοσιν ὑμῶν in v. 9. In v. 8 the Pharisees ἀφέντες (abandon) the command of God, while in v. 9 they ἀθετεῖτε (remove) it. By contrast, in v. 8 they κρατεῖτε (observe) the tradition, while in v. 9 they στήσητε (establish) it. Indeed, the vocabulary does sharpen from v. 8 to v. 9, bearing in mind also the sarcasm of καλῶς in v. 9, but only mildly so. Would a redactor, having written or observed v. 8, have written so similarly couched a complaint as v. 9? We grant the different functions of the two verses: v. 8 underlines the application of the Isaianic text to the Pharisees, while v. 9 contains the general charge of the godless nature of the tradition, which is to be proved by the Korban practice. But, like v. 8 for the previous unit, v. 13 contains a similar underlining summary of the theological effect of the Korban unit. We are conscious here of straying into form criticism, but consider this to be an exceptional case where, correctly to identify redaction, we must contemporaneously use the form-critical tool.

Thus, if we place the two units in synoptic form, we find them to be almost identical:

Isaiah Unit	Korban Unit
A. He said to them.	A. He said to them.
B. (Charge). You are hypocrites.	B. (Charge). You abrogate the command of God to keep the tradition.
C. (Proof). Isaiah described in prophecy your hypocrisy.	C. (Proof). Your Korban practice breaks the 4th commandment.
D. Underlining summary.	D. Underlining summary.

We consider that a piece of evidence of the errors of Judaism, useable in anti-Jewish polemic, will normally have circulated in the churches, attached to an alleged saying of Jesus applying it to a current issue with the Pharisees or the Jewish Christians, as the case might be. But it appears more likely that the saying of Jesus will have *prefaced* the evidence by way of introduction or head-note, because unless at the oral stage the recipient is told first what the evidence (be it proof-text or incident) illustrates, it will fall awkwardly, even unintelligibly, upon his ears. However, a concluding interpretation is more likely to be, we think, a redaction of the tradition, driving home the point. Therefore, in the Isaiah and Korban units, we think that the proof-text and proof-practice respectively, at item C above, will have been attached in the tradition to the introductory charges of Jesus at item B above, but that the summary at item D is the redactor's work. We accordingly treat v. 8, the summary in the Isaiah unit, as redactional since we think Mark's evidence of Jesus' statement is outweighed by the evidence of the likelihood of Marcan summarizing; but v. 9, the introductory charge in the Korban unit, we believe to be traditional.[49]

Verse 10

Lambrecht (p. 53) comments that there is not much in this verse that can be called typically Marcan, and scholars, in general, agree that v. 10 is from the tradition. Pryke (p. 161), however, includes in his redactional text Μωϋσῆς γὰρ εἶπεν. Yet, if vv. 10-13a travelled as a unit of polemic, an expressed dichotomy of some sort between what the Pentateuch says and what the Pharisees say is surely essential, and Μωϋσῆς γὰρ εἶπεν seems as likely to be genuine as any other form of preface to a citation from the law; we are surprised that Pryke should attribute the phrase to Mark.[50] Admittedly, the use of γὰρ is one of the Marcan literary idiosyncrasies observed by Pryke, but it is here used in an entirely orthodox manner to express cause.[51] What other conjunction would be more natural?

The Decalogue command in this verse is given without the reason which accompanies it in Deuteronomy (and Exodus), but otherwise LXX Deut. 5.16 is transcribed. The penal provision of Exodus 21.16 is abbreviated, and differs slightly from the LXX which reads τελευτήσει θανάτῳ: this is not evidence of Mark's work, we feel, as it is probably due to use of a different version of the LXX. In fact, the B (Vaticanus) manuscript of the LXX does have Mark's reading.

Verses 11-13

Lambrecht (p. 53) is confident of Marcan redaction in these verses. He mentions the continuation in λέγετε of the second person plural used in vv. 8 and 9 (κρατεῖτε and ἀθετεῖτε). Turner,[52] Sundwall[53] and Zerwick[54] have drawn attention to Mark's preference for direct speech, and Pryke (pp. 73-74) observes that when Mark does attempt to sustain indirect speech, it soon breaks down, and he resorts to direct speech. As a consequence of Mark's prolific use of direct speech, Zerwick[55] stresses the importance of the little indirect speech in Mark as, at least, confirmation of the use by him of a source. We agree that this predilection for direct speech may indicate that when Mark does use indirect speech, he is following a source, and, perhaps, that the source is oral rather than written, for if he were copying, there would be less cause for his syntax to break down; if the author of a written source were also unused to indirect speech, that speech would possibly not have been employed by him in the first place. The converse, however, that where Mark uses direct speech he is not handing on tradition, does not seem justified: it is more likely that Mark is putting the tradition received by him into the verbal form which is more natural to him. While this rephrasing is a kind of redaction, it is not the creation of *new material* which is the main concern of our enquiry.

That Mark has rephrased his inherited material in these verses is further indicated by the anacoluthon in v. 12 which we mentioned earlier; after the ὑμεῖς δὲ λέγετε of v. 11, we would expect in v. 12 'he is not permitted' or equivalent, rather than the direct address by Jesus of οὐκέτι ἀφίετε αὐτόν. This inconsistency does, we think, show ὑμεῖς δὲ λέγετε as editorial, for Mark has probably, for anti-Pharisaic polemic, inserted the emphatic ὑμεῖς δέ to contrast with Moses' words in v. 10, and has forgotten to alter the syntax correspond-ingly in v. 12. If we remove ὑμεῖς δὲ λέγετε, vv. 9-12 constitute a unit of polemic which could well have been handed down on its own; to create the necessary contrast with Μωϋσῆς γὰρ εἶπεν in v. 10, we would in v. 11, after the first ἐὰν, add δέ, for some such adversative particle, we think, was probably in the tradition, to indicate the contrast.

We also exclude from v. 11 as redactional, in common with Pryke (p. 161) and most critics, the explanatory words ὅ ἐστιν δῶρον, and are slightly reinforced by this explanation in our belief that the Korban pericope was in Mark's source: if it had not been passed to him, he might well have directly substituted δῶρον for κορβᾶν, although customary use of that term and a concern for technical accuracy might have occasioned initial mention of it.

Our comparative analysis of the Isaiah and Korban units caused us to remove the summarizing v. 8 (item D) from the Isaiah unit, and we would similarly remove the summarizing v. 13a from the Korban unit, as Mark's work. Were we not excising the whole participial phrase, we would in any case remove the ἣ παρεδώκατε as tautolo-gous, and consequently unlikely to have existed in an oral tradition which for mnemonic reasons would tend to conciseness. Pryke (p. 161) rightly includes v. 13b in his redactional text for we clearly see here the work of the generalizing editor who was active also at vv. 3 and 4.

Verse 14
Taylor (p. 343) writes that the introduction at v. 14a consists of

common Marcan words, and is almost certainly the Evangelist's free composition. The summoning of the crowd, indeed, is generally considered to be Marcan redaction. Wrede used the artificiality of Mark's introduction of the crowd as one of his arguments to show that this Gospel, like the others, was an interpretation of the life of Jesus, and contained its own theological slants. He relates how at the beginning of ch. 7 Jesus disputes with the Pharisees and scribes about handwashing, and then calls the crowd to him and tells them the parable: but after that he enters the house, away from the crowd, and explains the parable only to the disciples. Wrede writes, 'Clearly it is only the parable which has produced the crowd from the wings, as parable and crowd belong together . . . The crowd has not heard of the dispute with the lawyers, but then comes to hear a parable related to something which it has not heard, and must content itself with the parable alone for the interpretation and significance are not for it!'[56] In view of the conjunction of this internal improbability and the Marcan vocabulary, we remove the summoning of the crowd, as being redactional; Mark's evidence is outweighed.

Regarding ἔλεγεν αὐτοῖς, however, which follows in this verse, we must again distinguish between substantive and verbal redaction. It can hardly be denied that the phrase is frequently used by Mark, yet the following words of Jesus would naturally be passed on in the tradition with a preface stating that Jesus was the speaker, and to whom he spoke (since whether he spoke to the Pharisees or the Sadducees or the disciples of John the Baptist, for example, would affect the significance of his words). Thus, while the frequency of ἔλεγεν αὐτοῖς may indicate that its use is redactional in the sense that Mark has rephrased the tradition to his own verbal usage, it is not redactional in the sense important to us, namely that Mark created its substance. And regarding Mark's frequent use of the phrase, if the occurrence of an oft-repeated act, like a preacher preaching, is to be reported, why should the reporter on each occasion strive for a different verbal permutation in recording the occurrence? The fact that he uses a customary formula should not prejudice the validity of its content.

Lambrecht (p. 58) denies that the purity logion was preceded by the call in this verse to hear and understand, but Paschen (pp. 162-63) notes the history of this kind of imperative in Isa. 6.9, 1 Macc. 2.65 and the repeated שמעו שמעו at 2 Sam. 20.16. He concludes, 'So in his mother tongue will Jesus of Nazareth have turned to the people when he sat down at a village well, at the market or at the town gate, and solicited the curiosity and attention of the crowd'. We preserve these words for the tradition, for although we doubt that Jesus *summoned* the crowd, we do not deny the possible existence of a crowd whose attention could be claimed by these words.

Verse 15

Most scholars consider the purity logion constituting this verse, to be genuine in substance, although some, like Lambrecht (pp. 59-60), think that Mark has affected its final wording. Pryke (p. 161) does not include this verse in his redactional text, but Lambrecht points to εἰσπορεύομαι, ἐκπορεύομαι and the 'antithetical and progressive' οὐδέν . . . ἀλλά as frequent in Mark. In view of Lambrecht's repeated references to Mark's verbal use-rate as a guide to his redaction, it is refreshing to read his acknowledgment (p. 60) that it is methodologically inadmissible to say on the basis of the Marcan character of εἰσπορεύομαι (as Merkel[57] partly does), that the idea contained in this verb was not already present in the original saying.

Paschen (pp. 173-74) also notes the 'Komplex' of Marcan expressions in the logion and explanations (vv. 18b-21a), and removes εἰσπορεύεσθαι (together with εἰς αὐτόν in 15a and εἰς τὸν ἄνθρωπον in 18b), and ἐκπορεύεσθαι. He argues that these verbs have a purely explanatory function, and can be removed without real loss, and almost without injury to the grammar. But real loss of meaning is caused by the omission of εἰσπορευόμενον εἰς αὐτόν in v. 15; the presence of those words restricts the denial of defilement to things entering man (presumably food and drink) while their absence extends the denial to everything outside man. Merkel also would omit those words in v. 15 and translate the remainder, 'Es gibt *nichts* ausserhalb des Menschen, das ihn verunreinigen kann!'[58] Yet 'ausserhalb' hardly translates ἔξωθεν which, as an improper preposition with the genitive, means 'from outside (man)',[59] and thus needs a verb of motion, and usually a noun of destination, with it. Indeed, Merkel's translation emphasizes how different the meaning is without the verb of motion and the destination (εἰς αὐτόν)—*all* external defilement is denied. Similarly, in v. 15b τὰ ἐκ τοῦ ἀνθρώπου is too elliptical if unaccompanied by ἐκπορευόμενον or a synonym. Moreover, while possible Greek, it has a strange ring. Similar observations apply to the other excisions of these verbs as proposed by Paschen: we accordingly do not assign their substance to redaction.

In connection with οὐδέν in v. 15, Paschen (pp. 174-76) examines the use of the negative pronoun οὐδείς in words of Jesus in the Gospels, and finds that it is more frequent in John (31) and Luke (18) than in Matthew (10) and Mark (10). He notes Matthew's Jewish manner of composing, and concludes that use of οὐδείς is produced by facility in Greek. Being concerned only with the original Sitz im Leben, he does not enquire whether οὐδέν in v. 15 belongs to church tradition or redaction, but he considers that the πᾶν . . . οὐ construction of v. 18b is a translation of the Aramaic לא . . . כל, and is thus the earlier form of the first limb of v. 15. He also sees ἐστιν τὰ κοινοῦντα in v. 15b as a translation of the Aramaic use of the participle as predicate, although in the present tense the Aramaic auxiliary הוא (εἶναι) is not usually employed, and may have been inserted later to accord with Greek syntax. GK (§ 116m) confirms that the use of the participle as predicate is very frequent in noun-clauses in Hebrew; the use of the participle as a *finite* verb is attributed by Moule,[60] in at least some instances, to semitic influence. However, Paschen (p. 176) is right to caution that the use of semitisms does not identify the voice of Jesus for a semitizing tradent or one imbued with the LXX might be responsible. Indeed, if Aramaic was the first language of Mark, he might have produced these semitisms himself. We are nevertheless disinclined to attribute the ἐστιν τὰ κοινοῦντα to Mark in view of the significant semitic construction.

Verse 16
Aland does not include this verse in his text, although it is present in the majority of witnesses. It is, however, absent from important Alexandrian texts, and Metzger[61] believes it to be a scribal gloss, derived, perhaps, from the analogy at 4.9. From considerations of context we are inclined to agree; it seems unlikely that Jesus would urge attention immediately *after* an important statement, since the time for the preacher to waken his audience is *before* the climactic words, not after them,[62] and if he has urged them beforehand, he is less likely to repeat it afterwards.

Verse 17
Paschen (p. 159) identifies as editorial work of Mark, the parataxis with καὶ εἰσερχέσθαι εἰς οἶκον and introduction of direct speech by the present historic λέγει. He agrees with Gnilka that the indirect formulation of the disciples' question is also Marcan. Gnilka,[63]

however, concludes from his linguistic analysis that Mark has taken the complete structural statement constituting v. 17 from his source, and he cites μαθητής and ἐπερώταν as words from a fixed vocabulary of disciple-questions. Against this, Paschen cites 4.10 where the periphrasis οἱ περὶ αὐτὸν σὺν τοῖς δώδεκα and the simple ἐρώταν are used instead. Paschen thinks it more likely that 4.10 containing ἐρώταν (only used by Mark again at 8.5), κατὰ μόνας (only use by Mark), and οἱ περὶ αὐτόν, was in the tradition, and that Mark has adopted from that tradition the mechanism of the private question by the disciples and created the other private questionings at our v. 17, 9.28 and 10.10 which contain vocabulary more clearly Marcan. He later comments, however, that 9.33 may be pre-Marcan, for only here is γινέσθαι used in the sense of being locally present, and ἐν τῇ οἰκίᾳ in a structural statement. By the latter term, Paschen thinks an actual house in Capernaum is meant, perhaps the house of Peter. He concludes from 4.10 and 9.33 that in Mark's sources the discussions of Jesus with his attendants took place 'at home' in Capernaum, and that from this datum Mark has constructed his 'wandering-idea' which produced the εἰσῆλθεν εἰς οἶκον for his structural remarks at 7.17. But, it might be argued, if the private teaching 'at home' was in the tradition at chs. 4 and 9, it is logically possible that it was authentic, so that if Jesus is said to explain parables privately at 7.17, it is as likely as not that this report is similarly traditional and authentic.

Paschen's attribution to the tradition of the private teaching at 4.10f. and 9.33f. influences us towards preserving this verse also for the tradition. We think it likely that the disciples did ask for an explanation of the παραβολή which, as Taylor (p. 344) points out, is here used in the sense of משל, a 'dark saying'; the disciples would have been intuitive, indeed, to have understood the purity logion without explanation!

We accordingly judge that the evidence in v. 17 that the disciples asked privately about the parable, supported by the above considerations, is stronger than the opposing evidence of the Marcan editorial practice in the verse. We postpone final judgment, however, until we have considered the Explanations in vv. 18-23, for if these are redactional, then the 'scenery' of v. 17 will collapse with the 'script'. Judgment of v. 17 is unaffected by our assignment to Mark of the summons of the crowd in v. 14, for a crowd may well have gathered spontaneously, as the debate with the Pharisees probably proceeded in a public place.

Verse 18

Lambrecht (p. 62) notes the characteristically Marcan theme of the disciples' lack of understanding in the first of the two questions here, and Pryke (p. 161) includes both it and the καὶ λέγει αὐτοῖς in his redactional text. Neirynck[64] sees Mark's hand in these double questions in which the second clause says more than the first, and concretizes it, 7.5b and c being another example. Not all the double questions serve this purpose, however, for at 4.13 the second question is less concrete and more generalized than the first: 'Do you not understand this parable? How then will you understand all the parables?' It seems unlikely that Jesus would have upbraided the disciples as ἀσύνετοί for failing to understand the enigmatic logion. We think it was Mark rather than the tradition which introduced the theme of the dullness of the disciples. An artificial theme is more likely to be the creation of one man than a community, and the theme of the disciples' dullness assists the preservation of the Messianic Secret which, with Dibelius,[65] we also think was Mark's creation.

We conclude that Mark's evidence here is overborne by this evidence of internal improbability, supported by the evidence of Marcan syntax in the double question, and we remove the first question as redactional. On balance, we retain the milder οὐ νοεῖτε of the second question, and we retain καὶ λέγει αὐτοῖς, for there would be some formula at this stage for introducing Jesus' further speech.

Verse 19

Pryke (p. 161) treats all this verse as redactional, and as the syntactical features to which he refers (p. 143) all relate to 19c, we assume that his reason for excising the remainder of the verse arises from the probably Marcan vocabulary in it—εἰσπορεύεται, ἐκπορεύεται. This is strange because he does not consider the possibly redactional nature of v. 15 which contains both these verbs, or of v. 18b which contains εἰσπορευόμενον and δύναται. As the redaction in v. 19 (apart from 19c) was probably only rephrasing (for we believe the substance was in the tradition), we preserve 19a and b.

Many scholars consider v. 19c to be an early gloss despite 'the overwhelming weight of manuscript evidence'[66] in its favour. But Cranfield[67] and Taylor (p. 345) consider it Marcan, and Zerwick,[68] who terms it stylistically 'eine Härte und ein Unicum', attributes it to careless comment on Mark's part.

Since this phrase is clearly comment on the preceding explanation, it must emanate from the early church or Mark. If the phrase had formed part of the traditional material, we do not think it would have been passed on in this awkward structure; frequent repetition would have caused a smoothing of the syntax in and near it. The preservation of καθαρίζων, notwithstanding its grammatical difficulty, argues for Mark's hand, and places the phrase on a par with the anacoluthon in v. 12 and the interrupting parenthesis in vv. 3 and 4. Moreover, its character of Marcan summary is so akin to the others in our passage that we think this, too, is Marcan.

Verse 20
Pryke (p. 161) considers ἔλεγεν δὲ ὅτι τό in this verse to be redactional. The residue is ungrammatical without τό, but we agree that once v. 19c is removed, the introductory ἔλεγεν δὲ ὅτι here is unnecessary, although a δέ would suitably connect and contrast with v. 19b. There is no cause to consider the rest of the verse redactional, since a substantial repetition of v. 15b is necessary to contrast with the preceding explanation of what does not defile, and to preface the detailed explanation of what does.

Verses 21 and 22
Pryke (p. 161) notes ἔσωθεν γὰρ ἐκ τῆς καρδίας in v. 21 as Marcan redaction, and considers (pp. 126f.) the explanatory γάρ as one of the features of Mark's style. He suggests (p. 130) that Mark inserts ἔσωθεν under the influence of ἔξωθεν in v. 15. Lambrecht, also (pp. 59-60), muses on the origin and relationship of these two terms. Did Mark insert them into our passage because he noticed them in the passage on purity in 'Q' (Mt. 23.25 par.)? We think not, since, if so influenced, he would surely have placed the terms in closer parallelism and proximity, rather than divided by an explanation. While the Marcan vocabulary in v. 21 cannot be denied, unless Mark created the explanation in these verses, some form of wording must have lain in the tradition to explain the point of the vices, namely that they come *from inside* (ἔσωθεν) man. Any redaction here is surely only rephrasing.

Whether the list of vices be derived from Greek philosophy and used in the Hellenistic synagogues, as suggested by Knox,[69] or is 'a thoroughly Jewish catalogue' as claimed by Cranfield,[70] there is nothing to suggest that it was created by Mark.

Verse 23

This verse seems to us a typical summarizing or 'signing-off' sentence of Mark; it introduces nothing new, generalizes, and would have been jettisoned by the tradents as 'deadweight'. We think it well described by Lagrange as 'Conclusion nerveuse de tout ce que précède . . . une sorte d'inclusio . . . le remarque de Mc . . .'[71]

Verse 17—a reprise

As we do not assign to redaction the explanations in vv. 18b-23, we are not obliged to assign to Mark also the preceding structural remarks in v. 17. We therefore confirm our judgment that this verse belongs to the tradition.

f. *Conclusion to Chapter 1*

We append below the text of our passage, and have underlined with a continuous line words which we deem redactional in the sense that neither they, nor synonyms thereof, were in the traditional material received by Mark. We have underlined with a dotted line words which we consider redactional only in the sense that Mark substituted them for synonyms in the tradition. We stress that, for the purpose of our enquiry, which is to trace the history of the *substance* of the units in our passage, the rephrasing or translation into his own vocabulary of traditional words of similar meaning is of little significance. The dotted underlining serves only to record formally that kind of redaction.

The general result of this redactional enquiry into our passage is that, while Mark has probably put much of the tradition into his own vocabulary, his actual additions are largely confined to parenthetical explanations, generalizing and summarizing sentences, and accentuation, against the Pharisees, of traditional argument. Two of the summarizing sentences, however, may be said to be creative in that they extend, or channel along a particular course, the thought in their respective units. For, although v. 13a substantially repeats the charge in v. 9, v. 8 clearly channels against the tradition the less precise attack in the quotation in v. 7, and v. 19c, by its interpretation of the explanation in v. 19a and b, extends, or directs, the application of the logion to the cleansing of *all* foods. Mark's redaction has also been creative in the summons of the crowd at v. 14, and the allegation of the disciples' dullness at v. 18.

It is not possible to decide whether the conjunctions δέ and καί, which link points of debate at the beginning of vv. 6 and 9 respectively, are Mark's redaction, until we have considered in the next Chapter the extent to which he received the tradition in our passage in separate units or joined together.

We have included and bracketed in v. 7 καὶ διδασκαλίας in order to show his omission of those words, and the second δέ in vv. 11 and 20 to show presumed Marcan omissions.

1. <u>Καὶ</u> συνάγονται πρὸς αὐτον οἱ Φαρισαῖοι καί τινες τῶν γραμματέων ἐλθόντες ἀπὸ Ἱεροσολύμων.

2. Καὶ ἰδόντες τινὰς τῶν μαθητῶν αὐτοῦ ὅτι κοιναῖς χερσίν, <u>τοῦτ'</u> <u>ἔστιν ἀνίπτοις</u>, ἐσθίουσιν <u>τοὺς ἄρτους</u>.

3. <u>οἱ γὰρ Φαρισαῖοι καὶ πάντες οἱ Ἰουδαῖοι ἐὰν μὴ πυγμῇ νίψωνται</u> <u>τὰς χεῖρας οὐκ ἐσθίουσιν, κρατοῦντες τὴν παράδοσιν τῶν πρεσβυτ-</u> <u>έρων.</u>

4. <u>Καὶ ἀπ' ἀγορᾶς ἐὰν μὴ βαπτίσωνται οὐκ ἐσθίουσιν, καὶ ἄλλα</u> <u>πολλά ἐστιν ἃ παρέλαβον κρατεῖν, βαπτισμοὺς ποτηρίων καὶ</u> <u>ξεστῶν καὶ χαλκίων</u> [καὶ κλινῶν].

5. <u>καὶ</u> ἐπερωτῶσιν αὐτὸν <u>οἱ Φαρισαῖοι</u> καὶ οἱ γραμματεῖς· διὰ τί οὐ περιπατοῦσιν οἱ μαθηταί σου κατὰ τὴν παράδοσιν τῶν πρεσβυτέρων, ἀλλὰ κοιναῖς χερσὶν ἐσθίουσιν τὸν ἄρτον;

6. Ὁ δὲ εἶπεν αὐτοῖς· καλῶς ἐπροφήτευσεν Ἡσαΐας περὶ ὑμῶν τῶν ὑποκριτῶν, <u>ὡς γέγραπται [ὅτι]</u>

οὗτος ὁ λαὸς τοῖς χείλεσιν με τιμᾷ,
ἡ δὲ καρδία αὐτῶν πόρρω ἀπέχει ἀπ' ἐμοῦ.

7.   μάτην δε σέβονται με
διδάσκοντες <u>διδασκαλίας</u> ἐντάλματα ἀνθρώπων (καὶ διδασκαλίας)

8. <u>ἀφέντες τὴν ἐντολὴν τοῦ θεοῦ κρατεῖτε τὴν παράδοσιν τῶν</u> <u>ἀνθρώπων.</u>

9. <u>καὶ ἔλεγεν αὐτοῖς·</u> καλῶς ἀθετεῖτε τὴν ἐντολὴν τοῦ θεοῦ, ἵνα τὴν παράδοσιν ὑμῶν στήσητε.

10. Μωϋσῆς γὰρ εἶπεν· τίμα τὸν πατέρα σου καὶ τὴν μητέρα σου, καί ὁ κακολογῶν πατέρα ἢ μητέρα θανάτῳ τελευτάτω

11. <u>ὑμεῖς δὲ λέγετε,</u> ἐὰν (δὲ) εἴπῃ ἄνθρωπος τῷ πατρὶ ἢ τῇ μητρί· κορβᾶν, <u>ὅ ἐστιν δῶρον,</u> ὃ ἐὰν ἐξ ἐμοῦ ὠφεληθῇς

12. οὐκέτι ἀφίετε αὐτὸν οὐδὲν ποιῆσαι τῷ πατρὶ ἢ τῇ μητρί.

13. <u>ἀκυροῦντες τὸν λόγον τοῦ θεοῦ τῇ παραδόσει ὑμῶν ᾖ παρεδώκατε·</u> <u>καὶ παρόμοια τοιαῦτα πολλὰ ποιεῖτε.</u>

14. καὶ προσκαλεσάμενος πάλιν τὸν ὄχλον ἔλεγεν αὐτοῖς· ἀκούσατέ μου πάντες καὶ σύνετε.
15. οὐδέν ἐστιν ἔξωθεν τοῦ ἀνθρώπου εἰσπορευόμενον εἰς αὐτὸν ὃ δύναται κοινῶσαι αὐτόν, ἀλλὰ τὰ ἐκ του ἀνθρώπου ἐκπορευόμενά ἐστιν τὰ κοινοῦντα τὸν ἄνθρωπον.
16. εἴ τις ἔχει ὦτα ἀκούειν, ἀκουέτω.
17. Καὶ ὅτε εἰσῆλθεν εἰς οἶκον ἀπὸ τοῦ ὄχλου, ἐπηρώτων αὐτὸν οἱ μαθηταὶ αὐτοῦ τὴν παραβολήν.
18. Καὶ λέγει αὐτοῖς· οὕτως καὶ ὑμεῖς ἀσύνετοί ἐστε; οὐ νοεῖτε ὅτι πᾶν τὸ ἔξωθεν εἰσπορευόμενον εἰς τὸν ἄνθρωπον οὐ δύναται αὐτὸν κοινῶσαι;
19. ὅτι οὐκ εἰσπορεύεται αὐτοῦ εἰς τὴν καρδίαν ἀλλ’ εἰς τὴν κοιλίαν, καὶ εἰς τὸν ἀφεδρῶνα ἐκπορεύεται, καθαρίζων πάντα τὰ βρώματα.
20. ἔλεγεν δὲ ὅτι τὸ (δὲ) ἐκ τοῦ ἀνθρώπου ἐκπορευόμενον, ἐκεῖνο κοινοῖ τὸν ἄνθρωπον.
21. ἔσωθεν γὰρ ἐκ τῆς καρδίας τῶν ἀνθρώπων οἱ διαλογισμοὶ οἱ κακοὶ ἐκπορεύονται, πορνεῖαι, κλοπαί, φόνοι.
22. μοιχεῖαι, πλεονεξίαι, πονηρίαι, δόλος, ἀσέλγεια, ὀφθαλμὸς πονηρός, βλασφημία, ὑπερηφανία, ἀφροσύνη.
23. πάντα ταῦτα τὰ πονηρὰ ἔσωθεν ἐκπορεύεται καὶ κοινοῖ τὸν ἄνθρωπον.

Chapter 2

THE HISTORY OF THE PRE-MARCAN TRADITION

A. *Identification of the original units of tradition*

a. *Scope*

In Chapter 1 we attempted primarily to identify creative additions and alterations made by Mark to the traditions which he received. In this Chapter, largely by the use of form criticism, we hope to determine whether the traditional material bequeathed to us by redaction criticism is unitary in the sense of containing discussion already connected in the tradition, or is composite in the sense of containing separate pericopae of tradition which were brought together by Mark. If the traditional material is composite, we hope to identify the original form of the dispute, and then to trace the history of that and the other pericopae in our passage by ascertaining the additions and alterations made to them by the early Christians and, indeed, whether the pericopae originated in the early church, or whether they go back to the historical Jesus.

This application of form criticism may demonstrate its interaction with redaction criticism, in that the former may show that a pericope had no function in the early church at all, or in that Marcan form, so that the pericope, or part of it, is cast out at this stage as editorial; alternatively, form criticism may show that words which we have already rejected as redactional are necessary to complete the polemical or other purpose of a pericope in the early church, and so are rescued for the tradition. But redaction criticism, also, may assist in the recovery of the earliest form of the tradition, for, in addition to laying bare the editorial work of the Evangelist, it may also expose the additions and alterations made to the original form of the tradition by the early church. Our final treatment of the tradition in this Chapter will be to apply to its earliest form the authenticating criteria for determining the mens ipsissima of the historical Jesus.

b. *Unitary or composite*

We now consider to what extent the narrative and discussions recognized in Chapter 1 as traditional were already connected together in the tradition received by Mark, or were collected by him as separate units, and put together by him. Nearly all scholars consider that the various units were not already connected when received by Mark.[1] One ground for this view, which immediately occurs to the modern Western reader, is that if the tradition was in oral form, it could not have been connected together, since the tradents would have been unable to memorize a passage of that length. In fact, this ground collapses, for Gerhardsson[2] has demonstrated the capacity of Jews of the first century to memorize long passages; their memories had not been weakened by reliance on the written word.

Gerhardsson,[3] indeed, believes that Jesus required his disciples, following the Rabbinic method, to learn certain of his sayings by heart; he thinks that the explanations of Jesus' sayings (as of the parables) derive in principle (for they were not learned by rote) from Jesus' own interpretation of his teaching. Further, the collegium of apostles in Jerusalem, he says, carried on as late as the fifties the work of collecting and fixing the tradition about Jesus, rather as the Rabbis formulated the traditions in the Mishnah. He thinks that tractates about Jesus were put together on factual or mnemonic principles, and instances the instruction of the apostles in Matthew 10, the parable tractate in Mark 4, and the bread traditions in Mark 6.31–8.26. 'It is probable', he writes, 'that relatively comprehensive tractates of Jesus-traditions had to be compiled at a fairly early stage for use of missionaries and teachers who went out from Jerusalem'.[4]

We are not sure that Gerhardsson's analogy of the Rabbis is appropriate, for they were trained in the use of mnemonics, and were a scholarly class, whilst, although most of the disciples and early followers would have been to synagogue schools,[5] they would not have been trained as Rabbis, and many, no doubt, followed manual occupations.[6] His theory seems unduly speculative for, apart from the linking of pericopae by subject-matter and 'catchwords', we have no evidence from the NT or early Fathers for a use of mnemonics, or for early compilations by a collegium.[7] Thus, while we would not deny that Jesus may have taught his disciples to memorize important units of teaching, we doubt that they learned long tractates such as Mark 4 or 6.31–8.26, as Gerhardsson avers.

Knox,[8] also, posits a number of 'tracts' containing accounts of Jesus' ministry, and either written or committed to memory, for he thinks that the Christian converts would want to know more about the life of Jesus, and the travelling evangelist would need more material for his work than was provided by the mission speech with its testimonia, or by the Passion story. Albertz[9] supposes these tracts to be a natural growth rather than a formal literary product, and to be of a length which could easily be committed to memory. He suggests that Justin Martyr's reference (*Apologia* 67.3) to the reading of the 'memorials' of the apostles at Christian worship may be an example of a practice which goes back earlier. But the reference hardly seems to support long, oral compilations, for Justin's words are, καὶ τὰ ἀπομνημονεύματα τῶν ἀποστόλων ἢ τὰ συγγράμματα τῶν προφητῶν ἀναγινώσκεται, μέχρις ἐγχωρεῖ.[10] Thus, the memoirs of the apostles (i.e. the things which, probably as participants, they remembered, but which had later been written down) or the writings of the prophets are *read* (ἀναγινώσκεται), so that it is difficult to deduce from this statement a practice of reciting by heart memoirs handed on *orally*. We can see more likelihood in Knox's proposal of written tracts containing accounts of Jesus' ministry, for it seems quite possible that Mark received in written form some of the traditional material in our passage.

We doubt, however, that the tradition in our passage was received by Mark wholly in written form, since in that event, instead of explaining phrases for his Gentile readers at vv. 2 and 11, Mark would surely have substituted the easier words. On the other hand, it is hardly credible that Mark's process of composition should have entirely excluded the written word. For, in order to arrange the traditional material into the correct sequences, and to insert the links and parentheses, it seems mechanically essential that he should first have put into writing the oral units which he had collected.

We also doubt that our passage was received by Mark in a wholly joined form, written or oral, because after the removal of Mark's redaction, the replies of Jesus give the impression of being disconnected from each other. To this it may be replied that the links whose removal demonstrate the previous disconnection have been removed largely on the ground of Marcan language, and may have lain in the tradition in different verbal guise, but we think this unlikely.

The questions of the extent to which the traditions were received by Mark in oral or written form, and the extent to which they were

joined when he received them, are thus fraught with difficulty, and
we can only attempt to summarize the position as follows:

1. We cannot, in view of Gerhardsson's work, deduce from the length
of our passage that Mark must have received its traditions in discrete
form, on the ground that first-century tradents could not have
remembered its entirety.

2. The notice of Mark's editorial work particularly at the seams of
pericopae indicates that Mark was joining pericopae which were
previously discrete.

3. The anacolutha involved in the insertion of the parenthesis at vv. 3
and 4, and in the following of 'you say' in v. 11 by 'you do not allow'
in v. 12, and the explanation rather than substitution of technical
words, may at first glance indicate that Mark was revising oral
traditions rather than written material, since he could probably have
edited writing more smoothly. Yet since he would presumably, as
mentioned above, write down the oral traditions in the course of
composition of the Gospel,[11] Mark would have the opportunity at
that stage to correct the anacolutha and substitute technical words. It
may therefore be that Mark so revered the tradition which he
received, whether it was written or oral, that he was willing to insert
additional words into it by way of parenthesis or explanation, but not
to alter its structure, even though that resulted in anacolutha and the
need for explanations. For we concluded in Chapter 1.f that while
Mark has probably put much of the traditions of our passage into his
own vocabulary, his other redaction is largely the addition of
parenthetical or summarizing sentences.

4. It is very likely that Mark found some of his material in written
form. The reception of both oral and written tradition by the
Evangelists seems to be recognized by Gerhardsson when he writes
of them, 'They worked on a basis of a fixed, distinct tradition from,
and about, Jesus—a tradition which was partly memorized and
partly written down in notebooks and private scrolls . . . '[12]

c. *The contribution of form criticism*
In addition to the above considerations, the discrete nature of our
passage is supported by the results of form criticism. The division of
the synoptic material into small separate units each having a
liturgical, catechetical, evangelistic or polemical function in the early
church has been the achievement of the form critics. Dibelius[13]
traces the pericopae in the Gospels from the earliest form in which

they were handed on by Christians to each other, until they reach the style in which they appear in the Gospels. Dibelius notes that some narrative stories appear so united in the Gospel that they can hardly have originated with Mark in that form,[14] but that Mark, also, interwove stories, is shown by Mark 6.45f. where, after the walking on the water, he harks back at v. 52 to the preceding Feeding story. However, Dibelius believes that the sayings of Jesus were originally independent, and were cast, either by Mark or earlier, into a dialogue so as to form a conversation scene, and he thinks this is especially true of the disputes over being in league with the devil (3.23-30), divorce (10.2-12) and handwashing (our passage).

He argues that our passage is composite by pointing to the lack of direct connection between the various parts of it.[15] The accusation of breaking the fourth commandment by the practice of Korban (vv. 9-13) has nothing at all to do with the question about handwashing, and the saying about true cleanliness (v. 15) relates to eating, he says, and not to washing, and he considers the individuality of these verses is further shown by their special introductions. The two explanations of the purity logion in vv. 17-19 and 20-23 do not suit its radical character, and are church doctrine, because they are given esoterically to the disciples and arise from the interest of the churches in the food question. Nor does the reply in vv. 6-8 that the Pharisees break the command of God and hold the tradition of men, supported by the Isaiah quotation, answer their question about handwashing. He consequently considers that the words of Jesus do not deal at all with the question at v. 5 which has probably been placed in front of the composition by the Evangelist. Conspicuously, Dibelius thinks that the joining of the replies of Jesus may have taken place *before* Mark received them (at least as regards vv. 6-15), starting with the quotation at v. 6.

Bultmann,[16] on the other hand, starts with the tradition in its most developed form, i.e. in the Gospels, and by form-critical analysis and dissection attempts to trace back the tradition to its earliest form. One species of the sayings of Jesus which Bultmann identifies is the apophthegm, by which he means a saying of Jesus set in a brief context where the whole concern of the unit is the pointed declaration or apophthegm of Jesus (which Dibelius terms a paradigm). Bultmann describes how, in the case of speech material, one mashal was joined to another and small groups were formed, but that there was a natural limit in the oral tradition to the size of such groups (presumably imposed by memory). This limit could be exceeded when the tradition came to be written, but, at that stage also, the larger units were formed by the process of adding one small unit to another. He terms this primitive stage 'serializing the dominical sayings without reference to their context'.[17] Thus, in our passage, to the apophthegm about handwashing (vv. 1-8), which leads to the pronouncement of Jesus at v. 8, have been added, on account of their kindred subject-matter, the units about outward observance of the law (vv. 9-13) and inward defilement (vv. 14-23).

The explanations of the form critics as to how Mark's Gospel and, in particular, our passage were assembled seem more natural and realistic than Gerhardsson's theory, partially supported by Knox, of memorized tracts. In our passage five subjects are introduced— handwashing, the Pharisees' religious hypocrisy, their infringement of the law of God by adherence to tradition, defilement by eating and defilement by evil thoughts. We do not believe that such a complicated structure, combining teaching on different, albeit connected, themes would be assembled by the apostolic collegium, as Gerhardsson proposes, or by the churches for the use of evangelists, as Knox suggests: it is difficult for the preacher to memorize, together with much other teaching, if oral, and is too diffuse in content for the recipient to comprehend easily, whether oral or written. We further doubt whether the units in our passage were linked together when Mark received them (apart from the purity logion with the two explanations), as Dibelius proposes, because while we acknowledge that the church influenced the content of the units by the impress of its own needs and issues, we think that those needs caused the units to be preserved, but not necessarily to be linked together.

d. *Units of debate*
Following our acceptance of the composite argument of the form critics, we now set out the tradition shorn of the redaction which we identified in Chapter 1. Our task is now to separate this tradition into the individual pericopae which have been separately used and handed on in the church. First, however, we separate the material not into units of tradition, but into units of debate.

This analysis[18] will assist us in deciding which question(s) and replies formed the original dispute, for it will indicate which of them dialectically correspond as units of debate. This correspondence need not be logical, for argument is not always logically based, and the first-century Jewish concept of consistency in debate may differ from our own, as shown by Stendahl.[19] Yet, there must be some 'intersection', to use Neusner's word, between question and answer, to produce a credible argument.

We will not learn from this analysis whether the original form constitutes an historical dispute between Jesus and the Pharisees, but we can discover which replies *cannot* be historical because there is no correspondence in debate between them and the question(s).

The following units of debate constitute one, or two, questions (dependent on analysis of v. 5), and three replies which are shown to be individual by the independent content of their argument. Dependent upon these basic units are an introductory description of the incident which provokes the debate, a change of scene after the third reply, and the private explanations of the two halves of the third reply.

Introduction (vv. 1, 2 and 5)
Συνάγονται πρὸς αὐτὸν οἱ Φαρισαῖοι καί τινες τῶν γραμματέων ἐλθόντες ἀπὸ Ἱεροσολύμων καὶ ἰδόντες τινὰς τῶν μαθητῶν αὐτοῦ ὅτι κοιναῖς χερσὶν ἐσθίουσιν τοὺς ἄρτους ἐπερωτῶσιν αὐτόν

Question(s) (v. 5)
Διὰ τί οὐ περιπατοῦσιν οἱ μαθηταί σου κατὰ τὴν παράδοσιν τῶν πρεσβυτέρων, ἀλλὰ κοιναῖς χερσὶν ἐσθίουσιν τὸν ἄρτον;

Isaiah Reply (vv. 6 and 7)
ὁ δὲ εἶπεν αὐτοῖς· καλῶς ἐπροφήτευσεν Ἡσαΐας περὶ ὑμῶν τῶν ὑποκριτῶν ὡς γέγραπται ὅτι

οὗτος ὁ λαὸς τοῖς χείλεσιν με τιμᾷ
ἡ δὲ καρδία αὐτῶν πόρρω ἀπέχει ἀπ᾽ ἐμοῦ
μάτην δὲ σέβονταί με
διδάσκοντες ἐντάλματα ἀνθρώπων καὶ διδασκαλίας

Korban Reply (vv. 9-12)
καὶ ἔλεγεν αὐτοῖς· καλῶς ἀθετεῖτε τὴν ἐντολὴν τοῦ θεοῦ ἵνα τὴν παράδοσιν ὑμῶν στήσητε. Μωϋσῆς γὰρ εἶπεν· τίμα τὸν πατέρα σου καὶ τὴν μητέρα σου, καὶ ὁ κακολογῶν πατέρα ἢ μητέρα θανάτῳ τελευτάτω. Ἐὰν δὲ εἴπῃ ἄνθρωπος τῷ πατρὶ ἢ τῇ μητρί· κορβᾶν ὃ ἐὰν ἐξ ἐμοῦ ὠφεληθῇς οὐκέτι ἀφίετε αὐτὸν οὐδὲν ποιῆσαι τῷ πατρὶ ἢ τῇ μητρί.

Purity Reply (vv. 14 and 15)
καὶ ἔλεγεν αὐτοῖς ἀκούσατέ μου πάντες καὶ σύνετε. οὐδέν ἐστιν
ἔξωθεν τοῦ ἀνθρώπου εἰσπορευόμενον εἰς αὐτὸν ὃ δύναται κοινῶσαι
αὐτόν, ἀλλὰ τὰ ἐκ τοῦ ἀνθρώπου ἐκπορευόμενά ἐστιν τὰ κοινοῦντα
τὸν ἄνθρωπον.

Scene-change (v. 17)
Καὶ ὅτε εἰσῆλθεν εἰς οἶκον ἀπὸ τοῦ ὄχλου, ἐπηρώτων αὐτὸν οἱ
μαθηταὶ αὐτοῦ τὴν παραβολήν.

Medical Explanation (vv. 18 and 19)
Καὶ λέγει αὐτοῖς· οὐ νοεῖτε ὅτι πᾶν τὸ ἔξωθεν εἰσπορευόμενον εἰς
τὸν ἄνθρωπον οὐ δύναται αὐτὸν κοινῶσαι ὅτι οὐκ εἰσπορεύεται
αὐτοῦ εἰς τὴν καρδίαν ἀλλ' εἰς τὴν κοιλίαν, καὶ εἰς τὸν ἀφεδρῶνα
ἐκπορεύεται;

Ethical Explanation (vv. 20-22)
Τὸ δὲ ἐκ τοῦ ἀνθρώπου ἐκπορευόμενον, ἐκεῖνο κοινοῖ τὸν ἄνθρωπον.
ἔσωθεν γὰρ ἐκ τῆς καρδίας τῶν ἀνθρώπων οἱ διαλογισμοὶ οἱ κακοὶ
ἐκπορεύονται, πορνεῖαι, κλοπαί, φόνοι, μοιχεῖαι, πλεονεξίαι,
πονηρίαι, δόλος, ἀσέλγεια, ὀφθαλμὸς πονηρός, βλασφημία, ὑπερηφανία, ἀφροσύνη.

We can assume, in determining which units of debate together
formed a separate unit or pericope of tradition, that the question
would be accompanied in the traditional unit by at least one of the
replies. Against this, however, it is argued by Dibelius that Mark,
having received various sayings on the traditional law and purity,
some of which were linked before he received them, transformed
them into a dispute partly by placing the question of v. 5 in front of
them. Our stated view, that vv. 3 and 4 are a parenthesis inserted by
Mark between an *existing* narrative introduction and question, denies
to us this possibility. Since we deny both that the whole of the
question was constructed by Mark, and that a question could survive
in the tradition without a reply attached, our next step must be to
elicit the original form of the Question, and then to identify the Reply
which was linked to that Question.

e. *The Question*
We must first consider whether v. 5 was originally constructed as one

or two questions, for if, in substance as contrasted with form, it contains two questions, they probably comprised, with their respective replies, two separate units of tradition. Construed as one question, the verse asks, 'Why do your disciples eat with unclean hands— which is contrary to the tradition of the elders?' Here the question only relates to the washing of hands, for the reference to the tradition only describes the consequence of the failure to wash. Construed as two questions, the verse asks, 'Why do your disciples (1) not live in accordance with the tradition of the elders, and (2) eat with unclean hands?' Whether there originally lay in the tradition a question relating to the tradition or to handwashing or to both will affect which of the Replies were part of the original dispute, and is, therefore, important. We suggest that whether one or two questions are involved in the verse depends on the value to be given to οὐ . . . ἀλλά. Blass–Debrunner, § 448, classify ἀλλά as an adversative conjunction, and note that it appears most frequently as the contrary to a preceding οὐ. Mark thus uses οὐ . . . ἀλλά in his Gospel to point a contrast.[20] Sometimes it is a parallel contrast in which the second limb reflects in a positive form almost the same statement as the first, negative limb. An example of this is 2.17, 'Those who are well have no need of a doctor, but those who are sick'. The parallel contrast may be more circumlocutory, as in our purity logion. In other cases, the contrast produced by this construction is not parallel because it introduces a different idea, as in 12.25, 'They neither marry nor are given in marriage, but are like angels in heaven'. The contrast is similar at 1.44 (the use of μηδέν here does not affect the adversative element), 'Say nothing to anyone, but go, show yourself to the priest'. The distinction between Mark's two uses of the negative followed by ἀλλά is that in the first use described, the positive limb is just the converse of the negative limb, while in the second use, a fresh statement is made by the second limb. There is not a complete dichotomy between the two uses, however, for even in the first use of the construction the second limb will sometimes not merely reflect the negative limb, but will amplify it, as at 4.17, 'They have no root in themselves, but endure for a while', and at 10.40, 'to sit at my right hand is not mine to grant, but it is for those for whom it has been prepared'.

We believe the use of this construction in the question at v. 5 to be an example of the second use, whereby two statements are made. The second limb, about eating with common hands, does not merely express the converse of the first limb, or simply amplify it, but is an independent statement particularizing the general allegation of infringement of the tradition contained in the first limb.[21]

It is thus possible that two questions were created in separate circumstances, and were brought together to form this dual question in v. 5 by the use of the οὐ . . . ἀλλά construction. We must, therefore, enquire whether the two limbs of this joint question were already joined in the earliest form of the tradition, or whether one or both of them were created by Mark[22] or the early church. Kümmel[23] claims that the Korban dispute was originally handed down as the reply of Jesus to the question about handwashing, which indicates that the question mentioned the tradition, and that both limbs therefore composed the original question. Hübner (p. 146), who also sees the Korban Reply as the original reply of Jesus, notes that the v. 5 concept 'tradition of the elders' is missing in that Reply which refers only to the devalued form, 'your tradition'.[24] The polemic of Jesus in vv. 9-13 is thus completely intelligible only when linked with the whole of the v. 5 question. He argues that the dispute was about the tradition of the elders, and that the Pharisees had referred in their question to that tradition, thus producing the best sense for the Korban Reply interpreted as, 'On what basis, then, do you, who have discredited your tradition by the infringement of the fourth commandment, propose to my disciples this handwashing, and thus the performance of your discredited tradition?' On this argument for the original unity of the two limbs of the question, Jesus is not discussing the validity of handwashing per se, but is claiming that the whole tradition (which includes handwashing) is invalid, because it breaks the commandments of God, as illustrated by the Korban practice of the scribes.

Hübner's reconstruction of the dispute does not persuade us. Since handwashing, although arguably a practice of the tradition, does *not* infringe a commandment of God, it does not ring true that Jesus should have argued against the whole tradition by pointing to an instance (Korban, hardly a fundamental one) wherein the tradition *did* infringe a commandment. Admittedly, we must not assume that only watertight arguments were used by the early church or Jesus, or that Western concepts of dialectic are necessarily applicable, but even allowing for this, the reconstruction seems to lack cohesion as the original debate.

We think it probable that the Question's second limb alone

constituted its earliest form. It seems unlikely that either Mark or the early church should have created a question about handwashing, for it can hardly have been the most conspicuous or contentious example of a legal system which covered comprehensively almost every aspect of Jewish daily life. Handwashing is not specifically referred to again in our passage, so it has not been mentioned in the Question in order to 'link up' conveniently with a Jesus logion. Indeed, the very relation of handwashing to the purity logion and its explanations is not a straightforward matter. We think that Mark, as indicated by his editorial hostility towards the traditional law in vv. 3 and 4, inserted the first limb of the Question to stress that the handwashing deprecated by Jesus in the Purity Reply was imposed by that law. We accordingly consider Mark's evidence as to the dual form of the Question to be outweighed by the opposing evidence, and see its earliest form as: διὰ τί οἱ μαθηταί σου κοιναῖς χερσὶν ἐσθίουσιν τὸν ἄρτον;

f. *The Reply*

Having identified the handwashing limb as probably the earliest form of the Question in the tradition, we now seek to know what was the Reply to it in the earliest stratum of the tradition. Although handwashing was connected with the traditional law, as Mark indicated by adding the first limb of the Question, and although all three Replies attack more or less vehemently the traditional law, a dialectic gap exists between the Question in its restricted form and both the Isaiah Reply and the Korban Reply. For, since we have deleted the first limb which refers to the tradition, there is insufficient correspondence between the truncated Question and either of these Replies for them to be credible. Mark's addition of the reference to the tradition in the first limb was instrumental in welding the three Replies into a unified response which interfaced with the Question; the removal of that reference shows the originally discrete nature of the Replies. In short, it does not 'ring true' to us that Jesus, asked only why his disciples did not wash before eating, should condemn the Pharisees as hypocrites (Isaiah Reply), or condemn the tradition, citing Korban.

However, scholars, while generally agreeing on the composite nature of our passage, have differed substantially over the form of the original dispute. We have already discussed and rejected the views of Kümmel and Hübner that the original reply (to a twofold question) was the Korban Reply. Bultmann[25] and Taylor (p. 334) recognize the original dispute in vv. 1-8. They also acknowledge a twofold question, and Bultmann rejects the purity logion as the original reply because, unlike us, he sees the tradition as the prime concern of the question. But while Bultmann attributes the original dispute in vv. 1-8 to the Palestinian church because no real answer is given to the question in it, Taylor believes the dispute authentic, and that the Isaiah Reply involving the charge, 'You abandon God's commandments, and hold men's precepts', 'comes to grips with the main issue and answers with a decisive "No"'. Perhaps Taylor does not intend his résumé of the argument to be construed too literally for, strictly, the question does not permit the answer 'no'; it seeks a positive reason *why* (in its full form) the disciples break the tradition, and neglect washing.

On substantive grounds, however, we cannot agree that the Isaiah Reply was the original one. First, for the reasons discussed above, we believe that the Question in the earliest tradition consisted only of the handwashing limb, so that the charge of hypocrisy which prefaces and describes the Isaiah quotation has little direct connection with the Question. And with regard to the closing participial phrase of the quotation and v. 8,[26] which alone refer to the commands of men or the tradition, there is the dialectic gap from handwashing mentioned above. Secondly, even if, as assumed by Bultmann and Taylor, the Question contained both limbs, the quotation (especially in its pre-Marcan form) does not correspond very neatly to it, in our view. The preface and the quotation are principally concerned with the hypocrisy of the Pharisees; it is mainly Mark's alteration of the participial clause of the quotation, and v. 8 which we have also attributed to Mark, that interpret the quotation as an attack on the tradition. We think that the Isaiah Reply was a separate unit of polemic alleging hypocrisy, and was used by Christian Jews against the non-Christian Jews in the synagogue.[27] Mark added v. 8 when embodying it in his Gospel, for (in addition to the reasons discussed in Chapter 1.e) the quotation does not refer to 'the command of God', and the claim that handwashing infringes such a command is extravagant. Thirdly, the changing of the position of διδασκαλίας in the quotation, which we have attributed to Mark (but acknowledge it might have been the work of the early church), indicates the employment of implicit midrash which, while it could have been the work of Jesus, is more likely to stem from Mark or the early church, straining to see authority for their polemic in the fulfilment of OT prophecy. Certainly, Paul used OT texts which he applied to the current situation by verbal alteration.[28]

Positing, as we do, the original form of the Question to be the handwashing limb, we see the *Purity Reply* as the original reply in the tradition. The first limb of that Reply, i.e. that there is nothing outside a man going into him which can defile him, is a direct reply to the Question enquiring why the disciples eat food with common hands. For food enters man from outside when he eats it, and it was at least arguable[29] that cultic impurity passed to a man who ate food suffering from a sufficient degree of impurity. To neglect to wash hands might cause them to defile cultically the food. Thus, question and answer logically interface, and Mark's evidence of the tripartite Reply of Jesus is outweighed by the opposing dialectic evidence.

We must, however, consider what was the original form of the first limb of the Purity Reply in case the correspondence of the Question and this Reply has only been achieved by subsequent adaptation in the tradition (or by Mark) of a less convenient form of purity logion. It has been suggested[30] that this first limb might originally have expressed a wider application, unrestricted by the words εἰσπορευό-μενον εἰς αὐτόν which confine its ambit to the consumption of food and drink. Certainly, the early Gentile church possessed motive to give the logion a pointed application to food, for the application of the dietary laws to Gentiles was a serious and early cause of dissension with Jewish Christians.

Paschen (pp. 173f.) looks for the earliest form of the purity logion by identifying expressions which may be literal translation of Aramaic into Greek. He notes that this process may only reveal the Aramaic of an early tradent, but it must surely be a step nearer the mens ipsissima, even though both the Aramaic and its re-translation into Greek must, as Lambrecht stresses, be highly speculative. After this exercise, Paschen (p. 177) proposes the following as the original Greek form of the logion:

πᾶν τὸ ἔξωθεν τοῦ ἀνθρώπου οὐ δύναται κοινῶσαι αὐτὸν ἀλλὰ τὰ ἐκ τοῦ ἀνθρώπου ἐστὶν τὰ κοινοῦντα τὸν ἄνθρωπον.

He thus sees v. 18b as closer to the original form of the first limb of the logion. Hübner (pp. 166-67) agrees, and, unlike Paschen, sees v. 20b as closer to the original second limb, due to its Semitic casus pendens. We doubt, however, whether Mark, on finding Paschen's form of the first limb in the tradition, would have altered the πᾶν . . . ου construction to οὐδέν; in view of his redactional πάντα τὰ βρώματα in v. 19c, he would have favoured the exclusive πᾶν equally with οὐδέν.

Although we concluded earlier that εἰσπορευόμενον εἰς αὐτόν in the first limb of the logion, or some synonym, was contained in the tradition received by Mark, we are inclined to agree with Paschen that neither those words nor a synonym were contained in the earliest form of the tradition. We confirm, however, our previous disagreement with Paschen that those words can be removed without loss of meaning: we believe that they or a synonym were inserted by a Gentile Christian to emphasize the point that things going into a man, i.e. food, cannot defile him.

The identification of redaction in the course of transmission of this limb is assisted by the unconventional use here of ἔξωθεν. The Gentile Christian who inserted εἰσπορευόμενον εἰς αὐτόν into the first limb, has also, we believe, altered the static ἔξω (outside) into the mobile ἔξωθεν (from outside). Bauer, *s.v.* ἔξωθεν, terms its use as a preposition with the genitive 'improper', and in the sense of 'from outside' cites only its use here in the NT. The insertion of εἰσπορευό-μενον εἰς αὐτόν by the redactor has probably suggested to him a corresponding change of ἔξω to ἔξωθεν in order to convey 'nothing *from outside* a man going into him'. That -θεν was not present before εἰσπορευόμενον εἰς αὐτόν was inserted, is suggested by Bauer's further note that in the static sense of 'outside' (like ἔξω), ἔξωθεν in the NT is only found at Rev. 14.20 and 11.2a, when employed as an improper preposition. The rarity of the use of ἔξωθεν as a preposition in either sense strengthens the impression that the tradition has here been amended.[31] We consider Mark's evidence of the form of the first limb of the Purity Reply to be outweighed by the opposing evidence of the Gentile Christian polemic and of the syntax. We accordingly see the first limb of the Purity Reply as: οὐδέν ἐστιν ἔξω τοῦ ἀνθρώπου ὃ δύναται κοινῶσαι αὐτόν.

However, the first limb of the reply in this unqualified form still constitutes a credible reply to the Question since the food which the Pharisees fear is defiled by common hands is undoubtedly 'outside a man'; the limb just loses its pointedness as polemic against the dietary laws in particular.

g. *The extent of the Reply*
Did the original Reply include the second limb of the purity logion?

It can be argued that as the first limb is negative in content, it requires a positive reason (which the second limb affords) to make it a satisfactory refutation. Admittedly, the fact that things going out from a man defile him does not logically entail that impure things going into him, like defiled food, do not defile him, but this is perhaps too strictly analytic a criticism to place against the credibility of argument used in the cut and thrust of debate.

Support for the inclusion of the second limb in the original Purity Reply may lie in the likelihood of Jesus intending a relative, rather than an absolute, denial of the defiling power of external things; for if Jesus only meant that things outside a man do not defile him *as much as things inside him*, then the logion must have contained both limbs in order to make the comparison. But support for the second limb from this quarter is impeded by the difficulty of showing whether the syntax indicates a relative denial in this sense, or an absolute denial that external things defile. Neirynck[32] mentions that the οὐ . . . ἀλλά[33] antitheses at Mark 9.37 and 13.11b have been suggested by Schürmann[34] to possess a relative meaning following the Semitic dialectic negation. Kruse[35] wrote regarding this idiom that the significance of the relativity of the denial must be given expression through 'not so much as', or through an 'equally' or 'rather' in the positive limb. But Winer[36] had recognized this relative meaning of οὐ . . . ἀλλά more than 100 years previously, and had stressed that only careful consideration of the context could determine whether an unconditional denial was intended or whether, for rhetorical reason, an intended relative denial has been expressed as an unconditional denial not in order to cancel the first statement, but to direct all attention upon the second. He pointed out that in every place where, according to the logical sense, οὐ . . . ἀλλά means 'not so much . . . as', it involves a rhetorical colouring which must be retained in the translation.

The relative sense of οὐ . . . ἀλλά is also attested by Blass-Debrunner, § 448, which also cites 9.37 as an example, yet the recognition of the relative usage is a highly subjective matter. For we would have expected the sentence at 9.37, 'And whoever receives me, receives not me but him who sent me', to have been generally acknowledged as a relative use of the construction, since Jesus admits that he is received, before the antithesis with God is expressed; surely the sense is 'he receives not so much me as (God)'. Yet, while Schürmann[37] and Blass-Debrunner, § 448i, support the relative sense, Neirynck and others[38] support the absolute. And when we note that Lagrange[39] interprets that sentence in the most relative sense of 'not only . . . but also', the wide variation of meaning which οὐ . . . ἀλλά may express is plain.

Westerholm[40] inclines to interpret the purity logion in a relative sense on the ground that it may reflect this semitic idiom of negation, and Rawlinson[41] expresses no doubt that it is to be interpreted in this way. But in view of the subjectivity which must attend a choice of the relative or absolute sense of the οὐ . . . ἀλλά construction, we hesitate to rely on the semitic idiom entirely, and on Winer's advice look to the context for support. The importance of the choice of meaning to be given to this construction cannot be over-stated, for upon it may depend whether Jesus is considered to abrogate, or merely depreciate the cultic law of Israel.

The contextual evidence of the correct meaning lies mainly, in our view, in the unlikelihood of Jesus making an unqualified abrogation of the cultic law in response to a question about handwashing, which appears a minor feature of purity law in comparison with the Levitical methods of purification and the more serious defilements which they would remove. It may be argued that the Pharisees asked about handwashing because it was characteristic of Jewish purity practices; Mark's reference at v. 3 to 'all the Jews' washing before eating, and the story at Numbers R. XX.21 of the Jewish shopkeeper, who recognized Jewish customers by their handwashing, might be cited in support of this argument. We oppose such a view of handwashing, however, on the grounds that Mark's verse is greatly exaggerating the extent of the practice, and that the Rabbah story belongs to a later period.[42]

We are also supported in a relative understanding of the οὐ . . . ἀλλά construction here by the evidence of Jesus' upbringing and behaviour within the law, which we set out at section C.e. below.

A further supportive point is Neirynck's suggestion[43] that the οὐ . . . ἀλλά construction is so suited to Mark's proclivity to progressive double phrases that he may have often by this device 'reinforced the antithetical character of the sayings of Jesus'. This may apply to our logion, for we have already noted other Marcan vocabulary in it. If so, the logion had a more relative and less absolute tendency before the insertion of this construction.

We are strengthened by the above considerations in our preference for the relative understanding of the construction, and accordingly interpret the Purity Reply as meaning that things outside a man do not defile him *as much as* things coming from him. The second limb of the logion is therefore necessary to complete the comparison.

Regarding the detailed wording of the second limb, we find Paschen's rejection of ἐκπορευόμενα difficult to accept. For the omission produces a rather unsatisfactory ellipsis in that the need is felt for some participle of motion after τὰ ἐκ τοῦ ἀνθρώπου both for the sake of style and to avoid ambiguity. The only use noted by Bauer, *s.v.* ἐκ, of τό followed by ἐκ and the genitive noun without a participial verb, where ἐκ is used in the sense of 'the source from which something flows', is τὰ ἐκ τοῦ ἱεροῦ at 1 Cor. 9.13. And there the nuance of the use sounds almost possessory, 'those who work with holy things, eat the things from (of) the holy place'. We consequently think that ἐκπορευόμενα, or another appropriate participial verb of motion, is required in this limb, and we preserve it.

Mark's evidence that there was in the tradition available to him a second limb, and his statement of its form, is thus supported by the syntactical and contextual evidence.

Regarding the Medical Explanation and the Ethical Explanation, we think that these may be later teaching tacked by the early church onto the Purity Reply, and we therefore doubt that they formed part of that Reply. We previously preserved the introductory Scene-change on the grounds that the tradition probably contained a theme of private teaching, and that such teaching was an intrinsic likelihood. If, however, we credit to the early church the teaching there given, then ipso facto we must treat the Scene-change as a creation of the early church also. We must accordingly study the origin of these Explanations.

Regarding the interrogative introduction, καὶ λέγει αὐτοῖς· οὐ νοεῖτε, to the Medical Explanation, it is hard to assess whether in the earliest tradition this Explanation was linked (apart from the Scene-change) to the logion by this introduction, or whether it started after ὅτι with a γάρ, or other conjunction, after πᾶν. For whether the Explanation derived from the early church or from Jesus, some form of connection with the logion was necessary, assuming, as we have done, that the logion was the original Reply, and was not extrapolated from the two Explanations by Mark. We think that this introduction also must stand or fall as part of the earliest tradition according to whether the Medical Explanation forms part of the Purity Reply.

Similarly, the repetition of the first limb of the logion, starting with πᾶν, seems an integral part of the Explanation, and must stand or fall with it. For since the medical explanation of why things outside *do not* defile follows the second limb assertion in the logion that it is things from inside which *do* defile, it was necessary that the denial in the first limb of the logion be repeated in some form, before the explanation of it (even if the Scene-change did not intervene).

The Medical Explanation is that things entering man cannot defile him because they enter not his heart but his stomach, and are then evacuated. Berger (pp. 470f.) claims that the whole theme of our passage comes from a Jewish-Hellenistic source which, contrary to the Jewish circles emphasizing food prohibitions and cultic purity concepts, proclaimed the God-willed nature of the order of creation, and the catchword, 'everything is pure'. He thus sees this Explanation which is based upon the natural process of the bowels, as springing from popular medical 'wisdom' knowledge, and as constituting an argument founded on the order of Nature. He describes this mode of thought as a basic Judaism influenced by Gnosticism. This diagnosis is supported by the recognition that the view of the heart (which the Explanation contrasts with the stomach) as the seat of thought and emotion is an essentially Jewish view. The kernel of the Explanation, however, requires neither Gnostic nor Jewish influence: a Gentile mind unaffected by Jewish purity concepts but possessed of popular medical knowledge, could well have observed that if hygienically dirty hands make food dirty, and the food then enters the body, no harm may be done, because the dirt will be excreted. We agree, though, that such an argument could not proceed from a Jewish Christian church conformant with orthodox thinking on purity, for man if *cultically* defiled cannot evacuate the impurity through the bowels. The most likely cultic purification for a man defiled by food eaten would be immersion in a miqveh followed by waiting until sunset (cf. Lev. 17.15). Thus, whatever the attitude of Jesus may have been towards the Jewish purity law, he is, in our opinion, unlikely to have grounded a denial of it upon an argument taken from a totally different conceptual world. For the same reason, we think that this argument would be alien to the Palestinian Jew, and could only have originated amongst Gentiles, or Jews who had been exposed to the thought-forms of Hellenism. Despite possible Jewish influence in the contrast with 'the heart', we credit this explanation to a member of the Hellenistic Gentile church, and exclude it from the earliest tradition, and from the Purity Reply.

We think that the Ethical Explanation also stems from the Hellenistic Gentile church. Certainly, the two Explanations must have the same provenance, both for structural and conceptual reasons. For the Explanations are complementary: the Medical explains the first limb of the Purity Reply, while the Ethical explains the second limb. Both limbs of the Reply were difficult to understand, since the Medical Explanation probably mistook the reason why things outside a man do not defile, and the Ethical Explanation possibly (as we investigate in Chapter 5) mistook the reason why things leaving man do defile him. We believe the function of the Explanations in the life of the church to have been partly catechetical, and that it would be unlikely for a teacher to explain incorrectly one limb of a saying, and then to consider that the almost equally elliptical content of the other limb did not need clarification. For an Hellenistic student applying the biological thinking in the Medical Explanation to an unexplained second limb might conclude that the defiling things which leave a man were excreta and urine. The conceptual reason for the unity of the two Explanations lies in the continuation in the Ethical Explanation of 'the heart' theme (from v. 19a) as the source from which evil things emanate.

As indicated previously, scholars differ over whether the list of vices in this Explanation originated in a Palestinian Decalogue-based list or in a Greek domestic list of sins. Our treating of the two Explanations as a unity leads us to regard the list also as having an origin in Gentile thought.[44] And, considering the content of the list, we think that such a juxtaposition of merely social sins with offences against the Decalogue would not have been tolerated in Palestinian Judaism. Indeed, Matthew's revision of the list towards a more Decalogue-like form perhaps indicates Jewish dissatisfaction at this confusion. An Hellenistic origin is supported by Taylor's analytical table of the vocabulary, which shows it to be predominantly Pauline (p. 346).

We therefore consider Mark's evidence that Jesus gave the Explanations to be outweighed by the evidence of the error in the Medical Explanation and its inconsistency with Jewish thought.

We thus remove the Explanations from the earliest tradition of the Purity Dispute and, with them, the dependent Scene-change.

h. *The Introduction*

Bultmann[45] stresses the tendency in the Gospels to present the opponents of Jesus as scribes and Pharisees. But even he would not exclude scribes and Pharisees from all controversy dialogues, and they are very likely opponents to Jesus in the original Dispute which we have determined above to concern purity. We believe that an introduction of this nature lay in the earliest tradition, for when the story of the Dispute was passed on for the first time, some formula, elaborate as here, or brief, would indicate the questioners and their addressee. Similarly, we preserve the link and call to hear in v. 14, as explained at Chapter 1.e.

i. *Conclusion regarding earliest form of the Dispute*
We thus conclude that the form of the Dispute in the earliest tradition comprised the Introduction and the following forms of the Question and Purity Reply:

Διὰ τί οἱ μαθηταί σου κοιναῖς χερσὶν ἐσθίουσιν τὸν ἄρτον; καὶ ἔλεγεν αὐτοῖς· ἀκούσατέ μου πάντες καὶ σύνετε. οὐδέν ἐστιν ἔξω τοῦ ἀνθρώπου ὃ δύναται κοινῶσαι αὐτόν, ἀλλὰ τὰ ἐκ τοῦ ἀνθρώπου ἐκπορευόμενά ἐστιν τὰ κοινοῦντα τὸν ἄνθρωπον.

j. *Other independent units*
We believe that the Explanations could not have survived as an independent pericope apart from the purity logion. Admittedly, the two limbs of the logion are repeated before their respective Explanations, but the Jesus logion would be an essential preliminary in the tradition to give the teaching in the Explanations point and immediacy. Whether the logion travelled separately at the earliest stage, as Bultmann[46] and others think, or whether it travelled as the Purity Reply in the Dispute, as we have concluded, the Explanations, when created, were dependent on that logion and, in our opinion, would have withered without it.

In contrast, the Isaiah Reply and the Korban Reply were, in our view, each used as separate units in the polemic of the early church. The earliest form of these units was probably similar to that set out in section d above, after the removal of Marcan redaction, except that the introductions would specify that Jesus was speaking to the scribes and Pharisees, and would not include the linking conjunctions δέ (v. 6) and καί (v. 9).

k. *Excursus. Bultmann and the Sitz im Leben of the Dispute*
At this juncture, we are halted in our tracks by Bultmann,[47] who

claims that to seek first the original dispute is an incorrect method: we should start by asking in what historical setting the controversy dialogues have their proper place. By this, Bultmann apparently intends an enquiry as to who used these stories, and for what purpose. He answers that the Palestinian church used the stories in its apologetic and polemic with its opponents (presumably Pharisaic)[48] over questions of law, and in similar debates within its own body. He states that in the Gospel form the controversy dialogues are imaginary scenes illustrating by an actual incident a principle which the church ascribed to Jesus. Bultmann then uses the form of the controversy dialogues to show why they constitute imaginary scenes created by the early church.

He points out that the dialogues start with some action or attitude of Jesus or the disciples, which is seized upon by the opponents for attack by accusation or question. The reply of Jesus is more or less standardized, often being a counter-question or metaphor, although sometimes, as in vv. 6-7 of our passage, a scriptural quotation. Since Bultmann avers that to carry on disputes in this way is typically rabbinic, he concludes that the Palestinian church, having argued with the Rabbis of its own day according to this form, has cast fictitious arguments of Jesus with the Pharisees into a similar form. Therefore, Bultmann would conclude, it is in vain that we enquire concerning the original question and answer in our passage, since the question and answers were created by the church to express dramatically a principle believed to stem from Jesus.

We are dissatisfied with this hypothesis of Bultmann for two reasons, the first challenging its basic premise, and the second assuming the premise but denying the validity of the parallel.

First, we believe that the first question to be asked of the material is a redactional one, seeking to remove the accretions of Mark and early Christians during the development of the tradition. We do not find it a logical or persuasive progression to argue that, because a literary form contemporaneous with the early church is similar to the form in which Gospel disputes appear, the Gospel cannot contain in substance the original question put to Jesus or his original reply. Yet this seems to be Bultmann's thesis in his section (pp. 39f.) on Controversy Dialogues. He makes occasional statements, however, which soften this radical view. Thus, although he writes (p. 51), 'It is quite impossible any longer to suppose that Jesus used to engage in harmless debates', yet at p. 40 he admits it to be 'very probable' that

Jesus sometimes healed on the Sabbath, and used a particular expression in a Controversy Dialogue. And after referring to the use by the church of proof-texts in its debates, he acknowledges (p. 49) that this use does not exclude the possibility that occasionally there was historical truth in the claim that the text was employed by Jesus. But, he stresses, it is no longer possible to establish that.

But is the difficulty of proof that it was the early church which created a debate attributed in the Gospels to Jesus and the Pharisees, any less than the difficulty of proof that the Gospel record of that debate is, in substance and after redactional surgery, authentic? We grant without reservation the conjectural and subjective nature of an attempt to penetrate back to the original debate, but is it less conjectural or more objective to attribute dialogue to the church, against the overt Gospel evidence, on the ground that its style resembles the Rabbis' debate-form? We thus demur at Bultmann's basic premise of method.[49]

For the purpose of our second reason, we will assume the validity of Bultmann's claim that to find the origin of the Gospel material we must first look at the use made of it in church history. Bultmann claims that the Gospel disputes resemble the rabbinic disputes because both start with an accusation or question arising from some act or attitude. But there is surely nothing significant in this similarity. An action or attitude of one party must be one of the more common provocations of discussion, and the commencement of the discussion by accusation or question can hardly be so rare a feature as to constitute an identifying characteristic.

Bultmann's next point of similarity is that in both kinds of dispute the reply is a counter-question, often in the form of a metaphor. But, in our view, the variety in the kinds of reply employed by both Gospel and Rabbis is too wide to permit a meaningful comparison to be drawn. Bultmann (p. 41) refers to a more or less set form of reply in the Gospels with special preference for the counter-question, metaphor or, sometimes, scriptural quotation. So he admits three different kinds of reply. And if it be said, with Bultmann, that they all have a common hallmark, in that they reduce the question to absurdity, this must be denied: at Mark 10.3 the counter-question of Jesus elicits a factual reply from scripture which Jesus opposes by another argument from scripture. Again, at 8.12, the reply to the Pharisees seeking a sign is a question asking the reason for their request, followed by a simple denial of it.

There is still more variety in the rabbinic debates. Muddiman[50] who, against Dibelius,[51] Albertz[52] and Hultgren,[53] considers the parallelism with rabbinic debates to be obvious, stresses, against Bultmann, that the rabbinic form has an extended structure beyond the first reply of Jesus; the counter-question, instead of terminating the discussion, is used as a means to continue it. Daube[54] describes a common rabbinic sequence as: 1 Hostile question by outsider, 2a Counter-question, by his answer to which the opponent becomes vulnerable, and 2b Triumphant conclusion from the opponent's answer. There are examples of this sequence in the Marcan debates at 3.1-5, 11.27-33, and 12.14-17, but they do not seem sufficiently numerous or stereotyped to establish influence from the rabbinic form.

The ten examples which Bultmann cites (pp. 42f.) as his rabbinic parallels in his main text are mainly Talmudic or Midrashic *baraithoth*. But it is doubtful whether the forms of debate to be found in the Talmud correctly record the style of debate actually in use before 70 AD. In the case of the Mishnaic traditions, Neusner[55] has argued convincingly that the debate forms which appear in the Mishnah were standardized by Rabbi Judah the Prince in the final compilation of it in about 200 AD. Similarly, the forms of the Talmudic and Midrashic *baraithoth* may not represent the forms which the discussions historically took, and may thus be an unrealistic comparison with the Gospel debates.

Further, the forms of debate in the Talmud are more multifarious than Bultmann indicates. The recorded disputes, for example, between Hillel and Shammai and their respective Houses contain many forms beyond the question and counter-question style.[56] And regarding the Gospel disputes, Bultmann admits (p. 47) that he has not prescribed a recipe for dealing with them all, for each one requires special treatment. This individual nature of the Gospel dialogues militates against the validity of rabbinic parallelism. Again, Muddiman claims that the Gospel dispute is particularly close to the rabbinic form 'when allowance is made for the variety that is a feature of both'.[57] But this very qualification undermines the parallelism.

If we apply Bultmann's thesis to our passage, it would presumably produce the argument that because (1) the question at v. 5 stems from the disciples' neglect to wash their hands, and (2) the reply at vv. 6-8 contains a scriptural quotation, and (3) both a question arising from an incident, and the quotation of scripture are features of rabbinic debates, *therefore* vv. 1-8 are an unitary creation of the early Palestinian church. But can we safely admit an influence of one literary form upon another on the basis that two religious groups, the authority for whose faith lay in the same scriptures, were each asked hostile questions arising from an incident, and sometimes referred to those Scriptures in reply?

From the methodological viewpoint, we therefore resist Bultmann's claim that we should not seek first the original dialogue, and we are unable to accept a creation of vv. 1-8 of our passage by the early church under the influence of rabbinic parallels.

B. *History of the original units of tradition*

a. *Introduction*

In Section A we identified, and determined the earliest form of, the three independent units or pericopae of tradition in our passage. We will now consider more closely the history and provenance of those units.

Since this will involve examination of the possible use of the units in a particular church, be it the early Palestinian (i.e. Jewish Christian), or Hellenistic Jewish (i.e. Jewish Christian in the Diaspora), or Gentile, we must first hearken to the caveat of Catchpole.[58] For he has warned of the difficulty of establishing criteria by which traditions may be attributed to one of these sources or to Jesus. He emphasizes the very fluid state of early Christianity in all quarters. Certainly, even Palestinian Judaism cannot be treated as 'pure' Judaism, unaffected by Hellenistic thought and culture. Following the conquests of Alexander, Hellenism had infiltrated Palestine. 1 Macc. 1.15 and 2 Macc. 4.12-15 relate the establishment of a gymnasium in Jerusalem in the time of Antiochus Epiphanes, and even the abandonment by the priests of the Temple sacrifices in order to participate in the games. Acts 6.9 mentions Hellenistic synagogue(s)[59] in Jerusalem, and the propinquity of the Greek cities of the Decapolis and of the trade route from Egypt to the north are evidences of a continuing Hellenistic influence. Catchpole mentions the wide adoption into Hebrew and Aramaic of non-Semitic loanwords.

Catchpole[60] also draws our attention to the distinctions within communities. At 1 Cor. 1 Paul complains at the party animosity and asks, 'Is Christ divided?', and both his letters to the Corinthians contain a large measure of justification of his own teaching in contrast to that of other missionaries. He repeatedly battles with 'the Judaizers', and, writing to the Galatians, he argues with those who desire to be 'under the law'. In his correspondent communities, however, it is clear that, apart from those who had been 'bewitched' by Jerusalem missionaries, there were many who had been won from the law by Paul's preaching. But Paul's polemic shows that in Hellenistic Judaism there were many Jewish Christians who clung to an orthodox attitude towards the law, in addition to the more liberated members.

Indeed, Weeden[61] maintains that it was a radical divergence of view within Mark's own community which provoked the writing of his Gospel. He sees Mark's community as, forty years after Easter, troubled by the delay of the parousia. Mark counters this by formulating the function of the church to be to suffer, and so follow the ideal of Jesus as the Suffering Servant. The Messiah suffered on the cross, and his followers must take up their cross until the return of Jesus in glory. But 'interlopers' arrive with a θεῖος ἀνήρ Christology, proclaiming Jesus as a miracle worker who imparted secret teaching about God and himself. Following this model, they claim that genuine faith is shown by miracle-working ability, and by pneumatic experience of the risen Lord. To demonstrate the position of these enemies as heresy, Mark dramatizes the Christological debate in an 'historical' drama in which Jesus, pro Mark, preaches and acts the suffering-servant theology, while the disciples, pro Mark's opponents, articulate and act the θεῖος ἀνήρ theology. Thus here, according to Weeden, we see in a single community vital distinctions concerning the nature of the faith.

These illustrations serve to underline the diffidence which must accompany attempts to assign the creation, or the amendment, of tradition to a particular branch of the early church. In view of the difficulties, it is not surprising that critics have differed widely in the allocation of our passage to authors. Thus, while Weeden sees the whole Gospel as a unitary composition, Crum and Hirsch see successive authors at work. Crum[62] posits Mark I and Mark II. The first Mark is less theological, and tells a simple story of Jesus. He is one of the first Jewish Christians, and Crum thinks he may have been the young man at 14.51, and Peter's friend. Mark II, who works over the first writing, belongs to a later church of Hellenistic Jews in Rome, writes in LXX Greek, and makes use of a document closely related to 'Q'. Crum briefly allocates the whole of our passage to this second Mark who, however, amplified early tradition.

Hirsch[63] also identified a Mark I who had contact with Peter, represented the Palestinian Jewish church, and wrote his stratum in the first year after Jesus' death. But his Mark II, although thinking in LXX Greek, and writing at Rome in the seventh decade, is a Gentile Christian. He further posits a third hand, a redactor living also in Rome who, shortly after 70 AD joined together the two Marks. Of our passage, Hirsch ascribes v. 1 from τινες, v. 2, vv. 9-13a, the singular vices in v. 22, and vv. 14, 15, 21a and 23 to Mark I, which attributes to the historical controversy far more material than most critics would allow.

We agree, however, with the division of the material by Crum and Hirsch into at least two layers, but our reasons lie, as noted above, mainly in the dual-pronged nature of the v. 5 question, and the diverse nature of the argumentation.

Bearing in mind, therefore, the diversity of thought within early Christian communities, we will attempt to trace the history of the three independent units of tradition.

b. *The history of disputes over purity and law*
In order to assign each of our units to Jesus or to a section, or particular viewpoint, within the early church, it is necessary to propose a tentative outline of the history of disputes about purity and law. We admittedly derive our evidence concerning this history from NT passages to which we have not space to apply traditio-historical criticism. While the passages, particularly in the Acts of the Apostles, may thus be challenged for historicity, we believe that they are representative of trends of polemic in the early church, and we think of Peter's vision, the Council of Jerusalem, and the Apostolic Decree, as examples in this regard. A history of this polemic, however brief and tentative, must be attempted, since the cause of the creation and preservation of these units is probably to be found within it.

For convenient reference, we set out the history in stages, although the historical process is gradual, and the polemical trends would fluctuate in intensity.

1. Purity obstacles to Jesus' ministry. c. AD 27-30
Pharisees, probably *haberim*, object to Jesus eating and drinking with tax-collectors and *'am-ha'ares*, presumably on the grounds (inter alia) that he may eat untithed food, and may incur impurity from

them or their garments. Since his hosts were Palestinian Jews, Jesus would not be offered prohibited or non-kosher food. The criticism of his ministry by the Pharisaic *haberim* on the above grounds at Mark 2.15-17 may explain Jesus' logion at 7.15 and his justification there of the the neglect of a purity practice.

2. Justification of Jesus as Messiah. From AD 30
After Jesus' death, the Palestinian Jewish Christians, and perhaps the Hellenists at Jerusalem in particular, argue with the Jews in the synagogue that Jesus was not recognized by them as Messiah because of the hardness of their heart, and their apostasy from God. For this purpose, they use texts such as Isa. 6.9f. and the quotation in our Isaiah unit. Thus, Stephen in Acts 7 describes how the Jews rejected Moses (vv. 27, 39), the prophets and the Just One, of whom they have now been the betrayers and murderers (v. 52). At vv. 44-50 Stephen attacks the Temple, as not ordained by God, and at v. 53, the failure of the Jews to keep the law (presumably the written law since it is εἰς διαταγὰς ἀγγέλων). Since the Korban unit involves an alleged misuse of a Temple-vow and denial of the fourth Commandment, it is possible that this unit originated among, or was preserved by, Hellenistic Jews of Stephen's persuasion.

3. Justification of Mission to Gentiles. From c. AD 33
Although the disciples who were dispersed after the death of Stephen into Judea and Samaria (Acts 8.1) probably preached originally only to the Jews of the synagogue (Acts 11.19), disciples from Cyprus and Cyrene convert Gentiles at Antioch (Acts 11.20). These Hellenistic Jewish missionaries then come into conflict with the Jewish Christians at Jerusalem concerning whether the gospel should be preached to the Gentiles. The Jewish Christians there oppose the mission because of the likelihood of the missionaries being given non-kosher food and food sacrificed to idols (Gal. 2.12, 14; cf. Acts 15.20, 29; 1 Cor. 8). But they also object on the ground that Jews should not associate with Gentiles (Acts 10.28a; John 18.28) since they are ritually unclean according to the tradition. Thus, Peter's interpretation of his vision, according to Luke, is that although it is unlawful for a Jew to associate with a Gentile, God has thereby shown him that he must not call any *man* unclean (Acts 10.28b).

The Hellenistic Jews, in response to this argument based on Gentile uncleanness, may have used the Isaianic unit for a second and different purpose, i.e. not to show that the Jews' rejection of Jesus is another example of their apostasy from God, but to prove that the Jewish Christians at Jerusalem by their adherence to the traditional teaching (ἐντάλματα ἀνθρώπων) about uncleanness, contravene the will of God. These Hellenistic Jews had good cause to preserve the Korban unit also, for the sake of its attack upon this tradition.

4. Application of the Law to Gentiles. From c. AD 44

When the evangelization of Gentiles abounds, notwithstanding the opposition to it, Pharisaic Christians (Acts 15.5) claim that the converts should be circumcised and observe the Mosaic law. As Paul points out at Gal. 5.3, circumcision involves a man in keeping the whole law (ὅλον τὸν νόμον), and almost certainly that term is intended to include the unwritten law.[64] Paul and his supporters deny the need for circumcision of Gentile converts, arguing (inter alia) that each man should lead the life which God has assigned to him (1 Cor. 7.17). Thus, Gentiles could eat prohibited diet, or non-kosher diet or cultically contaminated diet (1 Cor. 10.23-25; Rom. 14.1-3, 14). At Antioch, Peter apparently adopted this view, and ate non-kosher food with Gentiles until emissaries arrived from James (Gal. 2.12, 14).

The relationship between this dispute and the Council of Jerusalem reported at Acts 15.6f., the Apostolic Decree reported at Acts 15.20 and 29 and Acts 21.25, the meeting of Paul with James, Peter and John at Gal. 2.1f. and the above dispute with Peter, is difficult to gauge exactly, but, with Haenchen,[65] Dibelius[66] and Goulder,[67] we think that Luke's 'history' in Acts has been greatly influenced by his theological motifs, and we prefer Paul's first-hand evidence in Gal. 2, where it conflicts with Acts (although we think that Paul went to Jerusalem by summons rather than 'revelation', Gal. 2.1). However, we agree with Dibelius[68] that Luke did have documentary evidence of a Decree, since the more faithful textual evidence of the Decree emphasizes its Levitical contents, which Luke would probably not have done unless faced with unambiguous evidence. We are also attracted by Catchpole's suggestion[69] that the men who came to Antioch from James (Gal. 2.12) brought the Decree, since it requires abstention from blood and strangled things, i.e. non-kosher food which Peter was presumably eating.

Whatever be the exact sequence of these events, it seems fairly clear that, probably from the date of his preaching at Antioch (Acts 11.25f.) shortly before the famine (11.28) in c. AD 45, Paul had preached that the Gentiles were not required to become Jews, i.e. be circumcised, in order to become Christians. At some stage (perhaps about AD 49 if we adopt Gal. 2.1, and accept that the Decree was brought by James's men at 2.12) the Apostles at Jerusalem attempted to compromise between Paul's views and those of the Pharisaic Christians by a Decree, which did not require the Gentile converts to be circumcised, but, regarding ritual obligation, required them to abstain from non-kosher food.[70]

This attempt at compromise was not accepted by the 'Judaizers', however, who continued their missions urging the Gentile converts to be circumcised and accept the whole law. That the 'Judaizers' tried to force the whole law onto the Gentiles is shown by Col. 2.8, 11, 13 and particularly vv. 20-21 where Paul, or one of his persuasion, writes, τί ὡς ζῶντες ἐν κόσμῳ δογματίζεσθε; μὴ ἅψῃ μηδὲ γεύσῃ μηδὲ θίγῃς . . . .[71] The battle between Paul's followers and the 'circumcision party' was still being fought at the time of the letter to Titus,[72] as we see from the reference to that party at 1.10 and from the condemnation of Ἰουδαϊκοῖς μύθοις καὶ ἐντολαῖς ἀνθρώπων, which latter is clearly intending the tradition at 1.14.

We see the two Explanations of the purity logion as created by Gentile Christians of Paul's persuasion, believing that they were not bound by the law; similarly, we see Mark's editorial accentuation of the attack on the traditional law, particularly on purity, as aiding this Pauline battle.

Having sketched these four historical stages, we will now study the history of the three Units in more detail.

c. *The Dispute Unit*

We believe that this Unit formed part of the earliest stratum of tradition, and was preserved by Hellenistic Jews at Jerusalem of the same liberated attitude towards the law and the Temple (and thus, cultic purity) as Stephen (Stage 2 above). It was later used by those Jews, in defence of the mission to the Gentiles, against the Pharisaic Christians who opposed it on the ground that Jewish evangelists would be cultically defiled by the uncleanness of the Gentiles (Stage 3 above). This Unit disparages such external purity. But those Jewish Christians, we think, would not countenance the possibility that Jesus intended to abolish the kosher laws, so that the explication of that idea by the insertion of εἰσπορευόμενον εἰς αὐτόν in the first limb of the Reply would stem from a Gentile Christian community.[73] For even Paul, to judge from 1 Cor. 7.17-20, did not urge the Jewish Christian to abandon the written law.

Berger (pp. 461f.), who considers the purity logion in its full Marcan form to be a wisdom saying, attributes it entirely to Hellenistic Judaism. He thinks that it originally circulated independently, and that vv. 1 and 5 were subsequently constructed to form a concrete life-situation for it. We stress that Berger, accepting the Marcan form as original, does not eliminate εἰσπορευόμενον εἰς αὐτόν; a logion which thus emphasizes that food cannot defile, is, we agree, more likely to originate in Hellenistic rather than Palestinian Judaism, but a Gentile origin seems the most probable for such a view.

Berger mentions (p. 465) that the closest comparison to the purity logion in Hellenistic Judaism is in Philo, *De Specialibus Legibus*, 3. 208-209 where, commenting on Num. 19.22 concerning defilement by touching a corpse, Philo writes, 'Everything else too, he [Moses] says, that the unclean person touches, must be unclean, being defiled by its participation in the uncleanness. This pronouncement may be thought to include a more far-reaching veto, not merely stopping short with the body, but extending its enquiry to matters of temperament and characteristics of soul. For the unjust and impious man is in the truest sense (κυρίως) unclean.'[74] Thus, argues Philo, every action of the unjust man is reprehensible (ἐπίληπτα), changing with the worthlessness of the doer. Conversely the actions of good people are praiseworthy, gaining merit through the virtues of the doers, since πέφυκε πῶς τὰ γινόμενα τοῖς δρῶσιν ἐξομοιοῦσθαι.

Philo thus explains the defilement effected by the touch of the unclean person in terms of the Greek concept of the similarity of the deed to the doer. We believe that Philo is depreciating the Jewish purity law only in the relative sense that we have suggested Jesus did, and it is instructive to compare the οὐκ . . . μόνον ἱστάμενος, ἀλλά comparative syntax of the penultimate Philonic sentence quoted above, with the similar οὐδέν . . . ἀλλά of our logion. The sentence of Philo reads in Greek (our underlining):

καθολικωτέραν δ᾽ ἀπόφασιν ὁ χρησμὸς οὗτος ἔοικε πῶς δηλοῦν, <u>οὐκ ἐπὶ σώματος αὐτὸ μόνον ἱστάμενος, ἀλλὰ ἤθη καὶ τρόπους προσδιερευνώμενος ψυχῆς</u>.

Philo is not here denying the Levitical concept of bodily defilement, rather does he expressly admit its validity; he is indicating, as does Jesus in our logion, the comparatively greater importance of defilement of the soul, inner defilement. The problem of determining whether Philo intends a law to be observed literally as well as allegorically often arises in his writings. It seems clear from *De Praemiis et Poenis*, 2, however, that he considered the Pentateuchal laws discussed in his *De Specialibus Legibus* to require literal observance. He also writes at *De Migratione*, 89, 'There are some who, regarding laws in their literal sense in the light of symbols of matters belonging to the intellect, are overpunctilious about the latter, while treating the former with easy-going neglect. Such men I for my part should blame for handling the matter in too easy and offhand a manner: they ought to have given careful attention to both aims, to a more full and exact investigation of what is not seen and of what is seen, to be stewards without reproach.'[75]

There is thus good reason for believing that Philo's attitude was similar to Jesus' in not denying cultic, but placing greater emphasis on ethical, rather than cultic purity, and this Philo achieved by the use of allegory. It is difficult to know to what extent the views of Philo in Alexandria were typical of Diaspora Judaism in this regard, but in his allegorizing of the law he had both predecessors and imitators.[76]

Berger (p. 467) finds another link between the purity logion and Hellenistic Judaism in verse 228 of the *Sentences* (Γνῶμαι) of Pseudo-Phocylides, which Codex Baroccianus reads as, Ἁγνείη ψυχῆς, οὐ σώματός εἰσι καθαρμοί, and we may translate as, 'Purifications of the soul, not of the body, make atonement'. This abrogation of the need for bodily purification is weakened, however, if the textual variants of σου (M) or τοῦ (P) are substituted for οὐ. Van der Horst[77] reads ἀγνειῇ which he thinks makes better sense than ἀγνείη, and he translates, 'Purifications are for the purity of the soul, not (for the purity) of the body'. He acknowledges that there is no manuscript support for this reading, which is based on a conjecture of Ludwich,[78] and the dative of purpose adopted by van der Horst seems unusual. We think we would be closer to Phocylides' intent if, with the majority of texts, we read ἀγνείη and valued it as an irregular nominative plural (which is supported in substance by P's reading of ἀγνεῖαι). This quotation is a very relevant comparison to the purity logion since, as van der Horst points out,[79] it is probable that the *Sentences* were written in Alexandria between 30 BC and AD

40, and that the author was a Hellenistic Jew. Admittedly, the identification of the place of writing is based on only a single statement (v. 102) in the *Sentences*, that it is not right to dissect a human body, the view being that only in Alexandria was human anatomy studied by means of dissection. But similarities in the *Sentences* with Philo also indicate this centre of Hellenistic Judaism.

Whichever reading of the first word is adopted, the juxtaposition of ψυχῆς and σώματος and the most likely reading, οὐ, before σώματος clearly demonstrate a contrast between soul and body. The exact meaning to be given to ἁγνείη and καθαρμοί is explained by Wächter, who writes, 'The ἁγνεῖαι determine that and from what, one must be pure before or during involvement in cultic matters; the καθαρμοί declare the necessary purifications in the case of a defilement'.[80] In this spiritualizing of the cult the terms are perhaps being used in a looser sense and, whatever the exact nuance of meaning intended, the basic idea of the verse is clearly that purity of the soul rather than of the body is important.

With this verse, van der Horst compares the Letter of Aristeas, another Hellenistic Jewish text, where the king asks at 234, 'What is the highest form of glory?', and the guest replies, 'To honour God, and this is not done with gifts and sacrifices, but with purity of soul (ψυχῆς καθαρότητι) and holy conviction...'[81] In view of the Hellenistic provenance of both the phrases from Phocylides and Aristeas, we would not be justified in proposing a Semitic original for either. Thus, viewed as absolute denials of cultic purity, they would support an origin in Hellenistic Judaism for the absolute form of the purity logion, rather than the relative form which we posited. It can, of course, be urged that the difference between the absolute and the relative denial of cultic purity is only one of degree, but to us the distinction appears cardinal: in the one case the whole system of cultic purity is condemned, while in the other case priority only is stated.

Berger (p. 469) thinks that an apocalyptic provenance of the logion in our passage is indicated by the position of purity in the apocalyptic dualism as a power sitting in the hearts of the godless producing corruption. He sees this provenance as confirmed by v. 16, if original, whose terms proclaim the logion as a 'Rätselwort', since these 'enigmatic words' generally contain teaching about apocalyptic mysteries. Berger's conclusion is that a Hellenistic logion of a wisdom nature has been framed in an apocalyptic tradition. We grant the possibility of a Hellenistic Jewish origin. The evidence adduced above from Philo shows that at least a section of that culture allegorized the purity laws and, while not denying literal validity, emphasizes the internal aspect. But the evidence quoted by Berger for the apocalyptic connection is not convincing.

Berger supports his claim that the purity theme of our passage stems from Hellenistic Judaism by tracing the attitude to purity which he finds in Philo and Ps.-Phocylides into gnostic-influenced Judaism which emphasizes the order of creation, and whose key-phrase is 'everything is pure'. This view, he says, spread into Hellenistic Jewish Christianity, and is found in the New Testament and early Christian writings. He refers to Tit. 1.14, 15a where the ἐντολαῖς ἀνθρώπων are condemned, and the precept πάντα καθαρὰ τοῖς καθαροῖς is enjoined. Among other citations, he mentions the πάντα μὲν καθαρά of Rom. 14.20 (and v. 14 is similar) as showing a pre-existing catchword. While these citations indicate a common philosophy based upon the validity of *all* creation, we do not assess this thought to be consonant with our logion since it denies the Levitical purity laws while our logion, according to our relative interpretation of the οὐ . . . ἀλλά construction, merely depreciates those laws. Nor do we see this thought as a conceptual descendant of Philo who does not deny external purity, although similarity to Phocylides, who denies bodily impurity, is evident.

Of the various analogies which Berger posits for our logion, the only one which we find persuasive is that of Philo. But before we can treat Hellenistic Judaism of the Philonic kind as as a potential source for our logion it must be asked whether a Jew could remain in the synagogue, even in the Diaspora, and sit so lightly to the Levitical idea of purity as Philo. We think the answer to this question is 'yes', because Philo did not deny the literal validity of the purity laws, but by allegorical treatment emphasized their ethical interpretation. But it seems less likely that a Jew could remain in the synagogue, and *absolutely* deny Levitical purity. Berger construes the first limb of our logion as an absolute denial, but argues that neither by affirmation of the logion nor by the rejection of handwashing did a Jew place himself outside the framework of Judaism or even against the authority of Moses. He writes that a man had to justify views such as our logion but that, as in the case of Philo, this could be effected by exegetical methods like allegory. Philo did remain within the bounds of Hellenistic Judaism, but only, we believe, because his denial of

Levitical purity was *relative* and not absolute.

Secondly, Berger (pp. 476-77) claims that his absolute interpretation of the purity logion was tenable in Hellenistic Judaism because the authority of the Mosaic law was not that of a canon, but was of a much more variable weight. He writes, 'Da der Kanon nicht im Ganzen und vor allem nicht in gleichmässiger Weise als Autorität galt, waren Reinheitsgesetze wohl in hohem Masse prinzipiell diskutierbar'. But he does not quote any authority for this theory, which the available evidence appears to contradict. According to Pfeiffer,[82] the Pentateuch had achieved canonical standing in 400 BC so that it would be surprising if in the first century AD a Jew could gainsay its purity laws with impunity.

We next consider whether the attitude of the Qumran community to purity is analogous to our logion. According to Davies,[83] although the Zadokite Documents (CD[C]) and the Rule of the Community (DSD or 1QS) constituted an interim programme pending the advent of the Messiah, until that advent strict observance of the Mosaic law was required. 1QS IX (Vermes,[84] p. 87) reads, 'They shall depart from none of the counsels of the Law, to walk in the stubbornness of their hearts, but shall be ruled by the primitive precepts in which the men of the Community were first instructed, until there shall come the Prophet and the Messiahs of Aaron and Israel'. Many cultic purity rules are reiterated in the Damascus Document, such as at XII (Vermes, p. 114), 'All wood and stones and dust defiled by the impurity of a man shall be reckoned like men with regard to conveying defilement; whoever touches them shall be defiled by their defilement. And every nail or peg in the wall of a house in which a dead man lies shall become unclean as any working tool becomes unclean.' Purity is, indeed, used sometimes with an ethical meaning but, as in the prophets and Psalms, generally by way of metaphor. It is stated in Hymn 17, 'For the sake of thy glory thou hast purified man of sin that he may be made holy for thee with no abominable uncleanness and no guilty wickedness' (Vermes, p. 186).

There are texts in the Scrolls, however, which appear to gauge the purity of a man by his inner, ethical condition, and to relegate the purificatory rite from an efficacious to a symbolic function. The Community Rule, III, provides that a wayward member shall not enter the Council 'for whoever ploughs the mud of wickedness returns defiled . . . He shall not be reckoned among the perfect; he shall neither be purified by atonement, nor cleansed by purifying waters, nor sanctified by seas and rivers, nor washed clean with any ablution. Unclean, unclean shall he be . . . ' (Vermes, pp. 74-75). Here, the cultic rite is not to be performed if the subject is ethically defiled. Again, the wicked (Community Rule, V, Vermes, p. 79), 'shall not enter the water . . . for they shall not be cleansed unless they turn from their wickedness'.[85] It is rather the spirit of holiness, uprightness and humility which purifies. The exact function of the outward rite is not clear; as it cannot be performed unless the soul is re-aligned to the ways of God, it is, perhaps, the outward manifestation of the purified inner state. The most explanatory passage is again in the Community Rule, III, 'For it is through the spirit of true counsel concerning the ways of man that all his sins shall be expiated . . . He shall be cleansed from all his sins by the spirit of holiness uniting him to his truth, and his iniquity shall be expiated by the spirit of uprightness and humility. And when his flesh is sprinkled with purifying water and sanctified by cleansing water, it shall be made clean by the humble submission of his soul to all the precepts of God' (Vermes, p. 75). This Qumran statement is essentially the converse of the second limb of our logion: the soul becoming righteous un-defiles, i.e. purifies, according to Qumran, while the sinful soul (producing the evil things that come out of a man) defiles, according to the logion.

It would be rash, however, to judge the theology of Qumran upon the basis of a few selected verses, and the dominant feature of the Scrolls with respect to purity is one of scrupulous adherence to ceremonial purity. This marks the difference between Qumran and our logion: the over-all verdict of the Scrolls is in favour of Levitical purity, but there are passages where a metaphorical application to moral sin of the language of ceremonial purity spills over into a view of inner righteousness as the purifier of moral uncleanness. In these passages the language of ceremonial impurity does not seem simply to be employed metaphorically; impurity is genuinely considered to be an ethical state. But our logion is weighted otherwise: Levitical impurity is acknowledged, but is considered of less gravity than the defiling effect of impurity in a moral sense.

To summarize, therefore, assuming the purity logion to have been handed on as a saying of Jesus, by itself, but possessing a *relative* depreciation of external purity, either with the Marcan form of the first limb or with the abbreviated form we adopted above, then we consider Hellenistic Judaism of the Philonic persuasion to have been a possible origin. But we disagree with Berger that, as an independent saying constituting an *absolute* denial of cultic purity, it could have originated in Hellenistic Judaism. For, unqualified by the circumstances of a particular question to which it stands as reply, the logion, with either form of the first limb, is too drastic a denunciation of basic tenets of Judaism to have been countenanced by any Jew other than a complete apostate. And, particularly in view of Paul's injunctions to remain in the state in which they were called (1 Cor. 7.17), it is unlikely that there was a sufficiently cohesive body of apostates to have preserved the heretical saying.

Also in contrast with Berger, we have determined that in the earliest tradition our form of the logion was not an independent saying, but was the Reply to our form of the Question about handwashing. It is unlikely that a dispute about handwashing was created or preserved by Hellenistic Christian Jews of the Diaspora. They are unlikely to have created it, since handwashing can hardly have been a serious point of conflict with the Jewish Christian missionaries. Even though they did urge circumcision, and thus the keeping of the whole law (Stage 4), their teaching probably did not descend to the relatively unimportant particularity of handwashing:[86] it is thus unlikely that this church in the Diaspora has put a dispute of its own into the mouths of Jesus and the Pharisees. Nor is it likely that this church has preserved the Dispute, since, as our historical sketch indicates, there was considerable motivation for its preservation, originally in Jerusalem by Stephen and his followers, then the supporters of the Gentile mission (perhaps the same 'party'), and finally in the Diaspora by Gentile Pauline opponents of circumcision, all of whom had cause to depreciate the cultic law and purity; and, if the Dispute is authentic, it would naturally be handed down originally in Palestine, where it took place.

d. *The Isaiah Unit*
When considering the units of debate at b. above, we suggested that the harsh polemic constituted in this Unit by the charge of hypocrisy supported by the Isaianic quotation was likely to have been used by Christian Jews against non-Christian Jews in the synagogue.

Although the quotation, in the contrast between lips and heart, does itself allege hypocrisy, yet the introductory charge of hypocrisy did, we believe, travel with the quotation in the substantial form of v. 6. It is interesting that Papyrus Egerton 2[87] contains an introductory charge by Jesus (almost certainly against the Pharisees) in the same words as here, except that τῶν ὑποκριτῶν is omitted, and there is one change in the word-order. The wording of Isa. 29.13, which also follows in Egerton 2, is essentially the same as in our passage except that the only word in the fragmentary last line is ἐντάλματα instead of διδάσκοντες. The Egerton pericope, however, is probably secondary, since it is dated up to eighty years after Mark, and the charge and Isaianic quotation are used in response to a question about paying taxes to the civil authority, which is very similar to Mark 12.14.[88] But it does seem that, as in the Egerton pericope, the charge and quotation in this Unit travelled together as a general accusation of hypocrisy by Jesus against the Pharisees, and were used by the early Christians as polemic against the synagogue.

It is, however, difficult to determine whether the charge and quotation were joined together in Palestine or the Diaspora. The use here of the LXX or another Greek version of the scriptures would not normally assist much for, as Catchpole[89] has pointed out, a writer will re-formulate a scriptural text into the version used by his community. Thus, the fact that Mark's Gospel contains the LXX version of Isa. 29.13 would normally only indicate that Mark or a tradent has, for the convenience of his community, used a Greek translation of the verse in the Hebrew Bible.

The use of the LXX in this Unit does, however, possess significance. For although the LXX of Isa. 29.13 supports in the participial clause the attack on the commandments of men (διδάσκοντες ἐντάλματα ἀνθρώπων καὶ διδασκαλίας), and Mark's version more so, the Hebrew Bible and, more importantly, the Aramaic Targum, do not. The relevant clause of the Masoretic text attacks an honouring of God which is commanded by men and learned by rote, while the Targum of Isaiah, as mentioned earlier, reads, ' . . . their fear of me is become as a precept of those that teach'; thus neither text assists the attack on the tradition of the elders. The earlier part of 29.13 is essentially the same in the Masoretic text, the LXX and Mark's version, for they all attack hypocritical worship. But the main function of the quotation in the Marcan debate is that, both in his version and in the LXX, it condemns in its participial clause those who teach the commandments of men (meaning, in Mark's context, the tradition of the elders).

Therefore, if Jesus did not quote 29.13 in the LXX or Mark's version, he did not utter the quotation in support of an argument against the tradition of the elders. The question of the language used by Jesus is now a much more open issue than it was, but it does seem unlikely that, brought up in the synagogues of Galilee, and working there and in Jerusalem, he would, in conversation, quote the LXX from memory, rather than the Targum.[90]

It is, of course, possible that Jesus spoke 29.13 in the form of the Targum, and that the Unit was preserved by Palestinian Christians as an allegation of hypocrisy only, against the Pharisees. It might later have been discovered that, using the LXX version, the quotation could be turned to a different polemical use, as condemnation of the tradition.

Dodd,[91] from the use of verses in the pericope Isa. 29.9-14 in the New Testament, infers that the pericope was brought together with other prophecies about the apostasy of Israel, to be used as testimonia in the argument about the extension of the Gospel from the Jews to the Gentiles. This may have been the primary use of the first part of the verse ('they worship me with their lips, but their heart is far from me'). But if we look at the verses surrounding 29.13 pursuant to Dodd's claim[92] that an OT quotation acted as a pointer to the whole passage, we see much useful material to fuel a campaign against the esoteric closed teaching of the scribes which kept truth from the people. 29.11-12 refer to the words of a sealed book which, if given to a learned man, he says he cannot read because it is sealed; if given to an unlearned man, he says he cannot read because of his ignorance. Again, after our quotation, Yahweh says in vv. 14-15 and 20-21, '... the wisdom of their wise men shall perish, and the discernment of their discerning men shall be hid. Woe to those who hide deep from the Lord their counsel, whose deeds are in the dark, and who say, "Who sees us? Who knows us?" ... all who watch to do evil shall be cut off, who by a word make a man out to be an offender, and lay a snare for him who reproves in the gate, and with an empty plea turn aside him who is in the right.'

Thus, by its implicit reference to these adjacent verses, the quotation in this Unit incorporates a wide attack on the teaching of the scribes (wise men) who obstruct the people from true learning and whose false teaching denies them justice. We therefore consider that Mark's evidence that Jesus gave this Reply is outweighed by the evidence of the likelihood that the Unit was not only used, but created by, the early Jewish Christian church as part of its polemical armoury against the synagogue. With its connotations to the adjacent verses in Isaiah, the quotation constituted a versatile weapon which could be used on diverse issues with the synagogue. Due to this versatility, it did not require a question to direct the scope of its attack. Nor did the introductory charge of hypocrisy limit the Unit's utility, for hypocrisy is a broad, generic, allegation. At Pap. Egerton 2, the hypocrisy charged involves calling Jesus 'Teacher' but not obeying his words, while in Clement's First Epistle to the Corinthians 15.2, the charge of hypocrisy, followed by the first line of 29.13, relates to upstart church leaders.

Lindars[93] has drawn attention to the shift of application of OT texts in the early church. He mentions[94] that our quotation was originally used for the same polemical purpose as Isa. 6.9f., namely to show that the Jews failed to accept the Christian message because of the alienation of their hearts from God. The re-application of 6.9f. was to show why the earthly Jesus had not been recognized as Messiah, and secondly, to justify preaching to Gentiles.

We think that the uses made of the Isaianic passage of which our quotation forms part were similar. The allegation of hypocrisy in our quotation was employed as the reason why most Jews in the synagogue refused to accept Jesus as Messiah (Stage 2), and later (Stage 4), the διδάσκοντες clause attacking the traditional law rendered it an effective verse, together with its neighbours cited above, for condemnation of the law in polemic with the Judaizers who wished to force the whole law onto the Gentile converts.

The use of the passage at Stage 2 is supported by the quotation of 29.10 in proof of the πώρωσις of the non-elect at Rom. 11.8 and by the use of 29.14b cited above, concerning the 'wisdom' of those to whom the cross is folly, at 1 Cor. 1.18-19. Use of the διδάσκοντες clause at Stage 4 is illustrated by the exhortation not to observe prohibitions against touching or tasting perishables κατὰ ἐντάλματα καὶ διδασκαλίας τῶν ἀνθρώπων, at Col. 2.20-22. Likewise at Col. 2.8 the author warns his readers lest anyone make prey of them through philosophy and empty deceit κατὰ τὴν παράδοσιν τῶν ἀνθρώπων. This phrase might have incorporated for the reader reference to the rest of the Isaiah passage discussed, philosophy being then represented by 'the wisdom of the wise' in Isaiah.

It is possible that our quotation, or the διδάσκοντες clause in it, was used at Stage 3 in the argument against the Pharisaic Christians who opposed the Gentile mission because of the defilement caused by Gentiles. However, there may have been the same conceptual gap between this attack on the tradition, and the Gentile impurity rule, as we discerned between the handwashing Question, and the attacks on the tradition in this Unit and the Korban Unit. Although, as we shall see in Chapter 6, the attribution of assumed impurity to Gentiles was connected with the traditional law, the sources of Gentile impurity were Levitically based, namely corpse uncleanness and menstrual uncleanness. There is thus no strong reason why the tradition of the elders, rather than the written law, should be depreciated because of this threat to the Gentile mission, so that an argument against the tradition, such as that in our quotation, might not have dialectically connected with the challenge to the mission, based on Gentile impurity. It rather militates against the use of the quotation at Stage 3, that Mark felt it necessary to accentuate the polemic in the διδάσκοντες clause for the purpose of the continuing battle against the attempt to impose the whole law (Stage 4). We accordingly incline to the view that our quotation was not used at Stage 3.

e. *The Korban Unit*
It is difficult to determine whether this Unit could have originated with the historical Jesus. It is arguable that the recorded sayings of Jesus indicate a greater concern with basic principles than with detailed practical points. Admittedly, at Mt. 23.16-19 Jesus displays knowledge of the nice distinctions drawn by the Pharisees in the kindred topic of oaths by the Temple and its altar, and at 23.23 and 25 he cites details of their tithing and washing practices. But nowhere else do we find Jesus providing almost an encapsulated law report! Hübner (pp. 153-55), however, maintains that Jesus *is* here concerning himself with a basic principle, that of God's dealing with man: the Torah must serve the God-willed welfare of man so that where its law requiring the observance of vows, is being applied so as to harm man, it is null and void. This interpretation, though, does not seem consonant with the way in which the Korban issue is expressed in this Unit; the command from Moses to honour parents is expressed as abrogated by the scribes' refusal to release a vow depriving parents. This issue is thus shown as God's laws against man's laws, not God against Torah. It is possible that originally the Unit addressed a different issue, for we have already removed Marcan redaction which accentuated the contrast between Moses and 'you', but there is little evidence in the immediate pre-Marcan form of the

Unit to support Hübner's interpretation of it.

It is probable that the Unit had a Palestinian Jewish provenance. For, although the vow of property to the Temple was known in the Diaspora (see Philo, *Hypothetica* 7.3-5) it is more likely that the devotion of property to the Temple by way of legal fiction[95] was practised in or near Jerusalem, where the actual vowing of property to the Temple (if only for practical reasons such as the carriage of the property) most probably originated.

In deciding whether this Unit was created by the early church, or should be reserved for consideration as potentially authentic Jesus-material, we have to weigh the evidence constituted by Mark's attribution of it to Jesus, against the opposing evidence formed by the unusual nature of the Unit, as a detailed statement of a legal practice, amongst the reported sayings of Jesus. In assessing the weight of this opposing evidence, we bear in mind that the Gospels obviously contain only a scintilla of the teaching and polemic which Jesus must have delivered during his short ministry. The weight of that evidence is also lightened through the preponderance of broader issues in the Gospels, being explicable by the church's concern to preserve such pericopae rather than criticisms of minor points of Jewish law. Even so, in view of the cited criticisms in Mt. 23, the criticism in our Unit is unusual only in its length and detail. We accordingly assess Mark's evidence that Jesus spoke this Unit to be stronger than the contrary evidence. If there were no motivation for the early church to preserve the Unit, then that, too, would form opposing evidence, but we believe that the church had good cause to treasure it.

For, as indicated above, we think that during Jesus' lifetime and the early period after his death (Stages 1 and 2), the Palestinian Hellenistic Jews of Stephen's persuasion would preserve the Unit, and use it, after Jesus' death, to show their opponents in the synagogues what was preventing them, and had prevented them, from recognizing Jesus as Messiah. The Unit's involvement of the Temple in the misuse of vows by the deprivation of parents, and its illustration of the breach of commandment caused thereby, would be useful ammunition to those Jews; it would show how their opponents, by attachment to the Temple and scribal law, had rejected Jesus, just as their forebears had rejected Moses and the prophets.

This Unit would also be preserved in Stage 3, since Jesus' pointing to the scribal tradition as infringing the commandment could be used against the Pharisaic Christians whose treatment of the Gentiles as impure was linked with the same traditional law. Having thus survived until Stage 4, it would again serve as a telling argument against the Pharisaic Christians: 'you should not attempt to impose the whole law on converts when the traditional part of it produces results which contravene the Fourth Commandment'.

C. *Mens ipsissima and the purity logion*

a. *Introduction*

It appeared possible, from our study of the three independent units of tradition in section B, that the Dispute Unit and the Korban Unit may have originated with the historical Jesus. We now proceed to examine whether the purity logion, which forms the Reply in that reconstructed Dispute, contains the mens ipsissima—by which we mean the substantial meaning of the words uttered by Jesus in that context. We will, while doing this, consider also the historicity of the Pharisaic Question, but space does not permit the study of the Korban Unit in this section.

The main problem in the search for the mens ipsissima is to distinguish the thought of Jesus from that of the early Christians, for the logion may contain the thought of Jesus, or that which the early Christians wished to attribute to him. We have, however, determined in section B that the only early Christians whose view of purity was similar to that of the logion were the Hellenistic Jews of the Philonic mould, and we deemed it unlikely that they should have created, or been early preservers of, a dispute over handwashing. Our task is to discover whether Mark's evidence that it was Jesus who spoke these words is stronger than the evidence constituted by any indications to the contrary.

We will accordingly apply to the logion 'authenticating criteria' which have been proposed by scholars for testing whether the substance of words belongs to the historical Jesus. McEleney[96] has applied most of these criteria to our passage, and we now consider with reference to the logion the more important and relevant ones.

b. *The Criterion of Style*

The evidence from style mildly favours Jesus' authorship of the purity logion. The negative (οὐδέν) limb and the positive (ἀλλά) limb are written in parallel, and Norden[97] wrote that parallelism of clauses was the second most certain semitism to be found in the NT.

Burney[98] concluded that antithetic parallelism characterizes Jesus' teaching in all the Gospel sources, and that in the case of marked antithetic parallelism we are nearer to the ipsissima verba than in any sentence otherwise expressed. Jeremias's[99] observation that antithetic parallelism in the sayings of Jesus places the stress on the second limb applies to our logion, for although the negative first limb is dramatic, it is surely subservient to the second limb which alleges the true source of defilement. However, Mark's frequent use of antithetic parallelism in non-Jesus statements, such as the Pharisaic Question at 7.5, must weaken its significance as a particular authenticator of Jesus' words.

Paschen (p. 176) notes a semitism in the use of the participle κοινοῦντα as a transitive main verb in the second limb, and both he and Hübner have identified Aramaic behind parts of the version of the logion in vv. 18b and 20b. But McEleney[100] draws attention to the circular weakness of the argument from style. To establish the peculiarities of language or syntax which indicate speech of Jesus, it is necessary to know that the material from which the peculiarities are drawn is speech of Jesus—which is the very purpose of seeking peculiarities of style. Perhaps the main difficulty of the criterion of style is that while the Greek may be shown to translate semitic idiom, this only indicates a Palestinian origin, and not necessarily the speech of Jesus.

In these circumstances we believe that, although the logion satisfies this criterion, the evidence in favour of authenticity thereby afforded is not strong.

c. *The Criterion of Attestation in Multiple Sources*
The premise of this criterion is that material which is contained in more than one independent Synoptic source is likely to be genuine. This premise is akin to the common-sense approach of the law courts that evidence which is corroborated by other independent testimony is more likely to be correct than uncorroborated testimony. Burkitt,[101] who posited two Synoptic sources, wrote, 'Where Q and Mark appear to report the same saying, we have the nearest approach that we can hope to get to the common tradition of the earliest Christian society about our Lord's words. What we glean in this way will indicate the general impression His teaching made upon His disciples.'

Clearly, this criterion is only valid to the extent that the strands of tradition usually identified as Mark, Q, special Lukan material (L) and special Matthean material (M), are, in fact, indepedndent. We see them as independent at the completed Gospel stage, in that together they make up the Gospel form, and do not generally duplicate each other. But we do not know to what extent separate strands of tradition stemmed from a common ancestor at the oral stage. McEleney[102] and Stein[103] rightly stress that this criterion only shows that the attested material was embedded in the early tradition; its antiquity rather than its authenticity is demonstrated, for the material might have entered the tradition as a very early creation of the church.

The number of witnesses competent to attest depends upon the critic's solution of the Synoptic problem, but if we follow Streeter's four-document hypothesis, we have four witnesses, to whom we can add John. But there is a certain circularity of argument in the application of this criterion to the common Synoptic sources. For the reason why we consider material to originate in common sources of Mark or Q is that Matthew and Luke both contain forms of their material. In some cases, the verbal similarity in the two Gospel versions is such that they *must* each have been copying from this common source; but in other cases, the similarity upon which a common source is argued may be caused by the derivation of essentially the same saying or narrative from independent sources, and thus may constitute multiple attestation.

This relationship between Synoptic sources and multiple attestation prevents the use of the parallel to our logion at Mt. 15.11 as an independent witness for its authenticity, even though the logion appears in Matthew in a slightly different form, since we have already determined that Matthew copied from Mark in his compilation of the parallel passage. The last sentence of Logion 14 of the Gospel of Thomas repeats Matthew 15.11 but this, also, is considered to be secondary.

Thus, this criterion may identify similar motifs in multiple sources more readily than similarly worded sayings or incidents, for a verbal similarity may well have resulted in the identification of a common source, such as Q or Mark. McArthur[104] notes that the identical incident or saying was generally not repeated in more than one source; but this may be because when such a repetition occurred, a common source was diagnosed. However, provided that the corroboration by motif is limited to the existence of the motif in separate strands of tradition, then the broadening of the criterion from multiple attestation of saying or incident to motif seems justifiable.

There is at Luke 11.38-39 independent attestation of the motif of the Pharisaic question in our Purity Dispute and of the logion of Jesus which forms the reply. According to our textual decision the Pharisee is amazed that Jesus did not *immerse himself* (ἐβαπτίσατο) before dinner. We also decided that this Lucan incident is not reliant on our passage; v. 38 is special Lucan material (L), v. 39 is 'Q'. Further, its circumstances are sufficiently dissimilar to disqualify it as attestation of the sayings and incident of our Purity Dispute in a literary sense. But there is, in our view, sufficient similarity for the corroboration of motif. For the motif of the Pharisaic question in our Dispute and at Luke 11.38 is attack by the Pharisees at neglect by the Jesus-circle of cultic purification; the difference, in that our Dispute mentions handwashing while Luke mentions immersion, hardly prevents similarity of motif. Also, the motif of our purity logion and of Jesus' reply at Luke 11.39 is the depreciation of external purity in favour of internal purity. Although 11.40 continues the contrast between inside and outside, its basis in the doctrine of creation prevents a true parallel of motif.

There are several verses in Acts 10 and 11, 1 Cor. 10, 1 Timothy and Titus, which deny external defilement, but they do not expressly appeal to the word of Jesus. However, at Rom. 14.14 Paul writes, 'I know, and am persuaded in the Lord Jesus that nothing is unclean in itself'. The continuation of the verse, 'but it is unclean for any one who thinks it unclean', which contains a different motif, should not be allowed to detract from the attestation in the first part of the verse. We think that the continuation is Paul's addition of the concept of brotherly tolerance which he enunciates in Rom. 14. While this statement of Paul that nothing is unclean in itself is an absolute denial of external purity rather than the relative denial we see in the logion, we count it as attestation of the first limb of the purity logion, since there would probably be a tendency during the mission to the Gentiles to intensify Jesus' relative denial into an absolute one.

To summarize, we do not find the criterion of attestation in multiple sources to be satisfied with regard to the actual Question or Reply in the Purity Dispute. However, we do find attestation of the motif of our Pharisaic question in the L strand of tradition at Luke 11.38. We also find the motif of our logion to be attested in the Q strand of tradition at Luke 11.39 (par. Mt. 23.25). There is further attestation of the motif of the depreciation of external purity in the Pauline tradition at Rom. 14.14.

Having asserted this attestation, we must lodge a caveat, for, in showing from other synoptic material corroboration of the motifs in the Purity Dispute, we have not exposed that seemingly independent material to any detailed literary criticism. We are thus testing the authenticity of partially tested material by its attestation in almost *entirely untested material*; yet, if the examination of the Purity Dispute is to be kept within reasonable bounds, it is impracticable to subject potentially corroborating material to the same literary tests as the Dispute itself.

However, subject to this caveat, we do have useful support from this criterion for the authenticity of the Question and Reply in our Dispute. An inherent danger of the criterion is usually the doubt as to whether the corroboration produced from independent sources for the primary logion or incident's motif, may only support the accurate representation in that logion or incident of a motif created by the early church. In the present instance, though, we are fortunate, for the express reference of the denial of external impurity to Jesus at Rom. 14.14 argues strongly for at least the logion, if not the Dispute itself, originating with the historical Jesus.

d. *The Criterion of Discontinuity*

This criterion was described as follows by Fuller[105] with regard to the sayings of Jesus: ' . . . traditio-historical criticism eliminates from the authentic sayings of Jesus those which are paralleled in the Jewish tradition on the one hand (apocalyptic and Rabbinic) and those which reflect the faith, practice and situations of the post-Easter church as we know them from outside the Gospels'.

At first glance this criterion appears excessively strict, in that two unlikely corollaries follow. The first is that although Jesus was a Galilean Jew, a reported attitude of Jesus, to be considered authentic, must differ from the thoughts of the other Jews of his day. Yet it is very probable that the views of Jesus did coincide on several points with those of other Jews. For example, Jesus' readiness to treat a rule of the tradition as invalid tends toward the Sadducean view reported by Josephus.[106] But why should we assume that the Sadducean view has been wrongly attributed to Jesus? Since it is equally likely that Jesus and the Sadduccees independently reached a common viewpoint, should not the burden of proof of wrong attribution lie on those who question the historicity of the Gospel statements?

The second corollary is that a reported attitude of Jesus, to be considered authentic, must differ from the views of the early church. While it is more credible that the early church should attribute its views to Jesus (to invest them with authority) than that the views of the Jewish opponents of Jesus should be attributed to him, we think that this corollary too is unrealistic. For would it not be very strange if the views of the early church did not in some respects coincide with the views of its founder? McEleney, who finds parallels for all the teaching in our passage in Judaism or elsewhere in the NT, concludes, 'Thus, by applying this criterion as its proponents wish, one cannot safely assign any part of the pericope to Jesus, for all that he taught in accordance with the views of his contemporaries is methodologically excluded. Obviously, then, use of the criterion in this way can lead to misleading and absurd conclusions.'[107]

However, as Stein[108] stresses, the criterion must be used as a *positive* tool. It does not follow that material which does not satisfy the criterion is not authentic; the small amount of material which does comply with this criterion is a 'critically assured minimum', and other teaching may then be shown to be authentic through coherence with this minimum.

A requirement for effective application of this criterion is that we should have an accurate picture of the Judaism and early Christianity with which the sayings of Jesus must be contrasted. Recent research has shown how wide was the diversity of belief amongst Jewish sects, and Hooker[109] has stressed scholarship's imperfect knowledge of Judaism and early Christianity. This imperfect knowledge may cause us to treat teaching as different from Judaism when we are unaware of some parallel strand of Jewish thought. We should not, however, discard the criterion for this reason, but rather, when the result of its use is positive, not treat the material, even though it is a minimum amount, as authenticated, unless the authentication is supported by the use of another criterion.

Applying this criterion, then, to our Purity Dispute, we noted earlier a point of contact between the logion interpreted in an absolute sense and the Hellenistic Judaism of Ps.-Phocylides and the Letter of Aristeas. Yet an absolute denial of the defiling capacity of externalities does, as Käsemann claimed, destroy the cultic foundation of Judaism. Admittedly, the concept of uncleanness had been used metaphorically of ethical wrong since the times of the Psalmists and Isaiah, but this had presupposed the continuance of the literal, primary sense of cultic purity. However, we have already discussed the grammatical and contextual considerations which have induced us to interpret the denial of external defilement in a relative sense. As we then admitted background considerations such as Jesus' upbringing and his instruction of the cleansed leper to make the Mosaic offering, we will consider further whether Jesus intended to deny *absolutely*, i.e. abrogate, cultic defilement. This enquiry is connected with the question whether Jesus intended in the logion that *nothing* from outside a man could defile him, or only that *some* things could not.

Hübner (pp. 166-69), who sees v. 18b and v. 20 as the original form of the logion, but thinks Mark had both that and v. 15 in front of him, believes that, by virtue of the πᾶν in 18b and οὐδέν in 15, both versions are exclusive in the sense that *nothing* from outside going into a man defiles him. He notes Lohmeyer's[110] support for an original Mt. 15.11 with the less rigorous οὐ, but, like ourselves, considers this secondary, and concludes that to postulate an older form without exclusive formulation is pure speculation.[111] However, Klostermann[112] does not accept the exclusive formulation, and considers that Jesus need not have intended the abrogation of the food laws. Klostermann is supported here by the absence of any reference to, or citation of, the Levitical food laws in the passage. If Jesus had in this context intended the abrogation of the food laws, it would surely, he urges, have been handed down with all clarity.

Hübner's conclusion also tends towards a relative view of the logion. But he first considers two possible attitudes of Jesus to the Mosaic law. First, Jesus may have fundamentally supported the Law, but have wished to radicalize it by laying bare its deeper sense, the love commandment. When the mission to the Gentiles was undertaken, the words of Jesus in support of the Torah were changed into words critical of the Torah. This hypothesis fits in with Paul's battles with law-zealous Christians as evidenced in his letters, and with the need for explanation to Peter in visionary form at Acts 10. The second possibility is that Jesus expressly abrogated the Torah. Hübner thinks the likelihood of this is supported by the many words critical of the Torah in the earliest stage of the Gospel tradition. But is this so? Certainly, at the Gospel stage, Jesus condemns Pharisaic interpretation and excess, and in Mt. 5 radicalizes the interpretations of the law, but he also affirms the greatest commandments (Mark 12.29-31), tells his inquisitor, 'You know the commmandments', and quotes them (10.19), tells a leper to observe the ceremonial law (1.44), and acknowledges the Sabbath commandment (2.27; 3.4).[113]

The difficulty in this second possibility is to explain why two battles over the law are necessary, the first that of Jesus, the second that of Paul who, in that he speaks at Gal. 4.4 of Jesus as γενόμενον ὑπὸ νόμον, is apparently unaware of Jesus' abrogation of the law. Hübner accepts this second hypothesis, and explains the two battles by the Easter event. The first conflict between the disciples and the Jews after, and because of, the Resurrection was over the Christian confession, 'Jesus is the Messiah, the Christ'. As the Christians tried to prove his Messiahship to the Jews through scriptural prophecies, a soft-pedalling of Jesus' condemnation of the Torah, also contained in those scriptures, was natural. Hübner suggests that the Palestinian Christians, after starting in Galilee, later became centred in Jerusalem, and that the dispute over the law then arose there between the Hellenists and the synagogue, as recorded in Acts 6f. Conzelmann[114] believes that these Hellenists continued the attitude of Jesus towards the law more accurately than the twelve disciples. According to Hübner this pressure on the Hellenists to observe the law arose before Paul's ministry, and Paul was probably fighting the effect on Christians which this synagogue pressure had already made. Jesus' critique of the law was probably combined with the nationalistic conviction of being sent only to the lost sheep of the House of Israel, and that only when the mission to the Gentiles was undertaken was the value of that critique fully exploited.

Hübner (p. 175) concludes that the purity logion is to be considered 'als ein Wort der Kritik an Lev 11 im eigentlichen, expliziten Sinn oder zumindest im *bewusst* impliziten Sinn . . . ' He thus supports an exclusive formulation of the logion which includes the food laws in its ambit. But as he understands the logion as a word of criticism (*Kritik*) only, he tends towards understanding the denial of external defilement in a relative sense, i.e. that it is *less* defiling than internal impurity.

Branscomb's[115] interpretation of the logion also gives it a relative sense. He starts with Jesus' view of the over-riding requirement of God that man should serve his fellows. Thus, Jesus is probably not saying that it is right to eat swine's flesh, but, according to Branscomb, Jesus would undoubtedly have declared that abstaining from meats was not God's aim for men, and that it was right to eat a rabbit if this was essential to service of one's fellows. He draws an analogy with Jesus' teaching on the Sabbath: Jesus did not urge men to work on the Sabbath normally, but stressed the primary duty to do good on the Sabbath, and if that involved work, then the primary obligation over-rode the secondary.

It is difficult to identify exactly how Banks[116] understands the purity logion. For he believes that it 'neither attacks nor, even in a qualified sense, affirms the Law' since it 'moves in a different realm altogether, expressing an entirely new understanding of what does and does not constitute difilement'. But, in general, how can an entirely new definition not attack or depreciate an existing one? And, in particular, how can a definition of impurity as arising from evil thoughts not detract from the previous definition of it as arising from external causes? Banks then quotes with approval Beilner's[117] statement that it in no way directly follows from Jesus' words that to observe the purity laws is forbidden, nor that he has with these words cancelled their binding force. But Banks adds that the latter is clearly latent in the saying. In an interpretation of such drastic import, however, we do not feel that abrogation of the purity laws should be deemed the intent of Jesus on the ground that it is implicit or latent— even Hübner's *conscious* implicit intent is hardly satisfactory, for what confidence can we have that an implicit intent was consciously experienced?

Although most critics think that the logion was spoken in response to a question on some specific issue, the meaning of the logion is often considered in the abstract. Similarly, although we decided earlier that the logion was the Reply to the handwashing Question, we do not think that it need be understood as referring only to food, since we determined that the original tradition of the first limb did not contain the words εἰσπορευόμενον εἰς αὐτόν which demand a dietary interpretation.

We accordingly understand the logion in an exclusive sense, in that we think its purport is not limited to food, but depreciates the whole range of cultic purity. And respecting our treatment of the logion as having a relative sense, we have found no cause from this further study to alter that view.

In comparing this relative depreciation of cultic impurity with contemporary Judaism, we must presumably consider any Jewish views which were known of in Palestine in the time of Jesus. As argued earlier, the view most compatible with our logion is that of Philo who, while not denying the literal application of the cultic law, stresses its ethical sense, as ascertained by allegory. It is uncertain whether the allegorical ideas of Philo were known in Palestine in

Jesus' time. In that he refers to himself as aged (ἡμεῖς οἱ γέροντες) at the time of the embassy to Gaius in AD 39-40,[118] he is thought to have been born about 20 BC. It does not seem likely, however, that the attitude to purity of a Hellenistic Jew living at Alexandria, or of the followers of that allegorizing tradition, would intentionally or accidentally be attributed to Jesus.

Branscomb,[119] however, maintains that, by the time of Jesus, Palestinian Judaism had developed to the extent that it was restrained only by the absolute authority of the word of scripture from approving the purity logion. Many writers quote the saying of Johanan ben Zakkai in this connection at Numbers R. 19.8, 'By your life! It is not the dead that defiles nor the water that purifies! The Holy One, blessed be He, merely says: "I have laid down a statute, I have issued a decree. You are not allowed to transgress My decree."'[120] This saying is similar to our logion if our logion is considered in isolation from the Question, for both qualify defilement from external causes. But while ben Zakkai affirms the binding nature of the purity rules as divine commands, Jesus accords them no such dignity, but depreciates their importance. Moreover, Jesus treats cultic impurity as less serious than ethical impurity, and this could hardly have been contemplated by ben Zakkai who treats cultic purity as the command of God.

With regard to the Sadducees, unless we limit the nature of the defilement depreciated in the first limb of the logion to defilement only by decree of the scribes, there is no similarity with their viewpoint, for they upheld the Pentateuchal purity law, but denied the traditional additions. And they denied absolutely, not relatively to ethical defilement, impurity ordained by the traditional law.

We mentioned earlier that the Psalmists and Isaiah speak of purity and washing metaphorically in an ethical sense, but without denying cultic purity. There is sufficient evidence in the prophetic writings, however, to indicate a strand of thought which considers moral wrongs more serious than cultic defilement. For the prophetic critique of sacrifice is a judgment on the value of the external or formal aspect of religion in general which includes cultic purity; indeed, sacrifice and purity are closely connected since the Israelite could not sacrifice unless he was cultically clean. Hos. 6.6, 'For I desire steadfast love and not sacrifice, the knowledge of God, rather than burnt offerings', and similar verses in the prophetic books and psalms are rightly interpreted as proclaiming that sacrifice is no *opus operatum*, that it is ineffective when offered by an unrighteous or unrepentant person. Indeed, the quotation from Isaiah in our passage says the same thing (and more pointedly in the Masoretic text) about formal worship generally.

The general tenor of this prophetic message is surely to place the importance of the inward or ethical condition of man above that of external or cultic observance. Jeremiah at 7.22-24 no doubt exaggerates the contrast between the ethical and the cultic in order to impress his audience, but after allowing for this, his message seems to summarize the priorities of the prophets, 'For in the day that I brought them out of the land of Egypt, I did not speak to your fathers or command them concerning burnt offerings and sacrifices. But this command I gave them, "Obey my voice, and I will be your God, and you shall be my people; and walk in all the way that I shall command you, that it may be well with you".'

This critique of the externalities of religion was continued in the inter-testamental literature,[121] and we have discussed above the evidence that at Qumran a repentant state of mind was required before lustrations were applied.[122] In that this critique subjects the efficacy of external observance to internal rectitude, its order of priorities is very similar to the relative depreciation of external purity in our logion. In view of its continuation through the inter-testamental period, and its influence, even if perhaps marginal at Qumran, it does seem feasible that this prophetic attitude could have been mistakenly or intentionally attributed to Jesus.

As the criterion of discontinuity is thus not satisfied by comparison with Judaism, we strictly do not need to compare the logion with the thought of the early church. Calvert,[123] however, treats the two comparisons involved in the criterion as separate criteria, yet if the criterion is to be viewed as a *positive* tool, we cannot see how this can be. For, if the thought in our logion may have been wrongly attributed to Jesus, since it coincides with views probably held by other Jews, then the logion cannot form part of that 'critically assured minimum' whether or not its thought was entertained by the early church and therefore, perhaps, wrongly attributed to Jesus. But while we acknowledge that the authenticity of the logion is not thus vindicated as a part of that minimum, its authenticity may yet be shown by a consideration of the cumulative effect of all the guides to authenticity; alternatively, of course, all the guides considered together may pronounce adversely on authenticity. So the possibility that the thought of the early church may have been assigned to Jesus, must also be weighted in the final balance, and we will now compare that thought.

Stein[124] suggests that in making the comparison with the thought of the early church we should seek evidence for that thought only in Acts, the Letters and Revelation, and any relevant non-canonical literature. We agree, for it hardly seems reasonable to test whether the early church created a saying which the Gospels attribute to Jesus, by assuming that the church created other sayings in the Gospels also attributed to Jesus. The best evidence for what the early church thought is surely to be deduced from letters written to it, and a document claiming to be a history of it.

We remind ourselves here that we interpret the logion to mean that nothing outside a man defiles him *as much as* the things coming from him. We also concluded that the intent of the logion was not limited to food, but was directed against external impurity generally.

There is considerable recorded teaching of the early church that external impurity does not defile. There are general statements to the effect that all things are clean or good at Acts 10.15, 1 Cor. 10.23, Rom. 14.14 and 20, 1 Tim. 4.4 and Tit. 1.15. At Col. 2.20-22 there is teaching against transferable impurity. Except in Titus, these denials of purity are not expressly contrasted with moral purity, and the denials of external purity are absolute in form rather than relative as in our logion. We believe, however, that the early church was so opposed to cultic purity that it had ample motivation to create our logion, and we must conclude that the criterion of discontinuity is not satisfied in relation to the thought of at least the Gentiles in the early church. We are strengthened in this view by Paul's reference of his denial at Rom. 14.14 directly to Jesus.

e. *The Criterion of Coherence*

Perrin writes that 'material from the earliest strata of the tradition may be accepted as authentic if it can be shown to cohere with material established as authentic by means of the criterion of dissimilarity'.[125] We think that the criterion in this form is too strict, for there is so very little material in the Gospels which can be held unquestionably authenticated, whether by the criterion of discontinuity or by other criteria. We think that some evidence of authenticity or otherwise could reasonably be obtained by enquiry into whether the thought in the logion coheres with the over-riding spirit or tenor evinced by the behaviour and speech of Jesus reported in the Gospels. For while it is difficult to be certain whether any *particular* saying is genuine, it seems to us more likely that an attitude which is attested in several different instances in the Gospels can with confidence be attributed to Jesus. Thus, Carlston,[126] from a study of the tradition of Jesus' teaching, found that an eschatologically based call to repentance was characteristic of it; he therefore required of an 'authentic' parable that it should fit into that theme. Sometimes the over-riding tenor we seek may be demonstrated by a motif with multiple attestation in the sources, but not necessarily so. For several separate incidents or sayings manifesting a certain attitude might show that general tenor, even though all the incidents or sayings are recorded only in the same strand of tradition. We also feel entitled to look for coherence in the largely undisputed facts of Jesus' background, such as his formative years in a Palestinian Jewish family in the early first century AD.

Having thus broadened the scope of material with which coherence may be sought, we make a less ambitious claim for the result of this criterion than does Perrin. For if material does cohere with an over-riding tenor of Jesus' teaching in some respect or a general attitude, it may only mean that the early church has created consistent material. Therefore, we only treat compliance with this criterion as *one* of the factors to be weighed in the balance when judgment on the cumulative evidence from the criteria concerning authenticity is made.

The most useful evidence for indicating a general trend of thought or attitude of Jesus, in our view, is, first, *actions*, because their nature is less open to misunderstanding by witnesses, and distortion during the oral tradition, and secondly, *speech of a mundane, practical character*, since this is, we think, less liable to be misunderstood than speech of a theological nature; the exact nuance of the latter may depend on inflection of voice, gesture or circumstance, which may be lost during the oral tradition, or which the written and then translated word may not recall.

In the application of this criterion we must study whether the logion whose meaning, broadly considered, is that cultic impurity does not defile so much as moral sin, accords with the general tenor of Jesus' behaviour and speech. We believe that his behaviour and speech were consistent with the logion if (1) he normally observed the cultic written law, if not the tradition, and (2) he disregarded that law if moral considerations demanded it.

We append below particulars of the background, behaviour and speech of Jesus which testify concerning his normal observance of the law:[127]

1. While some of the material in the first two chapters of Matthew and Luke concerning the infancy and childhood of Jesus is probably legendary, we see no reason to doubt that he was brought up in an orthodox Jewish home in which the Pentateuchal law, including the important provisions affecting purity, was observed. The strict orthodoxy of James the Just, the brother of Jesus, is some evidence of this.

2. There is abundant evidence in the Gospels of Jesus teaching in the Temple and in synagogues, and there is no record of him being cast out, except at Nazareth. His general acceptance in the synagogues is to be contrasted with the rejection of Paul who spoke against the law, and we do not know that the congregations of Palestine were more liberal than those of Asia Minor. It can hardly be doubted that Jesus also attended the Temple for some, at least, of the Jewish festivals, and that (whether or not the Last Supper was the Passover meal) he celebrated the Passover. Attendance at the Temple and celebration of the Passover are doubly important for they not only show a general compliance with religious custom but a particular compliance with the purity laws since cultic purity was required for both; except in Papyrus Oxyrhyncus 840 (discussed below in Chapter 6), it is not alleged that Jesus failed to respect purity in the Temple.

3. Jesus would observe some of the tradition as part of the customs of ordinary daily living as a Jew in Palestine.[128] Moore[129] notes that by the side of scripture there had always gone an unwritten tradition, in part interpreting and applying the written law, and in part supplementing it, and instances the priests' knowledge of traditional ritual which is assumed in the Pentateuchal laws on sacrifice. Thus, in the accounts of the feedings of the thousands, and of the Last Supper, Jesus blessed, broke and gave the food.[130] This benediction was ordained by the oral law, and detailed regulations are set out at Berakoth 6.1-8.

4. Although in this context we consider single instances of particular behaviour by Jesus to be less persuasive than a general line of conduct, we think that the report at Mark 1.44 of Jesus telling the leper after his cleansing to go to the priest, and make the offering required by the law, has some weight as evidence of Jesus' respect for the law.[131] Also of less persuasiveness for the same reason but of

some corroborative value is the reference at Mark 6.56 to τοῦ κρασπέδου of Jesus' garment which probably means one of the tassels (ציצת) which Israelites were obligated by Num. 15.38f. to wear on the four corners of their outer garment to remind them of the commandments.[132] Of similar value is Jesus' use of the law[133] to support his argument at Mt. 12.5(M) and his citation of the law at Mark 10.17-19 and 12.28-31 (which significantly incorporates the first part of the Shema).

5. Jesus' attitude of national exclusivity implicitly indicates support for the law, the possession of Israel. Mt. 10.5-6 (M) and Mark 7.27 attest to this attitude; also, perhaps, John 4.22.

That Jesus disregarded the law if moral considerations or the needs of his ministry demanded it, is indicated by his following behaviour and speech:

1. Jesus associated with tax collectors and sinners. This is so well attested in the Gospels that it constitutes a general trend of behaviour as defined above. The behaviour is evidenced in multiple sources, being in Mark (2.14-17), Q (Luke 7.34 par. Mt. 11.19) and L (Luke 15.1 and 19.2-7). The significance of this association is that Jesus befriended persons who were cultically impure, at least according to the Pharisees. To collect the Roman taxes, the collector had to come into contact with the Gentiles which rendered him presumptively impure since by the tradition Gentiles were deemed to be unclean[134] (according to Alon,[135] as an extension of the impurity of idols). The translation of ἁμαρτωλοί as 'sinners' by the RSV and other translators[136] is, perhaps, misleading since the 'sinning' did not only involve moral error but also non-observance of the cultic law, and of the purity laws in particular. It is unlikely that, when dining with the *'am-ha'areṣ*, Jesus would be offered prohibited or non-kosher diet, but it is certainly possible that he would eat produce from which the tithes had not been separated:[137] indeed, it is a premise of the Mishnaic tractate M. Demai that the *'am-ha'areṣ* were presumed by the Pharisees to neglect the Levitical law (27.30) requiring that tithe shall be paid on all the produce of the land. Neither Pentateuch nor Mishnah state that untithed food is impure, but M. Demai, *passim*, indicates that it should not be eaten. Thus, by eating with the *'am-ha'areṣ*, Jesus was liable to infringe these tithing regulations.

Further, he was liable to be defiled by *contact* with the *'am-ha'areṣ* who themselves were presumed to be impure.[138] The evidence that

Jesus dined and associated with tax collectors and the unobservant accordingly shows that the obligation of the law was for him subservient to the moral obligation to save men by calling them to repentance before the onset of the kingdom of God.

The moral obligation felt by Jesus to bring the Gospel to 'tax collectors and sinners' is, perhaps, indicated by Jesus at Mark 2.17, 'Those who are well have no need of a physician, but those who are sick'. Hübner (p. 166) mentions this verse in connection with our logion, and wonders whether our logion was intended to justify, from the standpoint of purity, the practice of seeking the lost. We do not believe this was the original purpose of the logion, but Jesus' order of priority as between legal obligation and moral imperative is well illustrated by his words at 2.17 on which Branscomb, appropriately in our view, comments, 'He conceived it to be His duty to save those who were not ready for the coming of the Kingdom, even at the risk of violating certain of the laws'.[139]

2. The attitude of Jesus to the Decalogue commandment on the Sabbath is also, we think, sufficiently attested to constitute an established trend of behaviour for our purpose. Thus, Mark 2.23-28 and 3.1-5, and Luke 13.10-17 and 14.1-6 (both L material), all evince the same approach of Jesus to the Sabbath, i.e. that if the doing of what is morally necessary on the Sabbath requires work, for example healing, then the Sabbath law must be broken.[140] Another incident testifying to Jesus' relative attitude to the Sabbath is found at Codex D after Luke 6.4 and Perrin, a cautious critic, accepts it as authentic. It reads, 'When on the same day he saw a man doing work on the Sabbath, he said to him: Man! if you know what you are doing then you are blessed. But if you do not know what you are doing then you are cursed and a transgressor of the law.'[141] This is a difficult saying, and Creed[142] notes Loisy's comment that it was, perhaps, too subtle to find a natural place in the Gospel tradition. It could mean that if the worker knew he was breaking the Sabbath, but believed he was breaking it for good reason, then he was justified; but if he was simply neglectful of the Sabbath, then he was unjustified. Whatever its exact meaning, it does affirm Jesus' general approach to the law—that he acknowledges its force unless there are special (generally, moral) considerations.[143]

3. Jesus' healing ministry is an undisputed trend of his behaviour as recorded in the Gospels. It is also well attested that in the course of this ministry he healed lepers. This is recorded in Mark (1.41), Q

(Luke 7.22 par. Mt. 11.5) and L (Luke 17.11-19), and is particularly relevant because a serious degree of impurity was transferred by the touch of a leper.[144] Jesus was also willing to risk defilement by a person thought to be dead (Mark 5.35-42 and John 11.43-4). Ceremonial defilement was thus of less importance to him than moral obligation.

We thus conclude that substantially attested aspects of Jesus' behaviour and speech support the view that he did normally observe the cultic law in the Pentateuch, but disregarded that law if moral claims demanded it. We accordingly believe this criterion of coherence, as defined by us, to be satisfied by the relative interpretation of the logion.

f. *Conclusion to Section C*

We can now review the results of the application to our purity logion of the four criteria of authenticity most relevant to it, namely those of Style, Multiple Attestation, Discontinuity and Coherence. We determined above that authenticity should be judged by the cumulative evidence provided by *all* the criteria. Thus, although the criterion of Discontinuity claims to *exclude* material paralleled in Jewish thought or early Christianity, we do not, ipso facto, deny authenticity to our logion, which is so paralleled, since we have noted good reasons for the parallels. We therefore weigh the evidence from this criterion together with that from the other criteria.

The evidence from the criterion of Style favours the authenticity of the Reply (and of the Question since that also contains Semitic antithetic parallelism), but this is not strong evidence for the reason mentioned. While we did not find Attestation in Multiple Sources of the *actual* Question or Reply, we did find the *motif* of the Question attested in the L tradition, and the *motif* of the Reply attested in both the Q tradition and in the Pauline corpus. We respect the warning that we are comparing partly checked with unchecked material, but feel that this criterion produces substantial evidence for the authenticity of the Question and even stronger evidence for the Reply in view of the attestation in *two* other traditions. Regarding the criterion of Coherence, we are impressed by the extent to which the relative depreciation of the cult, which we find in the Reply, is present in other *general trends* of Jesus' behaviour and speech, thus satisfying our re-formulation of this criterion.

We are of opinion that the evidence favouring the authenticity of the Reply, afforded by its compliance with the criteria of Multiple

Attestation of motif, and of Coherence, supported by the weaker evidence from the criterion of Style, outweighs the contrary evidence of failure to satisfy either aspect of the criterion of Discontinuity. Judged by the test of traditio-historical criticism, we thus find the Reply to be authentic.

Respecting the Question, its authenticity is indicated by its compliance with the criterion of Style and of Multiple Attestation of motif. But the criterion of Discontinuity is not relevant, since we would expect a genuine Pharisaic question to be consonant with some views within Pharisaism, and the Coherence of the Question with other Pharisaic views on purity waits upon our study of the history of purity in eating, in Chapter 4, and of supererogatory handwashing in Chapter 5. Traditio-historical criticism can accordingly only grant qualified approval to the authenticity of the Question.

While the Question (to this qualified extent) and the Reply are thus indicated by the tools of traditio-historical criticism to be authentic, it may yet be argued that we have not excluded the possibility that the Dispute might have been entirely created between AD 30 and 65-67, Mark's time of writing (see Chapter 3.g below), by the Gentile church or the Hellenistic Jewish church. The attack on cultic purity, and handwashing in particular, denies the possibility of its authorship by Judaizing Christians. We think it impossible to show conclusively that the Dispute could *not* have originated in Gentile or Hellenistic Jewish Christianity within that period, but it seems to us, for the following reasons, probable that the Dispute took place in Palestine:

1. It is unlikely that handwashing was ever an issue between the Gentile and the Judaizing Christians. Although the Judaizers probably tried during that period to impose on Gentiles both written and traditional law applying to all, it would have been most illogical for them to have required the observance of what, even in Mark's day, was probably a rule of the traditional law binding only upon those who chose to become *haberim* (see Chapter 5.d below) and during the earlier part of that period was probably only a custom of the *haberim* unsupported by Rabbinic decree. For the same reason it is incredible that Judaizers should have attempted to impose handwashing on non-*haberim* Dispersion Jews who would probably be aware of the supererogatory status of the practice. Admittedly, we concluded that it was possible for the relative interpretation of the purity logion to have originated as an independent saying in Hellenistic Judaism of

the Philonic kind, but if we are correct in thinking that the logion was part of the Dispute, then it cannot have arisen in Hellenistic Judaism for the reason just stated.

2. In our attempt to describe the history of the use of the Dispute in the early churches, we considered that it was preserved at Jerusalem by Hellenistic Jews of Stephen's persuasion, possessing his liberated attitude towards the law and Temple and hence cultic purity, shortly after AD 30. This view, if correct, supports a Palestinian provenance for the Dispute, since there was hardly time for it to have been created in the Diaspora, and then accepted into the Hellenistic corpus of tradition at Jerusalem at so early a date after Jesus' death.

3. We decided that the Medical and Ethical Explanations were the work of Gentile Christians. Because we considered that the Medical Explanation wrongly explains why unclean things entering man do not defile him, we think it unlikely that Christians who so misconceived the rationale of the logion could have created it.

4. When applying the Criterion of Style to the logion, we noted that Semitic idioms translated into Greek do not necessarily indicate the speech of Jesus, but do indicate a Palestinian provenance. There are several such idioms in the Dispute:

a. With Westerholm and Rawlinson we see in the οὐδέν . . . ἀλλά of the logion a use of the Semitic dialectic negation, and there is antithetic parallelism in the οὐ . . . ἀλλά of the Question, although we attributed its use there to Marcan redaction.

b. The use of the participle κοινοῦντα as a transitive main verb in the logion is noted by Paschen as a Semitism.

c. Mark's need in v. 2 to explain κοιναῖς in reference to hands indicates that in that context the adjective is unfamiliar to his, for the most part, Hellenistic readers.

d. While the reconstruction of an Aramaic original of the logion is admittedly speculative, Paschen and Hübner have shown that such an original form is very possible.

Mark's own evidence that the Dispute took place in Palestine, supported by the evidence constituted by the cumulative effect of the above considerations, persuades us that the Dispute had a Palestinian origin, and was not entirely created by Gentile, or Hellenistic Jewish, Christians.

PART II

Historico-Legal Criticism

Chapter 3

PRELIMINARY MATTERS

Our conclusion on the literary evidence that the handwashing limb was alone the earliest form of the question at v. 5 was pivotal to our reconstruction of the history of the tradition in our passage. We must now, therefore, attempt to test the accuracy of this conclusion by enquiring whether the handwashing question can credibly have been asked by the Pharisees and scribes according to any Pharisaic rules or customs which prevailed in the time of Jesus. As there were different views within Pharisaism on many matters, we will enquire whether *any* of their rulings could have supported the question, but we stress that we are concerned primarily only with the *Pharisaic* views on handwashing, because it was Pharisees and scribes[1] who asked the question. If *no* Pharisees in the time of Jesus considered themselves bound by a religious law to wash their hands before eating, or voluntarily chose to adopt that practice, then it is incredible that they could have asked Jesus why his disciples did not wash their hands. We accordingly investigate the legal credibility of the v. 5 question in Chapters 4 and 5.

In order to check the authenticity of the Purity Dispute by reference to legal history, we must also investigate whether, in the light of the then current views on purity law, the reply of Jesus in the modified form of v. 15 could credibly have been given by Jesus and, if it could, whether in the light of those views and of considerations of debate it forms an intelligible reply to the question. The application of the test of legal history to the reply will be different in that, while we expect the Pharisees, who ask the question, to conform to *some* Pharisaic view of the law, the reply of Jesus is credible if it either conforms to the law, or from ethical considerations exhibits a liberated or radical attitude to it. We investigate the legal credibility of the reply in Chapter 6.

An accurate comparison of the purity law implied in our passage with the evidence of such law in Jesus' time, gleaned from legal literature, demands that we identify the concept of purity involved in the v. 5 question, the exact meaning of the relevant terms in our passage, and also the principles underlying the detailed evidence. Further, since we will find a substantial difficulty in checking the legal credibility of the Purity Dispute to be the uncertainty of the date of prevalence of the law contained in the Talmud, we will also consider at this stage how we may safely assign dates to that evidence. But as Mark's Gospel both in our passage and elsewhere contains much earlier evidence of the traditional law than the Mishnah, we must consider the Gospel's date; also that of the Dead Sea Scrolls which contain valuable comparative evidence. Finally in this Chapter we look at the purpose of cultic purity.

a. *The Concept of Purity*

Correct understanding of the Pharisees' question about handwashing and of Jesus' reply defending the disciples' neglect demands that we determine the kind of cleanness to which question and answer repectively relate. For in Judaism, Hellenism and modern thought, cleanness can connote fitness for the cult, or moral rectitude, or the absence of physical dirt.

Both Bible and Talmud attest to several different motivations for cleanness. Washing for reasons of hygiene is attested in the OT, particularly in respect of the feet (e.g. Gen. 43.24).[2] Chemical aids to hygiene were used as today, 'though you wash yourselves with lye and use much soap . . . ' (Jer. 2.22). The Eastern custom of washing the dust from the feet of a guest is also attested at Luke 7.36f. and John 13.2f.

Cultic purification, however, is the most usual motive for washing in the OT and Talmud, and washing of the hands for this purpose is mentioned at Lev. 15.11. At Exod. 30.17-21 the Aaronites are commanded to wash their hands and feet before entering the tent of meeting or ministering at the altar. Since uncleanness is not expressly mentioned in connection with this washing, it may be that the reason was rather the sanctification[3] of their hands and feet for their holy duties, but the concepts of purification and sanctification seem to be closely related. Alon,[4] pursuant to his argument that the Temple was not the only cause for the maintenance of purity, refers to the customs of handwashing before prayer, and purification before the Sabbath. But these customs also can be explained as intended to sanctify or honour prayer and the Sabbath, not to remove impurity.

Another reason in the Bible for washing the hands was to reject symbolically involvement in ethical sin. Thus, it is decreed at Deut. 21.1-9 that when responsibility cannot be attributed for a murder in open country, the elders of the nearest city shall wash their hands over a heifer whose neck has been broken, and shall testify that their hands did not shed that blood. Similarly, Mt. 27.24 reports Pilate as adopting this custom when he washed his hands and declared himself innocent of Jesus' blood.

Since the complaint against the disciples in our passage is that they neglect to handwash before eating, the most relevant purposes of washing are the hygienic and the cultic. Mark's linking of the washing to the tradition of the elders in v. 5 need not postulate that the washing was cultically motivated, since the Rabbis recognized, and perhaps in the time of Jesus, a duty to keep the body free from dirt, since this was to honour God's creation (*baraitha* at Shab. 50b). Indeed, Maccoby[5] has warned against a too ready association of cleanliness in rabbinic matters with ritual purity: hygiene and ritual sometimes overlap, and Maine[6] claimed a hygienic origin for ritual purification.

Handwashing, in particular, seems to have hovered on the boundary between the hygienic and the cultic. It has been suggested that handwashing among the Jews may have derived from Roman table manners.[7] There is evidence from the Amoraim at Hull. 106b that the handwashing *after* the meal was to cleanse the hands of any salt of Sodom which would blind the eyes, and at 105a that cold water was to be used in order to remove the grease.

It is, however, clear from the Mishnah that in post-Temple days the hands were washed before ordinary food for reasons of ritual, and that prior to AD 70 the priests washed their hands before *terumah* for the same reasons. Mark shows by his description in vv. 2-4 of the Jews' cultic purifications, with specific reference to handwashing, that he intends the question at v. 5 to be understood in a cultic sense. Did the Pharisees, though, intend it in a cultic sense in AD 30? We believe they did. We doubt whether they would have made such an issue with Jesus about the disciples' neglect if it had involved hygiene alone, even if the practice were enjoined by tradition.

We accordingly conclude that the Pharisaic question lies in the realm of cultic purity.

b. *Definition of Greek terms*

Before we study the Jewish rules and practices about handwashing in the time of Jesus, we must define the terms used in our passage, so that we know exactly what neglect is complained of, and against whom the complaint is made.

(i) τινὰς τῶν μαθητῶν αὐτοῦ. The Pharisees saw only some of his disciples eating with unwashed hands. Does Mark mean that only some of the disciples neglected the washing, while others did wash, or that only some of the disciples were present, and they all neglected the washing? It seems more likely that the reference is to a few of the disciples all of whom neglected to wash since, as we shall discuss in Chapter 5, those who practised such handwashing probably would not normally eat with non-observers of the practice.

(ii) κοιναῖς χερσίν. The meaning of κοιναῖς in this phrase is important to the understanding of the premise behind the Pharisaic question. Does it mean ἀνίπτοις, as the redactor tells us in v. 2? Bauer, *s.v.* κοινός tells us that the basic meaning is 'common' in the sense of 'shared'. It is used in this sense by LXX and Josephus as well as by NT writers (e.g. Acts 2.44; 4.32). As with the English 'common', κοινός acquired a pejorative sense of 'ordinary' or 'profane', and is used in the NT with the meaning 'ceremonially impure'. But in Leviticus in the LXX ἀκάθαρτος, and not κοινός, is used to translate the Hebrew טמא. Bauer (*ibid.*) cites our vv. 2 and 5, Rom. 14.14a, Heb. 10.29 and Rev. 21.27 as examples of the use of κοινός with the meaning 'ceremonially impure'.

Paschen (p. 166) sees 1 Macc. 1.41-64 as illustrative of the development of this meaning in the Greek-speaking Jewish world. We are told here how Antiochus Epiphanes, in order to unify his kingdom, required that all its peoples should abandon their own customs and, in the case of the Jews, demanded that they slaughtered, for sacrifice, pigs and other κτήνη κοινά. But many Jews were faithful unto death μὴ φαγεῖν κοινά. Thus, κοινά indicates the animals whose edibility was 'common' to the surrounding peoples but which, according to the Torah, were cultically unclean and forbidden for eating. Thus, κοινά, from meaning meat the eating of which was 'common' to the Gentile neighbours, easily acquired a transferred meaning of meat which was unclean for Jews. Paschen's history of the word in Jewish speech-use does not, however, explain how the word came to mean 'defiled by impurity', so that persons (and, therefore, hands), and not only animals, could be classed as κοινοί. For, in the genus of the cultically unclean, there were three species: first, meat which was unclean because it was flesh of a creature prohibited for eating by Lev. 11, secondly, meat which was unclean because the creature had not been duly killed by ritual slaughter (Lev. 17.14-15), and thirdly, food, articles or persons which were unclean because they were contaminated by some transferable impurity. It seems possible that the use of κοινός to express the uncleanness suffered by things of the third species was by analogy to its use for the first species.

The correct meaning of the root κοιν- in our passage is thus defilement by cultic impurity. It seems probable that Mark by κοιναῖς χερσίν in v. 5 meant hands *assumed* to be impure, since at v. 3 he tells us that the Jews do not eat unless they (first) wash their hands. It also seems likely that the Pharisees were complaining at the disciples eating with hands *assumed* to be defiled, because they could not know whether the disciples' hands had been *actually* defiled, but they could easily have noticed that the disciples had not washed them. We shall accordingly treat κοιναῖς χερσίν as meaning hands assumed to be defiled.

(iii) τὸν ἄρτον. To gauge the conformity of the Pharisaic question with Jewish law, it is important to know what act must not be performed with defiled hands. This question refers to eating τὸν ἄρτον, but in the introduction at v. 2 the Pharisees see the disciples eat τοὺς ἄρτους. Because τὸν ἄρτον can mean bread, or a loaf of bread, or food generally (Bauer, *s.v.*), we need to know which meaning it possesses, since this will indicate whether removal of defilement is required before eating only bread, or before eating any food.

It is unlikely that τοὺς ἄρτους can mean food generally. Lohmeyer[8] writes, 'Man kann sagen ἐσθίειν oder auch ἄρτον ἐσθίειν (3.20), wenn nur die Tatsache des Essens bezeichnet werden soll, aber nicht τοὺς ἄρτους ἐσθίειν'. From the use of τοὺς ἄρτους in the feeding of the 5,000 at 6.41, 44 (and τοῖς ἄρτοις at v. 52), and at 2.26 regarding the Shewbread, to mean 'the loaves', it seems clear that this is the meaning to be given to these words in v. 2.

Regarding the singular τὸν ἄρτον in the Pharisaic question, Mark 3.20 and 6.8 suggest that when Mark intends food generally, he uses the singular without the article. At 7.27 Mark uses ἄρτον with the article perhaps with the sense of food generally, for Jesus has said that the children must first be filled (χορτασθῆναι). Admittedly, the Syro-Phoenician woman replies that even the dogs eat ἀπὸ τῶν ψιχίων; ψιχίον means 'a very little bit, crumb' (Bauer, *s.v.*). It is possible that the woman has understood ἄρτον in the 'bread' sense, while Jesus used it generally. But at Mt. 6.11 (par. Luke 11.3) there is support for the use of ἄρτον with the article in the sense of food generally.

The meaning which τὸν ἄρτον possesses in the Pharisaic question is important in assessing the relevant law, because there is late evidence that bread occupied a special position in relation to handwashing. In discussion between R. Shimi b. Ashi and R. Nahman (fourth-century Babylonian Amoraim), it is agreed that rinsing of the hands is required before eating bread but not before fruit (Hagigah 18b).

In view of the conflicting evidence as to the meaning of τὸν ἄρτον in the Pharisaic question, and the significance of the distinction between 'bread' and 'food', we will give it the inclusive meaning of 'food', but consider also any particular law relevant to the potential and more restricted meaning of 'bread'. Under either meaning only *solid* food is intended, which is significant for our examination of the purity laws which endow drink, like other liquids, with special properties (Lev. 11.34, 38; Parah 8.5-7).

c. *The Pharisaic system of cultic purity law*

Although we concluded in Section a. that the handwashing urged by the Pharisees in our passage was cultically motivated, yet in order to ascertain whether the v. 5 question is credible on the lips of Pharisees in AD 30, we have to consider what system of cultic purity was followed by Pharisees at that time. We wish to discover whether the rules of cultic purity observed by Pharisees generally, or a group of them, at that time required handwashing before ordinary food, for if they did, the question is realistic. But what sources have we for this information? Clearly the Pentateuch is a major source, and the Priestly Code in particular, and there are occasional relevant references in the Prophets and Writings.[9] For, while earlier laws and customs on purity may have been modified or developed before Jesus' time, they will be relevant to our historical enquiry, because they contain the basic structure of the system. Thus, from the fundamental rules in the Priestly Code different interpretative deductions were drawn by parties such as the Sadducees, the Pharisees and the Essenes/Qumranians. Our sources for these extensions of the basic system are the inter-testamental apocrypha and pseudepigrapha, Philo, Josephus, the Qumran writings and the NT.

But, for the purpose of this legal test of the results of literary criticism, we are concerned only with the *Pharisaic* views on hand-washing, and we do not find their purity system explained comprehensively until the Mishnah and Tosephta of about AD 200, and their system must be read largely as an adjunct to the Priestly Code upon which it is built.[10]

The utility of the Mishnah as a source for Pharisaic purity laws in the time of Jesus may be opposed on the ground that it is unlikely that such sophisticated rules governing the susceptibility to impurity and transmissibility of impurity as Mishnah contains pertained to the time of Jesus. It is clear that between AD 30 and 200 the decisions of Sages on doubtful points of detail greatly increased the regulations affecting purity; but we doubt whether the basic rules of susceptibility and transmissibility were much altered. For we see in the generative document, the Priestly Code, that clean or unclean already depends on definite rules. For example, distinctions affecting susceptibility are made in Lev. 11—a falling creeping thing defiles a vessel and everything in it, but not a spring or cistern; it defiles a water-affected seed but not a seed for sowing. In Lev. 15 sequences of transmissibility are ordained—not only does the *zab* defile his saddle, but the impurity is passed to a toucher of the saddle.[11] And at 15.11 we see that the washing of hands to prevent their touch transmitting impurity is already recognized in at least one situation. Since rules such as these were established at least 400 years before Jesus, we should not be surprised if even before his time Jewish purity rules had grown quite sophisticated.

But Neusner (*Purities*, XXII, p. 62) considers that the notion of removes of uncleanness (with which we are concerned, for we enquire whether hands can defile food, food defile the eater, and the eater defile holy persons or things) was developed after AD 70. Similarly, Hübner (p. 163) argues that the controversies about defilement in exactly differentiated grades arose after AD 70, and he supposes that the defilement of food by unclean hands was accepted in basically undifferentiated form by Pharisaic groups in the time of Jesus.[12] But unless (as may be the corollary of Hübner's supposition) the Pharisees of Jesus' time believed that impure things, before purification, defiled things they contacted in an indefinite sequence, which seems unlikely, then they must have accepted *some* limitations on the transmissibility of impurity. Such a limitation would naturally be the number of intermediate things between the source of the impurity and the thing potentially defiled. Although the Rabbis may not have analysed the rules of transmissibility to any great extent in Jesus' time, nor applied the terminology of 'first degree', 'second degree' (ראשון שני), etc., it seems likely that some limitations would evolve at an early date, perhaps allied, in the case of food, with some differentiation based on its holy or ordinary nature.[13]

We think it can reasonably be deduced from the Priestly Code that some impure things mentioned there are of greater defiling power than others; thus the *zab* and the *zabah* who are original sources of uncleanness (Lev. 15.2, 25), suffer uncleanness for seven days from the cessation of their discharge (15.13, 28), but anyone who touches him (15.7) or her bed (15.26-27) is unclean until the evening only (assuming immersion in each case).[14] These provisions, as just mentioned, indicate that impurity is transmissible in the Code, but also implicitly suggest that the receiver is less impure than the transmitter. This early evidence of differentiation in impurity on transmission renders it unlikely in our view that in any circumstances purity would be considered as transferred without regard to the intensity suffered.

Evidence of sophistication in purity rules at Qumran also argues for some qualification on the transmission of impurity in Jesus' time. Baumgarten[15] reads at Damascus Document XII.15-17, 'And all wood, stones or dust which are sullied by the defilement of man, having stains of oil[16] on them, according to their defilement, shall he who touches them become defiled'. He notes that the man is the source of defilement, but that the stains of oil are the agents of contamination enabling the impurity to pass from the materials to the toucher. The oil here affects the toucher with the same defilement as the materials (וכפי טמאתם). We discuss below (Chapter 4.b) how liquids act similarly as a medium of impurity in Mishnaic law. Elsewhere,[17] Baumgarten explains how the rule at Qumran (4QMisn[a]) that a clean vessel is defiled when liquid is poured from it to an unclean one, equates with the Sadducean view at Yadaim 4.7, and this is surely an advanced concept.

Directly within the Pharisaic sphere, we suggest below (Chapter 4.a) that the Houses' decrees at Shab. 13b, in which the defilement of the eater of *first or second degree* impure food is decreed, were made in about AD 51, and further we estimate that a Sage's question, which presupposes that the power to defile hands depends upon the *degree of impurity* possessed by the defiler, was asked before AD 66. Assuming that custom precedes legislative confirmation, it does not appear extravagant to suppose that limitations comparable to this system of 'removes' of impurity, affected its transmission in Jesus' time.

A further possible objection to the utility of the Mishnah for our purpose is the diversity of Judaism at the time of Jesus. We mentioned earlier the different views on purity held by Pharisees, Sadducees and Essenes/Qumranians, but stressed that we are concerned only with the views of the *Pharisees of v. 5*. The difficulty here is that there were divergent views on purity law even within Pharisaism, and we cannot test the v. 5 question's conformity, unless we identify the law which is to act as yardstick. It can be argued that the Mishnah presents only the 'orthodox' Pharisaism which the redactors of the Mishnah wished to survive, and that non-conformist views were suppressed. Commenting on an article by Neusner, Sarason[18] writes on the relationship between Mishnah and Tosephta, ' . . . sometimes Tosephta gives alternative versions of Mishnaic pericopae which contain information that cannot possibly be derived from Mishnah, indeed which contradict Mishnah . . . These sorts of materials suggest that Tosephta's framers had access to the same store of Tannaitic information out of which Mishnah was constructed. Indeed, this type of Tosephtan material sheds light on the extent to which Mishnah is a selectively edited document, one which does not simply formulate for effective transmission "the Tannaitic repository of information", but which picks and chooses and takes a position on mooted issues.' Similarly, Alon[19] argues that, contrary to the actual legal practice followed during the Second Temple period, the compilers of the halakhic tradition in Mishnah and Sifra prescribed that the Pentateuchal laws of Levitical cleanness applied only to priests, the entering of the Temple and the eating of consecrated foods. Scriptural verses indicating the contrary were deflected from their plain meaning and referred to the Temple and the priests.[20]

It seems almost impossible to prove that the editors of the Mishnah did not omit what they disliked; indeed this seems a natural function of an editor. But we do have evidence, scattered throughout the Mishnah, that opposing views on many topics were preserved. As examples we may cite the pericopae reporting the conflicts between the Houses (the School of Shammai say . . . the School of Hillel say . . .), between Shammai and Hillel themselves, and between later Masters (e.g. Eliezer and Joshua) and between a later Master and 'the Sages'.[21] And the contrary views preserved did not just affect unimportant matters. That refusal to accept the separate impurity of hands persisted into the second century is shown by the record at

Eduyoth 5.6 of the excommunication of Eleazar b. Enoch (a Tanna of the first to second century). At the other extreme, Akiba (fl. AD 120-140) could still, against the generally accepted view at that time, argue that the hands were, in special situations, separately susceptible to impurity in the *first* degree (Yad. 3.1). On a kindred issue, Rabbis Eliezer and Joshua (pupils of Johanan b. Zakkai) were debating at least a decade after the fall of the Temple whether the eater of first degree unclean food becomes impure of the same degree as the food or one degree less (Toh. 2.2-3), even though his impurity of the second degree is clear from the Hananiah decrees.[22] It is also implicit in the Hananiah decrees that second degree does not defile second degree, but it is argued by R. Joshua at Yad. 3.1 and by R. Eliezer (apparently) at T. Toh. 2.1 that second degree *does* defile second degree.

There is, however, evidence outside the Mishnah that the full range of views within Pharisaism is not represented there. In the Targumim there are early halakhoth which conflict with Mishnaic lemmas, and since the Pharisees greatly influenced the establishment and governance of the synagogues in which the Targumim were read,[23] it is probable that the legal variations from the Mishnah which they contain represent the views of *some* Pharisees. Thus Kahle[24] noted that in the Cambridge fragment and Neofiti I text of the Palestinian Targum to Exod. 22.4, 5 (vv. 5 and 6 in the RSV), the root בער is translated not in relation to eating but in relation to burning, so that in the earlier law the crop-destroying beast would not appear to be one of the primary causes of damage, as it is in the Mishnah (B.K. 1.1). Heinemann[25] argued that this deviation from the Mishnah made possible the conclusion that the Targum contained a pre-Tannaitic tradition. Jackson,[26] however, although he agreed it to be unlikely that the Targumic exegesis of Exod. 22.4 (RSV, 5) existed alongside this classification of the four primary causes, thought it more likely that the system of *'avoth nezikin* found in B.K. 1.1 is *late* Tannaitic, attributable, perhaps, to R. Judah the Prince. On this basis the exegesis of Exod. 22.4 as fire could well have been alive as late as the early part of the second century. Heinemann[27] also referred to the Palestinian Targum to Ruth 1.17, and argued that the inclusion there of hanging rather than strangulation in the list of death penalties shows that one of the four forms of capital punishment recorded at Sanh. 7.1 does not represent the earlier law. However, this view that what is anti-Mishnaic must be pre-Mishnaic has been contested by scholars such as York,[28] who have pointed out that the anti-Mishnaic rulings in the Targums may be simply private opinions from before or after the codification of the halakhah.

The above indications that the Mishnah may not contain the earliest or the only strand of relevant traditional law warns us against a too ready acceptance of the Mishnaic evidence, when dated, as representing the only prevailing legal views at that time. But to avoid an over-estimation of the importance of these contrary Targumic traditions, we must stress that we are not cognizant of any which conflict with the traditions which establish the Mishnaic system of purity, i.e. the susceptibility to impurity, the power of defilement and purification from it.[29]

There is, moreover, a methodological point which alleviates the difficulty over the use of the Mishnah as a source of Pharisaism in the time of Jesus. We deem it reasonable to deduce from v. 3 of our passage that at least as early as AD 65-67, when Mark wrote,[30] some Pharisees washed their hands before eating ordinary food. Therefore, if we find in the Mishnah (or other non-Marcan source) that the views held on purity law by *some* Pharisees in Jesus' time required them to wash before such eating, then the traditio-historical authenticity of their question at v. 5 is supported by legal history. The possibility that many, or even the large majority of, Pharisees did *not* feel legally obliged to wash their hands is not then important to our enquiry, for if *some* did, it is reasonable to assume that it was they who asked the question.

In short, the diversity of legal views within Judaism does not impede the application of a legal yardstick to the results of form criticism, for we only have to show that, however many and varied the views on purity in eating may have been, at least *one* of them demanded handwashing before ordinary food. Accordingly, we feel entitled to quarry the Mishnah with this end in mind.

We stress that our conclusion on the Mishnah is simply that it is a usable source, and that the sophistication of its regulations and the diversity of views within early Judaism do not exclude it as a *possible* source of law relevant to the Pharisaic question at v. 5. Whether its various lemmas *did* prevail in the time of Jesus raises the distinct problem of dating them, which we discuss in Section f. of this Chapter. But even if we find that its detailed rules affecting handwashing did not prevail then, they may facilitate plotting the law's later stages of development which, in turn, may suggest its stage at Jesus' time. This also we discuss in Section f. (v).

d. *The Mishnaic system of cultic purity*[31]

We have decided that the Mishnah is one of the usable sources for
enquiry into Pharisaic views in Jesus' time. To assist understanding
of our discussion of the Mishnaic evidence, we describe below its
basic rules on susceptibility and transmission of impurity. This
system was largely built on the foundations of the Priestly Code.

The system of cultic or ritual purity postulates that a person,
animal or thing can be in such a state of unholiness as to disqualify
him, her or it from having any contact with the Temple or persons or
things connected with the Temple. Except in the cases of the original
sources of impurity,[32] this state of unholiness is not connected with
the physical condition of the subject althought its purification, for
example by lustration or breaking, affects it physically. The condition
of unholiness, termed impurity, is transferable from an impure
subject to another subject normally by touching or pressure, but in
some cases simply by presence above or below the transferee, and in
the case of corpse-impurity by presence in the same confined
airspace.

The impurities decreed by the Pentateuch are the human corpse,
the dead body of certain other creatures, the discharge from human
sexual organs, and leprosy. These impurities (except the human
corpse) are called 'fathers of impurity'. A subject defiled by a father
of impurity is itself made impure of the first degree, and a subject
rendered impure by a subject of the first degree, itself becomes
impure of the second degree. The human corpse is so impure that is
is called a 'father of fathers', and a subject defiled by it becomes itself
a father of impurity.

A subject rendered impure by a father of impurity, or even by a
defiler of less impurity, is called an 'offspring of impurity'. A defiling
subject renders the defiled subject impure, but of an intensity one
degree less than itself. This rule, however, is subject to the following
qualification. A subject is defiled only if it is susceptible to defilement
from the degree of intensity of impurity possessed by the prospective
defiler. Thus, *hullin* (solid) can only suffer impurity of the first or
second degree, since it is, being secular produce, sensitive only to the
high intensity of impurity possessed by a father, or offspring of first
degree impurity. *Terumah* is susceptible to impurity of the third
degree, and *kodashim*, being the most sensitive subject, can suffer
impurity of the fourth degree. (For definition of these foods see the
next section.)

Only a subject which is impure (טמא), as opposed to unfit (פסול),

can defile another subject. A subject is rendered *impure* if it is defiled by a subject possessing impurity of an intensity higher by two degrees than the lowest degree of impurity to which the receiving subject is susceptible. If the impurity of the defiler is only one degree higher than that lowest degree of the recipient, then the recipient is rendered only *unfit* (or invalid)[33] and cannot transmit the condition. Thus, hands which are normally impure of the second degree can only render *terumah* (whose lowest degree of susceptibility is third) unfit, while *hullin* which has been defiled by a father of impurity, and is therefore impure of the first degree, can render *terumah* impure of the second degree; again, *kodashim* which has been rendered impure in the third degree can render other *kodashim* (but nothing else) unfit in the fourth degree.

A father of impurity renders men, garments and utensils, foods and liquids impure, but an offspring of impurity only renders foods, liquids and hands impure (B.K. 2b and Yad. 3.1). If the hands contact a father of impurity, the whole body becomes unclean in the first degree, and must be purified by immersion in a *miqveh*; if the hands contact only an offspring of impurity, they alone become unclean (in the second degree), and are purified by washing.

e. *Definition of terms involved in cultic defilement*

In our discussion of the effect of impurity, we will distinguish the susceptibility to impurity of food applied to different purposes. We therefore specify below the different purposes:

1. *Kodashim*. This food (animal's flesh or agricultural produce) being of the highest degree of sanctity, was the most susceptible to impurity. *Kodashim* was food which had been consecrated in the Temple for offering as a sacrifice there, and it became susceptible from the moment of slaughter (animals), crusting (bread), or sanctification (other things) (Meilah 2.1-9).

2. *Terumah*. This was agricultural produce or animal's flesh, so called because it was lifted or separated from the remainder of the owner's produce or his animal's sacrificed carcass, for the benefit of the priests. This food did not possess the same sanctity as *kodashim*, but possessed greater sanctity than Second Tithe or *hullin*. *Terumah* could be rendered not only impure (טמא) so that it could transmit its impurity to a food of greater susceptibility (i.e. *kodashim*), but could also be rendered unfit (פסול) (Toh. 2.3-7) so that, while unable to transmit its impurity to *kodashim*, it was rendered inedible by the

priest, and had to be burnt. There were three kinds of *terumah* relevant for our purposes:

i. *Terumah Gedolah* or 'First Fruits'. This comprised a fortieth to a sixtieth of the produce of each farmer's harvest, and was required to be given by the farmer to the priest outside the Temple.[34] Normally, it was given by the farmer to a member of the division of priests in his locality. Until the *terumah* was given, the rest of the produce could not be used by the owner (Num. 18.8f.; Deut. 18.4). The portion became *terumah* and, as such, more susceptible to impurity, from the moment when it was separated from the rest of the produce (Toh. 10.4).

ii. *Terumah* of Tithe. This was the tenth of the tithe received by the Levites from the people, which the Levites were obliged to deliver to the priests (Num. 18.25f.). There are indications in Josephus (*Vita* 63, 80), that in the first century the priests obtained these tithes direct from the people, perhaps because the people did not pay the Levites (cf. Neh. 13.10; contra Neh. 10.37).

iii. *Terumah* from Sacrifices. This was the portion due to the priests from various Temple sacrifices (Lev. 7.14, 32; Exod. 29.27). It is included within the term *kodashim* in the Mishnah (e.g. Hagigah 2.5).

3. *Second Tithe*. This was the tithe on agricultural produce which in every first, second, fourth and fifth year of a seven-year cycle had to be brought by the people to Jerusalem, and consumed there. If Jerusalem was too far for the produce to be carried, it could be sold locally and produce or peace-offering purchased with the proceeds in Jerusalem and eaten there (Deut. 14.22f.). This tithe was of less sanctity than *terumah*, but it had to be eaten by persons in a state of cleanness (M.S. 3.9).

4. *Hullin*. This comprised all flesh and agricultural produce not used as above, and is thus a residuary class. Although of no particular sanctity itself, *hullin* could contract uncleanness to a limited extent, and thus render *terumah* unfit, and *kodashim* impure. Liquid *hullin* had a greater defiling effect than solid *hullin* (Parah 8.5-7).

f. *The dating and assessment of Rabbinic material*

Legal rulings (halakhoth) and Scriptural exposition and homiletic (haggadah) of the Rabbis only assist us in judging whether statements in Mark's Gospel affecting the law originated with Jesus or the early church, if we know the time when the Rabbinic rulings were in force.

But how can we discover what the views of the Rabbis between, say, AD 30 and 70 were, when the Mishnah, the first written record of their views published by themselves, was not compiled till about the end of the second century AD? The credence which we can give to the contents of the Mishnah attributed to the early Rabbis and the Houses of Shammai and Hillel, depends on the reliability of their oral tradition in general, and of the assignment of material to individual authorities in particular. The extent to which there was written evidence of tannaitic teaching before the first compilation of the Mishnah has been disputed since the Middle Ages. Most recently, Baumgarten[35] has assigned the lifting of the ban on writing the oral law to the pressure of scholarly and political circumstances at about the time of R. Judah, the editor of the Mishnah. Neusner[36] challenged Baumgarten's view, arguing that it was only at Yavneh that the Rabbis introduced oral transmission and an interdict on writing to bolster their authority. Baumgarten[37] concedes that individual writings on halakhic matters were employed throughout the Talmudic period, though only for private use. It seems reasonable to suppose that the Rabbinic teachers supplemented their memories by some written notes. The existence of halakhoth in the Qumran writings[38] shows that such inhibition as the Rabbis entertained did not affect all Judaism.

Although the final compilation of the Mishnah was not completed by R. Judah until about AD 200, it contains sayings of Rabbis dating from about 200 BC. Indeed, some of the sayings may have originated with the *sopherim*, the expositors of the written Torah, who were established by Ezra[39] and ceased to function about 200 BC.

The Tosephta is another early collection of Rabbinic rulings, and its relationship to the Mishnah is 'one of the most vexing problems of modern scholarship'.[40] Scholars differ over both the date of its compilation and the date of its sources. Whether the Tosephta was, as its name suggests, written to complement the Mishnah does not necessarily affect the age of the materials in it, although the later the date of its writing, the more probable it is that early traditions have been corrupted. At Sanh. 86a R. Johanan says that the author of anonymous sayings in the Mishnah is R. Meir, and that the author of such sayings in the Tosephta is R. Nehemiah (Meir's contemporary in the mid-second century). Consistently with this, the Sherira Gaon in his Epistle, following tradition, takes the compiler of the Tosephta to be R. Hiyya, the disciple of R. Judah, the final editor of the Mishnah. On these views the anonymous contents of the Tosephta may reasonably be considered as old as those of the Mishnah. Indeed, M.S. Zuckermandel, who edited the Erfurt manuscript of the Tosephta, proposed that the Tosephta was the original Mishnah of Rabbi.[41]

Modern treatment of the Tosephta's age has swung to the comparison of individual tractates, and B. Cohen[42] has concluded from a comparison of Shabbat in Mishnah and Tosephta that the Tosephta frequently recorded halakhoth in a form earlier than that of the Mishnah even though the Tosephta was compiled later. De Vries,[43] who compared other tractates, decided that the Tosephta was even *written* earlier than the Mishnah. This view contrasts with that of Wacholder,[44] who believes the Tosephta was written after the Talmuds, and that of Herr,[45] who dates its compilation to the end of the Talmudic era.

Amid this welter of conflicting opinion, it is difficult to draw a conclusion concerning the Tosephta's age, but since it appears that some of its traditions may be older than those of the Mishnah, but that its compilation may have taken place after the Mishnah, it seems that a sensible working hypothesis would be to treat the dating of its halakhoth and their attribution to named authorities with neither more nor less caution than in the case of the Mishnah.

With regard to the Talmuds, the standard view is that the Palestinian one was finally compiled about 400 AD,[46] and the Babylonian about 550 AD.[47] Despite the distance in time between their compilation and our period, the Talmuds are valuable for our purpose because they contain *baraithoth*, statements by tannaitic Sages, some of which are not contained in the Mishnah.

Some rulings in the Talmudic literature are anonymous, and some are attributed to a named Sage, but even where they are attributed to a named Sage, how can we date the ruling unless we know a. that the attribution is correct, and b. the generation in which the Sage lived? Dating principles which would enable all rulings to be dated with confidence, cannot be formulated, but we set out below some of the recent approaches to the problem.

(i) *Bernard J. Bamberger*

In 1949 Bamberger[48] proposed the following guides to dating:
(a) 'The Mishnah, Talmuds and the standard Midrashim are generally reliable in their attribution of statements to the various Rabbis, although mistakes do occur.' If we accept this reliability, and can be sure of the generation in which a named Rabbi taught, then we can

assess the relevance of his legal statements to the Gospel evidence concerning the law in the time of Jesus. If a Rabbi taught in or around the third decade, then his teaching may support or prejudice the authenticity of legal views attributed by Mark to Jesus or the Pharisees. If a Rabbi taught at a much earlier date, then his teaching is still relevant, for later teaching develops, but does not usually cancel, earlier teaching.[49] If legal opinions in Mark's Gospel, however, coincide with the statements of a Rabbi who clearly taught after the death of Jesus, this may indicate that teaching attributed to Jesus or the Pharisees by Mark in fact stems from the early church.

The difficulty of using a lemma reliably attributed to a Rabbi of the First Generation (c. AD 10-80), is that, although we know that if his statement coincides with the Marcan legal evidence it may have been uttered before the destruction of the Temple, we can rarely say with confidence that the Rabbinical law *must* have originated before AD 30, i.e. in the lifetime of Jesus, and *not* between then and AD 70, i.e. in the period of the early church whose teaching would be known to Mark. This complicates the attribution to Jesus, as opposed to the early church, of views which Mark assigns to Jesus (cf. the Pharisees).

Even if the Talmudic literature is reliable in its attributions, this may confuse dating, for a Rabbi of the First Generation may only have been repeating the words of an earlier Rabbi without acknowledging the originator. Again, a lemma of a later Rabbi may have been put into the mouth of an earlier Rabbi in order to give the sanctity of antiquity to a new lemma. Bamberger acknowledges the first possibility, but not the second. Regarding the ascription of a statement to a named Rabbi, he writes, 'But such an ascription gives us only a terminus ad quem. The saying is surely no later than the man who is reported to have said it, but it may be much earlier. He may have neglected to mention the teacher from whom he heard it, or his reporter may have inadvertently omitted the name of the older authority; or perhaps the Rabbi was drawing on a widely diffused tradition which was not associated with any one teacher.'[50] In support, Bamberger mentions how in the Rabbinic literature the same opinion occurs in one place in the name of an earlier teacher, and in another place in the name of a later teacher.

Mielziner[51] cites Berakoth 9b, Taanith 10a and Sanhedrin 23a as instances of the presentation of the teaching of a post-Mishnaic teacher followed by תניא נמי הכי, 'we have a tannaitic teaching (i.e. *baraitha*) to the same effect'. The earlier statement then follows in full, and it is clear that the Amora was only quoting an older teaching, but this was not appreciated by the Talmudic compiler.

Further evidence that a saying may be much older than the Rabbi to whom it is attributed is derived by Bamberger from the existence of a common store of haggadic tradition.[52] While admitting that in a few cases the Rabbis actually borrowed, Bamberger considers that most parallels are due to this common stock. Thus, he says, R. Simeon ben Menasia would hardly be quoting Jesus (Mark 2.27) when he says 'The Sabbath is delivered unto you, and you are not delivered unto the Sabbath' (Mekhilta Shabbata 1). Similarly, Jesus is drawing on the common store of folk-sayings at Mt. 6.34; the Hebrew equivalent, 'It is sufficient for the evil to come in its time', is ascribed in Exodus Rabbah 3.6 to a fourth-century Palestinian Rabbi, while in the Talmud it appears anonymously, but in a context of sayings by Palestinian Amoraim (Berakoth 9b).

(b) 'Anonymous passages, especially in tannaitic literature, are frequently ancient.'[53] Bamberger maintains that this guide to dating is particularly reliable when no dissenting opinion appears in the context—a fact which indicates that the anonymous view was well known and generally accepted. He cites the beginning of Baba Kama and large parts of Tamid and Yoma as anonymous sections of the Mishnah which are very old as their content and style plainly indicate. He admits that other anonymous passages of the Mishnah emanate from the School of Rabbi Judah the Prince, in which the Mishnah was edited, but he denies that the anonymity of a passage is in itself evidence of lateness. He quotes Sotah 1.7, 'With the measure wherewith a man measureth, they measure out to him'. This emanates not from the second century but from an old proverb, as indicated by the parallel in Mt. 7.2, 'With what measure ye mete, it shall be measured out to you'. Against Bamberger's view, we must cite again the statement of R. Johanan at Sanhedrin 86a that R. Meir is the source of anonymous Mishnayoth (although, admittedly, Meir's collection may have contained earlier views).

(c) The lateness of an anonymous passage 'can be established only when the content reflects the conditions of a later period, or the interpretive methods of a late school'.[54] This guide must be qualified, however, for the Mishnah, and in particular the fifth Division, Kodashim, contains detailed regulations concerning sacrificial prayer and other cultic observances in the Temple, just as if the Temple were still standing when the Mishnah was written; yet R. Meir, to whom several opinions are attributed in this Division, is a Rabbi of the Fourth Tannaitic Generation (AD 140-165). It is, therefore, almost certain that some of the anonymous statements are late.

Further, it is argued by Neusner that after the destruction of the Temple in AD 70 the scholars at Yavneh, in recording the then existing traditions, used various forms both for concise expression and mnemonic value. Thus, the interpretive form of Yavneh may clothe a saying which was uttered by a pre-70 Sage. Neusner writes (*Traditions* III, p. 315), 'Clearcut and well-defined forms were used for the transmission of the Houses-materials, Hillel-pericopae, and related data... All are well attested at early Yavneh'. He also mentions the imposition at Yavneh of memory-aids in the form of balanced opposite opinions, or a balanced number of syllables, and contrasts such as clean/unclean. While the formulas used primarily affected attributed material, no doubt anonymous material was also editorially affected. Thus the impress of Yavneh was often put on pre-70 opinions, so that interpretive methods can be an unsound guide to dating.

To summarize, Bamberger's guides to dating manifest a less critical attitude towards the Rabbinic material than would be adopted today by many NT scholars. His acceptance of the general reliability of attributions, of the frequent antiquity of anonymous passages and the presumption of their early date unless rebutted by late conditions or interpretive methods, would all be questioned today.

(ii) *George Wesley Buchanan*

Buchanan's essay, 'The Use of Rabbinic Literature for New Testament Research', seems to have been provoked by the increased interest in Rabbinic literature following the discovery of the Dead Sea Scrolls, and by Sandmel's[55] castigation as 'parallelomania' of the resulting indiscriminate use of Rabbinic parallels to explain NT material without careful consideration of its contemporaneity with NT times. Sandmel rightly objected to the assumption that, in the case of true parallels, it was always Jesus who had influenced the Rabbis, and to the mis-use of alleged parallels to show that the teaching of Jesus was always superior to that of the Rabbis. Buchanan[56] suggests legitimate methods of using the Jewish sources, and makes the following points relevant to their dating:

(a) He acknowledges that the Rabbinic literature preserves some material which has been faithfully handed down from sources predating the NT. He denies, however, the point made by Bamberger above, namely that the latest date for any Rabbinic saying is the date of the Rabbi to whom the saying has been attributed. To indicate the fallibility of the Rabbis, he instances the occasions when the same statement is attributed to two different Sages.[57] Just as the early church is thought to have publicized some of its own teaching under Jesus' authority, so may later Rabbis have put their own teaching in the name of earlier Masters. He also stresses the element of sheer chance in attribution, quoting McNamara, '... the connection of any particular type of exegesis with a particular rabbi in rabbinic tradition may be merely due to an accident in the process of transmission. At some uncertain period it became a norm in rabbinism that, wherever possible, traditionists were to name their source and not hand on a tradition anonymously.'[58]

(b) Sayings alleged to be early but contained in later documents must be demonstrated as early, form critically, in relation to datable events or literature.[59] Towner, a pupil of Neusner, has done some rigorous form-critical work concerning numbered lists in Mekilta de R. Ishmael,[60] and Neusner himself has used this tool, but its assistance towards dating Rabbinic literature is limited, because of the paucity of datable events, and the stereotyped formulae placed upon much of the Mishnaic material at some stage.

(c) Obviously, Rabbinic material which has a demonstrably pre-Christian date can be considered for its influence on the NT.[61] But Sandmel complained that NT scholars tended to use Rabbinic literature as if all the tradition parallel to the NT must have been composed after the NT. Buchanan explains one situation in which the Rabbinic literature may assist the NT student even though he may be unable to date either set of material. Since both Rabbinic Judaism and Christianity developed from an earlier form of Judaism, an expression, custom or belief found in the literature of the one can sometimes be explained by the literature of the other.[62] Buchanan gives various instances of this mutual assistance, and the one most relevant to us is the rules of hospitality.

Demai 2.3 and T. Demai 4.9, writes Buchanan,[63] state the conditions under which an 'observant Jew' is permitted to receive guests into his home. He could admit another observant Jew at any time, and was obliged to admit him when travelling, to prevent him suffering through lack of approved food and undefiled quarters. But the observant Jew was not allowed to admit the non-observer into his house in the non-observer's own clothing.

Buchanan believes that this custom explains the instruction to the disciples not to greet anybody on the road (Luke 10.4), and only to

accept hospitality in the home of somebody who is worthy (ἄξιος)
(Matt. 10.11-12). This very example, however, illustrates the danger
of using a Rabbinic parallel without close prior examination of the
contextual and religious background. For Demai 2.3 applies to
המקבל עליו להיות חבר, one who undertakes to be a *haber*; we have no
evidence that Jesus or the disciples were *haberim*, so there is no
reason why Jesus should instruct the disciples to stay only with other
haberim. And while Bauer, *s.v.* ἄξιος, notes that it can mean fit or
worthy in the sense of deserving eternal life (Acts 13.46) or the
labourer deserving his food (Matthew 10.10) or pay (Luke 10.7), he
records no example of its meaning trustworthy or reliable in the
sense that the *haber* must be reliable (נאמן) as regards tithing and
purity (Demai 2.2). M'Neile[64] reasonably suggests that ἄξιος in this
context means 'readiness to receive the preachers and their message'.
Similarly, since the disciples were presumably not *haberim*, the
Demai passage does not explain the instruction not to greet persons
on the road.

However, Buchanan cites Demai 2.3 in support of his claim that in
some instances it is not necessary to know the date of a Rabbinic or
NT text for it to be useful to research: it is unimportant to know
when Demai 2.3 was composed because it records a rule taken for
granted by other Jews and Christians. But even if we accept that this
passage indicates that most Jews observed the purity rule mentioned
there, does the date of the law and practice not matter? Does it assist
exegesis of Jesus' reported instruction to his disciples, if the Demai
law was only evolved by the Sages of the second century or, to take
Buchanan literally, the tenth century? Common religious ancestry
does not predicate parallel legal development. Admittedly, Buchanan
proposes the Mishnaic legislation as a basis from which to begin
research into other Jewish and Christian literature, in order to check
the extent of application of the hospitality practice. But if we cannot
date our basic datum, the foundation for our research may be
unsteady.

(iii) *Jacob Neusner*
We can best begin to describe Neusner's contribution to the dating
and assessment of Rabbinic material by stating the nature of his
reaction against the traditional interpretation of Mishnah and Talmud.
He writes[65] that this interpretation is based on a false axiom that all
texts are to be interpreted in the light of all other texts. Thus,

Talmudic discussion of Mishnah and its meanings invariably shapes the received interpretation of Mishnah. But, he points out, nobody would argue that the original meaning of the Bible is shown in Midrash or medieval commentaries. The historian's question, says Neusner, is, 'What did these words of Mishnah-Tosephta mean to the people who made them up in the late first and second century?' Neusner then argues for a form-critical approach to the documents, which isolates the smallest units of tradition and, removing them from their redactional and exegetical-eisegetical framework, asks about their meaning and original intent.

Neusner condemns the traditional error of assuming that Rabbinic literature is timeless so that there is 'neither early nor late in Torah'. Since the traditional exegesis of Mishnah is non-historical, and not interested in what pericopae meant at the outset, Neusner maintains that it will not serve the historian's purpose.

Another vital historical question to which Neusner has proposed a new answer is, 'How can we discover how many stages of legal development precede c. AD 200, the time of the redaction of the Mishnah?'[66] The answer to this question is important to us, because the success of our attempt to check the results of tradition criticism by the yardstick of the law will depend on whether we are able to discover the stage of development which purity law and practice had reached in AD 30. Consequently, both here and in section f. (v) of this chapter ('Our Approach') we will attend carefully to Neusner's method of dating sayings attributed to named Rabbis in the Mishnah, a document which was written long after the generations of many Rabbis quoted in it. It is by consideration of, and in reaction to, Neusner's methodology that we will frame our own approach to dating.

Neusner's answer to the above historical question is his hypothesis that where a saying is attributed to a named authority, a correct assignment to the *period* in which that authority flourished may be assumed. For we can check by reference to the history of the concept whether the saying is conceptually contemporaneous with the period, but we cannot know whether a particular Rabbi uttered it. For example, if we are able to show that a saying assigned to a Yavnean contains an idea which is conceptually earlier than, and not dependent on, what is assigned to an Ushan, then, prima facie, the earlier concept is correctly assigned to a Yavnean. The development of the ideas of Rabbis on legal questions can in many instances be shown to take place through a sequence of logic in that the ideas of later

Masters are dependent on those of earlier Masters. Often the later Masters will be seen to assume the existence of the earlier ideas.

An apparent flaw in this method is that the assumption that a certain Rabbi belongs to a certain period may be false. While the hypothesis that the saying belongs to the period of the named Rabbi can thus be subjected to an intelligent form of checking, albeit imprecise, it may be difficult to check upon the placing of a Rabbi in a particular generation. Neusner is rightly cautious about attributions, for sayings have doubtless been placed in the mouths of earlier Rabbis than those who uttered them: but may not this free approach of Rabbinic tradents to historical accuracy have resulted in similarly unsound legend concerning the period when particular Rabbis flourished?

Nor does Neusner baulk at the challenge presented by anonymous sayings, since he claims that nearly all anonymous sayings in the Mishnah fall into the sequential-conceptual framework established by the attributed ones. He writes, 'Once, therefore, we are able to establish the stages by which the logic of the law unfolds, doing so, as is clear, with the help of attributions tested against the logical-chronological sequence of the substance of what is attributed, we are able to make provision for sayings which bear no attributions. In any event these sayings turn out upon careful study to form an inconsequential part of the whole . . . '[67]

A further assumption which Neusner makes is that the individual Rabbis would be consistent in their views.[68] For he deduces that if the sayings assigned to a Sage are consistent, then the attribution of sayings to that Sage would appear to be disciplined, so that the attributions can be accepted as probably correct. The best evidence of correct assignment, Neusner suggests, is where the sayings indicate that the Sage has determined several different issues in accordance with some general legal theory recognizable in those independent rulings. We think that this is a useful assumption even though the consistency may on occasion have been produced by careful editing.

In verifying the dates of sayings Neusner makes some assumptions which he admits to be unproved. For example, he assumes that later Masters commonly tried to assign sayings to the men who said them, rather than to some earlier, more prestigious authority. Thus, if something is attributed to Gamaliel II, Neusner assumes that Gamaliel II, or his circle with his consent, said it. Neusner admits that this assumption is not always reliable, but argues that the limited number of false attributions suggests that the attributions of tradition are generally reliable.

Despite Neusner's hypotheses, it is still difficult to know what Mishnaic rules originated before AD 70. According to Neusner (*Traditions* I, p. 6), the conditions for the redaction and transmission of sayings of pre-70 Masters differ from the conditions prevailing afterwards, and it is difficult to verify pericopae likely to have been given final form before the destruction of the Temple. He claims that the traditions about the pre-70 Masters do not indicate that the exact words of sayings preserved in the Mishnah were orally formulated and handed on from Master to disciple. He points out that none of the Masters prior to Gamaliel I (died c. AD 52) were personally known to post-70 authorities, so that nobody had heard exactly what they said. He deduces from this that the paucity of credible lemmas and tales about the pre-70 Masters is due to the fact that they were formulated mostly by post-70 Rabbis, who did not freely invent material about early teachers, but generally only reported what they had heard. It seems, therefore, that the war of AD 66-73 led to a radical break in the transmission of traditions since some authorities died in the war. The problem of determining what purity and other rules prevailed in the time of Jesus and the earliest church is thus increased by the fact that nearly all Mishnaic pericopae, according to Neusner, derive in their present form from after AD 70.

So revolutionary and far-reaching has been the critical work of Neusner that subsequent scholarship in this field can most conveniently be categorized as pro- or anti-Neusner.[69] However, we consider now a scholar who supports Neusner's critical approach, but detects some shortcomings in it.

(iv) *Anthony J. Saldarini*

In an article in 1974 reviewing progress in form criticism of Rabbinic literature, Saldarini[70] notes that Neusner's historical studies led him to employ form criticism, and then to move away from it towards methods more fruitful of historical results. Through form criticism, Neusner discovered that fixed forms of presenting sayings first appeared in material associated with Hillel and the Houses of Shammai and Hillel. As we have no evidence that the pre-70 Sages actually taught in set form (apart from this material), the teaching of Hillel and the Houses may have been put into set forms by the Yavneans who, Neusner thinks, have put their own disputes into this Houses-dispute form.

But form criticism did not assist Neusner to date teachings exactly, nor to distinguish the original teaching from later interpolation. So Neusner turned from form criticism to his system of dating by 'attestations'. This is the hypothetico-legal system to which we have already referred. On seeking to date a teaching attributed to a named Rabbi, Neusner checks whether the teaching belongs to the generation of the Rabbi. He does this by enquiring whether that teaching is referred to, or modified, or contradicted, by a named Sage of the same or next generation. If so, there is a 'double attestation' to the authenticity of the attribution to the period of the later, and perhaps of the earlier, Sage.

Saldarini points out, however, that the 'double testimony' on which Neusner is relying comes from sources which were all edited, according to Saldarini, after AD 200, and which may have been revised to form the harmonized structure in which Neusner finds credibility. Saldarini writes that, of the early Rabbinic sources, 'Neusner finds Mishnah and Tosepta materials most attested and reliable, but they also underwent the most intensive editing and, despite obvious redactional seams and differing views visible in the material, were edited into a relatively consistent whole'.[71]

Against the accuracy of attributions, Saldarini also notes that the Sage to whom a saying is assigned often varies between manuscripts; he admits that Mishnah MSS are fairly consistent, but thinks this is probably due to the close study and constant revision of them.

We may stress again here that Neusner's system of attestations relies heavily on the correctness of the placing of Sages in their generations, quite apart from whether the text adopted refers to the correct Sage. His claim that many of the Houses-pericopae are to be assigned not to the period following the death of Hillel, but to the Yavnean period when the Rabbis there put *their* disputes into Houses' form, shows the circularity of the problem. For how can we be sure of the generation assigned to a Sage when (1) that generation has probably been determined in part by the content of the teaching attributed to him, and (2) the accuracy of that attribution of teaching depends upon the teaching being logically prior to, or consequent upon, as the case may be, the teaching of another Sage presumably given a generation by the same method? The Generation Tables to which we can refer in Danby, and Strack,[72] and the generations assigned in the Soncino Rabbinical Index, have probably been influenced by the content of the respective teachings of the Sages. Neusner[73] points out that only two figures mentioned in the Mishnah are known outside the Mishnah as Pharisees—Gamaliel I

(Acts 22.3) and his son, Simeon, to whom Josephus refers (*Vita*, 190f., 216). He adds that he is inclined to work from the known— these two—to the unknown. Such is the chasm of uncertainty!

Baumgarten[74] has complained that Neusner has so occupied himself with formal criteria that he has neglected consideration of the meaning of the texts which he cites.[75] This may explain the cause of the failing which Saldarini notes[76]—that Neusner's interpretation of a particular passage is sometimes changed without re-integration into earlier discussion. Thus, Neusner originally interprets Kelim 2.1 at *JSJ* 4 (1973), p. 59, but in his three volumes on Kelim he produces two other interpretations which both differ from each other and from the original one![77]

Despite his criticisms, Saldarini[78] acknowledges that Neusner has made a 'methodological breakthrough'. Saldarini concludes, though, on a note of caution regarding the results of Neusner's method, for 'Neusner's method presupposes that attestation and consistency argue for reliability, but a later editor who subjected rabbinic traditions to close analysis may have imposed this consistency. Until we know why and for what purpose the rabbis valued attribution of a saying to a specific authority, we cannot be sure how these attributions were made and how reliable they are.'[79]

(v) *Our Approach*

Until about thirty years ago, the orthodox Jewish approach to the Talmudic literature, namely that each Sage had said what was attributed to him, and if there were apparent inconsistencies in the various teachings, the key to their harmonization had to be found, had passed virtually unchallenged; NT scholars, too, although aware of the need for critical treatment of their own literature, had accorded to the Talmud the same unquestioning credibility as had their Jewish colleagues.

Since that time, NT scholars have been treating the Jewish materials with increasing caution, which was turned to a rigorous scepticism by the revolutionary work of Neusner commencing with his *Development of a Legend: Studies on the Traditions concerning Yohanan ben Zakkai* in 1970.[80] Thus, while we may express surprise at Bamberger's ascription of reliability to attributions, and the treatment of an attribution as the terminus ad quem, we have to remember that he was writing apropos of Wolfson[81] who was treating as old Palestinian material on which Philo would have drawn, books compiled centuries after Philo's death.

But is Neusner sceptical enough? We are impressed by Saldarini's point that we do not have any Rabbinic sources from the first or second centuries which are free from possible later revisions. Further, the establishment and maintenance of their own judicial and legislative authority would provide sufficient motivation for the efforts of Judah the Prince and earlier collectors to harmonize the unwritten law, and exhibit it as a rational and internally consistent whole. It is, therefore, arguable that, in plotting the development of early Jewish law, we should give primary weight to the probable course of development of a legal concept, and only treat attributions of sayings to named Sages as support for, or detraction from, the conclusions thus reached. In short, we would reverse Neusner's hypothetico-logical method. For Neusner writes, 'The simplest possible hypothesis is that the attribution of sayings to named authorities may be relied upon in assigning those sayings to the period, broadly defined, in which said authorities flourished . . . This proposition can indeed be tested. We have laws which interrelate in theme and conception and which also bear attributions to successive authorities, e.g. to a Yavnean, to an Ushan and to an authority of the time of Rabbi. If we are able to demonstrate that what is assigned to a Yavnean is conceptually earlier than, and not dependent upon, what is assigned to an Ushan, then, on the face of it, the former indeed is an earlier tradition, the latter a later one.'[82]

Our own inclination, however, is to accord greater weight in dating to a credible development of legal history, than to an assignment to the generation of a named Rabbi. Our preference is influenced by the following considerations. First, the assignment of a saying to a particular Rabbi is open to doubt, as emphasized by Saldarini. Secondly, the assignment of teaching to the generation of a named Rabbi is based on a circular argument to the extent that the Rabbi has been placed in that generation on account of his teaching.[83] Thirdly, further doubt concerning the generation of a Rabbi arises when, as in the case of several important Sages, such as the Gamaliels and the Joshuas, it is uncertain which of the homonymous Masters from different generations is intended in a particular attribution. Fourthly, the length of years covered by the teaching of the Houses and Akiba respectively impedes the accurate dating of a saying correctly attributed to them.

In some places, Neusner himself seems to be moving towards an increased reliance on the evidence of dating afforded by legal history.

He writes (*Purities*, XVIII, p. 161), 'As our understanding of the character of the data has changed, we have tended to take diminished interest in the problem of the validity of attributions. We have learned to recognize that the logical structure and sequence of laws are to be discerned in their own terms, to be discovered within the conceptions of the laws themselves. Attributions therefore have proved interesting primarily as a way of checking upon the alleged sequences of logic.'

However, we treat our above preference for the evidence of legal history in dating as subservient to the over-riding principle of evidence which we have applied to the NT material, namely that a statement that a person (Rabbi A) said something (X) is evidence that Rabbi A did say X. That evidence will not prove that A said X, if it is intrinsically improbable, or if there is stronger evidence to the contrary. Contrary evidence may be either that it was not A who said X, or that A said not X but something else. Even if evidence in the form of a Talmudic statement that A said X is not intrinsically improbable and is not opposed by contrary evidence as strong, and the statement thus stands proved, it may be almost valueless as a guide to the state of the law in our period, if we cannot safely assign A's teaching to a particular generation.

Our above preference operates to the effect that the evidence constituted by the Talmudic statement will probably be overborne by any contrary evidence provided by the course of development of legal history.[84] For legal history may show that a Rabbi of A's generation is unlikely to have said X because in his generation the law was in a more primitive state. Our procedure in checking the statements on purity in our passage by reference to legal history will therefore be, first, to consider the evidence constituted by the more important attributed Talmudic statements, and, then, to assess whether that evidence is overborne by evidence from the development of legal history. Unfortunately, space does not permit us to subject Talmudic statements on less essential points in the passage to this procedure.

In our attempt to discover the state of the purity laws between AD 30 and 70 using, in part, the evidence constituted by the course of development taken by the law, we must start with *some* data; we can only progress from the known to the unknown. Fortunately, we do have some limited data. First, we know that the Priestly Code, which includes the law of purity in Leviticus 11–16 and a few texts on purity in Exodus and Numbers, received its final form after the return from Exile.[85] We can accordingly say that the law in that Code prevailed in 400 BC. Moreover, we have good reason to believe that, although that law was developed, its provisions were not abrogated, so that we can treat them as valid in the time of Jesus. The instances where Pentateuchal law was varied before or during our period, as was, for example, the seventh-year release of debts by Hillel's prozbul fiction, were rare and well-attested, and we are not aware of any such abrogation of a purity law.

Secondly, we know that Mark believed that certain provisions of purity law prevailed either in the time of Jesus, or at some time between then and the date of his Gospel, i.e. probably not later than AD 65-67.[86] Admittedly, express and implied legal statements in our passage must be treated with some reserve for Mark may simply have been mistaken, but he is unlikely to have invented *new* legal concepts. Thus, if Mark refers to handwashing before meals or bathing on return from market, it is very likely that at least *some* Jews did so at or before Mark's time of writing. We remind ourselves of Margoliouth's dictum that Mark and the Synoptic Gospels generally are at least as good an authority for the customs prevalent during the first 70 years AD as is the Talmud.[87] We also glean evidence on purity law from the Gospels of Luke and John, and from the inter-testamental literature.

Thirdly, we know from the Mishnah of a plethora of provisions which had been added to the purity law by c. AD 200. We can assume that the Mishnah usually does not speak of law which did not prevail c. AD 200; much of the law in it prevailed in earlier times also. But we must exclude from Mishnaic law prevailing in AD 200 its provisions relating to Temple matters, sacrifice and the like, which can only have been included for reasons of continuing academic interest, or to preserve them for the expected re-building of the Temple.

We thus have reasonable knowledge of the state of the law at each end of this 600 year span, and we also have evidence, primarily from Mark, concerning purity practices at a date between 30 and 70 AD. In our plotting of the course of development taken by the law within this span, however, we are assisted by the influence of logic upon that development. Neusner writes, 'The unfolding of the rabbis' ideas on legal and other questions may be shown to take place through sequences of logic, with what is assigned to later masters often depending upon and generated by what is assigned to the earlier ones. When we find a correlation between such logical (not merely thematic) sequences and temporal ones, . . . then we have history'.[88] Here again, we are stimulated by Neusner's approach, but it may result in a later dating of the commencement of rules than we would wish to adopt. For, if logic is the creative power in the development of law, then a new rule is unlikely to arise until the law-makers (the Sages) have decreed it. In reaction to Neusner, we stress the variety of influences in the development of law. What Holmes wrote of the English Common Law can be applied mutatis mutandis to other systems of law: 'The life of the law has not been logic: it has been experience. The felt necessities of the time, the prevalent moral and political theories, intuitions of public policy, avowed or unconscious, even the prejudices which judges share with their fellow-men, have had a good deal more to do than the syllogism in determining the rules by which men should be governed. The law . . . cannot be dealt with as if it contained only the axioms and corollaries of a book of mathematics.'[89] A more recent author, Recasens-Siches, writes, 'Legal rules are not the expressions of logical truths. On the contrary, legal rules are a human work, made by man under the stimuli of the problems raised by social living together and cooperation, in a certain time and in a certain place. Legal rules are the practical response to practical problems, under the pressure of the needs for order, security, peace and justice in social life . . . Consequently a legal rule can never be true or false. A legal rule can be just or unjust, adequate or inadequate, effective or ineffective.'[90]

That logic is only one of several forces in the development of law is shown not only by the need of the legislator and the judge to provide a satisfactory, just and practical answer to a social problem (whether logical or not), but also by the important function of custom in the growth of law. For custom does not flourish according to the dictates of logic. People's experience of social, religious and other influences gives rise to a preferred way of behaving, and this becomes a customary behaviour which, in turn, becomes law enforced by a social, religious or penal sanction. Ehrlich[91] stressed that in all ages the centre of gravity of legal development has lain neither in legislation, nor in juristic science, nor in judicial decision, but in society itself.[92]

It is thus possible to over-estimate the rôle of logic in legal development, since law arises from society, from the people themselves, and embraces all the innumerable customs, habits and practices which form the life of a society or group of people. And in the creation of these customs logic is only one of many influences.

Customs include what Sumner calls the 'ritual of the mores'. He writes, 'The mores are the social ritual in which we all participate unconsciously. The current habits as to hours of labour, meal hours, family life, the social intercourse of the sexes, propriety, amusements, travel, . . . and innumerable other details of life fall under this ritual. Each does as everybody does. For the great mass of mankind as to all things, and for all of us for a great many things, the rule to do as all do, suffices. We are led by suggestion and association to believe that there must be wisdom and utility in what all do. The great mass of the folkways give us discipline and the support of routine and habit.'[93] He then adds most perceptively in regard to the relative importance of expediency and logic in the formation of custom, 'If we had to form judgments as to all these cases before we could act in them, and were forced always to act rationally, the burden would be unendurable'.[94]

We see no reason to doubt that the pressure upon judges and legislators to provide expedient solutions of the people's problems, and also the force of custom have played an equally important part in the development of law affecting religious or sacred matters as it has in that affecting secular matters.[95] For example, it is likely that the members of the Sanhedrin who, following Deut. 17.11,[96] imposed the law not only between litigants, but with legislative effect, were similarly influenced by the need to find practical solutions in both the secular and religious issues before them; so also the individual Sages giving decisions. It was the interpretation of the relevant Scripture rather than logic which was the theoretical discipline followed by the Sanhedrin and the Sages. And the exegetical rules of Hillel (the Seven Middoth), for example, may be considered more arbitrary than logical.[97]

It seems clear that in early Jewish law custom could acquire the force of law. Cohn writes, 'in many instances, common usage as such, even without any underlying rule, acquires the force of binding law'.[98] He cites Baba Metzia 7.1 where the working hours and right to food of labourers is made dependent on local custom, and Baba Bathra 1.1 where the material of which a courtyard partition is built is said to depend on local custom.

Even in a theocratic society, such as Israel, where every act of daily living was to be performed in accordance with the will of Yahweh, the folkways, 'the rule to do as all do', were, we believe, the ancestors of what in time acquired the solemnity of traditional law.[99] For while the priest, and later the Sage, was available to advise on difficulties of clean/unclean, it is most unlikely that every doubtful point was submitted to them; no, in religious practice as in social, 'the rule to do as all do, suffices'.[100] Indeed, in some aspects of purity the folkways must dictate the effective scope of defilement even if this runs contrary to the decisions of the Sages. Thus, at Eduyoth 1.1 Shammai holds that a menstruating woman only defiles from the time of the first appearance of menstrual blood. Hillel holds that if a woman inspects herself, and finds a trace of menstrual blood, she has retroactively defiled all the clean things she has touched from the time of her last inspection when she was clean. The Sages whose opinion appears to prevail hold that if the menstruant last examined herself during the previous 24 hours, then she retroactively defiles the objects she has touched since that examination. If that last examination was not during the previous 24 hours, then her defiling capacity begins at the start of those hours. However, a woman with fixed periods is deemed to be unclean only from the first flow. But surely the view of Shammai must have represented the prevailing mores on the subject, whether or not a woman had fixed periods, for the practical uncertainty and inconvenience created by retroactive defilement is so immense. In the case of a woman with irregular periods, enquiry would have to be made as to what she had touched (and thus defiled) during the last 24 hours or less (the Sages) or during possibly the last few days (Hillel).

Again, the washing of the hands before eating, to which various origins have been attributed, may have derived not from any logical process but from a borrowing of contemporary Roman table manners. A practical origin is also provided for the ruling at Hullin 105a that the washing after the meal must be in cold water—'because hot water softens the hands and does not remove the grease'. And at 105b the reason for washing the hands after the meal is that salt of Sodom on the hands might otherwise touch and blind the eyes.

Finkelstein[101] has argued that many controversies between Pharisaic Sages were due not to differing interpretations of Scripture, but to different local or economic conditions or to professional allegiances of the Sages concerned. He counts eight controversies which, the Talmud maintains, reflect differences of background between Israel and Babylonia. For example, at Menahoth 13.6 R. Eleazer ben Azariah claims that to fulfil a vow to bring a whole-burnt offering, a pigeon or a dove must be brought, while other scholars said a lamb. The Talmud (Menahoth 107b) explains that both agreed that the least costly offering is required, but in the locality of Eleazar pigeons and doves were cheaper than lambs but more expensive in his colleagues' locality. Again, at TJ. M.S. 5.5, 56b, on the issue of whether the tithe should be given to the priest as well as to the Levites, the colleagues of R. Joshua ben Levi (who was a Levite) are astonished that he sides with the priests. This indicates that a scholar might be expected to be influenced by personal or tribal interests, and not only by logic and Scriptural interpretation.

A consequence of our insistence upon the rôles of custom and mores in the development of the law is a hastening of the time at which a law starts to operate. For we claim not only that custom, by which we mean 'what people actually do' is a source of law, but also that it *is* law.[102] So, for example, if we seek to know whether Jewish religious law enjoined handwashing in the time of Jesus, we ask whether Jews generally, or a section of Jews, did, in fact, wash their hands. For if they regularly washed their hands before meals, they felt some sanction (be it conscience, social disfavour or the compulsion to 'do as everyone does'), so that, for those affected, handwashing before meals was 'living law'. We therefore endorse the words of Margoliouth written in connection with handwashing, 'The strict codification of an ordinance is very often merely the final step in a course of development; and one has a right to assume that the formal extension of these rules of purification to the laity would not have been introduced, if they had not already taken root in the consciences and the conduct of the more pious of the people'.[103] The practical effect of this conception of law upon our dating of purity rules is that we deem them to be operative some time before they are declared by the Sages. For we doubt, for example, that the Sages would de novo declare handwashing obligatory before eating terumah: *some* priests, at least, would, we think, have been following the practice before it received judicial confirmation by the Sages, and the practice might have come to the Sages' attention either because a reluctant priest queried its necessity, or because some point on the manner or time of washing was submitted for decision.

Our procedure in charting the course of development of the early history of Jewish purity law will be to start with the early data, i.e. in the Priestly Code, and to progress towards the Mishnah using en route any available witnesses, such as e.g. the Apocrypha, Qumran, Philo, the NT, as intermediate guides.[104] For in assessing the law in c. AD 30, it is helpful to know its state both before and after that date; we can much increase the chances of approximate accuracy concerning the law at that time by having evidence of its state both before and afterwards.

Finally, we stress that we do not deny the part played by logic in the development of early Jewish law—in the deductions made from Scriptural texts and in relating new rules to other rules. We are impressed by Neusner's point that new rules are created from established principles by analogy or contrast. He writes, 'Something either is like something else, therefore follows the rule of that to which it is comparable, or it is not like something else, therefore follows the opposite of the rule of that to which it is contrasted' (*Purities*, XXII, pp. 69-70 n. 1). But we disagree with his view (*ibid.*) that very little in the system cannot be shown to emerge through these two methods of reasoning. We believe that in no small measure the Sages were influenced by social considerations, or were lending the weight of their authority to, or deciding marginal points affecting, law already constituted by the customary behaviour of the people or a section thereof, who were already 'doing' the law.

g. *The date of Mark's Gospel*

The difficulty of dating the Talmudic material increases the need to fix the date of Mark. The law expressed or implied in his Gospel is unlikely to have arisen at a later time than when Mark wrote, so that, depending on that date, if Mark's legal references are correct, their content may have prevailed, at least as custom, in the time of Jesus. There is possible inter-action here, for if we knew the earliest time at which Mark's law prevailed, that date would assist in fixing the earliest time of the writing of the Gospel.

In view of the evidence that Mark wrote after the deaths of Peter and Paul,[105] a terminus a quo of about AD 65 is indicated, and since Mark 13.14f. seems to lack knowledge of the capture of Jerusalem when compared with the actuality of Luke 21.20 and 24, Mark probably wrote before AD 70. For the purpose of using Mark's legal references as an intermediate guide to the state of the law in the time of Jesus, we would need no more precision than to place the Gospel in the seventh decade,[106] but we incline to Taylor's dating (p. 32) of AD 65-67.

h. *The date of the Dead Sea Scrolls*

While it is generally accepted that the Community took up residence at Qumran about 150 BC, and abandoned the site about AD 68, it is difficult to judge at what times within that period the various documents were written. Vermes (p. 71) considers the Community Rule to be probably one of the oldest documents, and to date from the latter part of the second century BC. In the Damascus Document, the reference to the New Covenant made in the land of Damascus, the chronological data, and the absence of any reference to the Kittim (the Romans, who invaded after 70 BC) suggest to him (p. 95) that the Document was written about 100 BC.

As these two are the main documents regulating the members of the Sect living at Qumran (Community Rule) and those living outside (Damascus Rule), we agree that they would probably be composed at a fairly early date within the first period of occupation of Qumran which was from c. 150 BC to c. 30 BC (Vermes, p. 54). Charlesworth,[107] however, notes the need to recognize that the Community Rule and the Damascus Rule obtained their present form through an evolutionary process mirroring the historical stages of the Qumran Essenes. Assuming the early origin of these two documents, and the cessation of activity at Qumran in 68 AD, it seems reasonable to suppose that most of the halakhoth therein had received final form by the time of Jesus' ministry.

i. *The purpose of cultic purity*

The exact question whose credibility we must now consider in the light of the law prevailing in the time of Jesus, is: 'Why do your disciples eat food with hands which are cultically defiled?' If it was neither legally required, nor customary, for Jews or a group of Jews to wash their hands before eating, then the previously posited authenticity of the earliest form of the dispute is seriously prejudiced. For we cannot accept that the dispute is authentic if the initiating question is nonsense because either a. there is no legal or customary cause for the disciples to consider their hands defiled, or b. there is no legal or customary cause why the disciples should not eat with hands defiled.

The nature and scope of cultic defilement are thus cardinal to a judgment of the credibility of the Question. The Scriptural sanction against cultic defilement was that no man who was unclean could offer sacrifice or take part in the worship of the Temple, and, according to 2 Chron. 23.19, the gatekeepers were intended to bar entry of the unclean. Regarding the priests, this sanction is expressed at Lev. 22.3, 'If any one of all your descendants throughout your generations approaches the holy things which the people of Israel dedicate to the Lord, while he has an uncleanness, that person shall be cut off from my presence'.[108] Regarding the people, after explaining how those suffering a discharge may be cleansed, the injunction follows at Lev. 15.31, 'Thus you shall keep the people of Israel separate[109] from their uncleanness, lest they die in their uncleanness by defiling my tabernacle that is in their midst'. Similarly, at Num. 19, after prescribing the purification for a man defiled by a dead body, v. 20 continues, 'But the man who is unclean and does not cleanse himself, that person shall be cut off from the midst of the assembly, since he has defiled the sanctuary of the Lord'.

Westerholm,[110] however, argues that there was a Biblical basis for many of the laws of purity being applied *without* reference to the Temple. He refers to the demand for separation from prohibited foods and from lepers, and to the defilement of non-cultic vessels in which food or liquids were kept. But it may be contended that the purpose of the Priestly Code in decreeing the defilement of non-cultic things or persons was not to attach importance to their own defilement, but only to their consequent power to defile other persons or things, and thus prevent their entry to the Temple, or usage for Temple-connected purposes. In contrast, Westerholm maintains that purification is required from all kinds of defilement when no visit to the Sanctuary is in view. But it is arguable that the express permission for both the clean and the unclean to eat meat which has not been sacrificed in the Temple[111] is implicit acknowledgment that a man needs to be clean only for Temple purposes.

It is possible that the Priestly Code accentuates the connection of the purity rules with the Temple because of its priestly authorship; neither the Covenant Code in Exodus nor the Deuteronomic Code states the defilement of the tabernacle to be the reason for the avoidance of impurity. A reason stated in Deuteronomy is that 'you are a people holy to the Lord',[112] but this does not necessarily imply disqualification from the Temple as the sanction for impurity.[113]

The correct solution to the ambivalence of Scripture concerning the purpose of purity may be that from early times there were two conflicting traditions. Alon[114] points out that there are Biblical passages which discuss impurity in the context of the priests, the Temple and holy foods, whereas other passages are addressed to all Israel and to the prohibition of uncleanness in all circumstances. Neusner lists several instances of extra-cultic uncleanness, and concludes, 'Clearly, the holiness of the cult is not the sole concern in regard to the preservation of cleanness. But Leviticus is explicit that the people and the land are deemed analogous to the cult... The various unclean people, in particular, produce consequences outside of the cult, principally in respect to the prohibition of sexual relations' (*Purities*, XXII, pp. 33-34).

It is undeniable that at a later stage of history the Pharisees did eat non-holy food in a state of levitical purity, and thereby created a focus of purity external to the Temple. We must elucidate the time at which this attitude to the domestic table arose, and amongst whom it prevailed. For if it prevailed in the time of Jesus amongst the Pharisees mentioned in our passage, then it is credible that they might suggest to Jesus that his disciples should do the same thing. Alon,[115] after examining the inclusion in the laws of impurity of unconsecrated objects and unconsecrated food, concludes that in the Second Temple period two conflicting trends co-existed: the 'expansionist' tendency established amongst the Essenes and the restrictive tendency dominant amongst the Sadducees.[116] Amongst the Pharisees neither tendency was able to oust the other entirely, though the tendency to limitation was stronger. Regarding handwashing before ordinary food (with which, recognition of the domestic table as a locus of impurity must be linked) Alon admits that till the destruction of the Temple and possibly even later, this practice was not accepted by all the Sages, nor observed by all Israel, and he cites Eleazar b. Enoch's doubts; he consequently regards our v. 3 that all Israel handwashed in Jesus' time as an 'exaggerated generalization'.[117]

At *Purities*, XXII, p. 89, however, Neusner considers that v. 3 attests to handwashing before eating 'at the earliest stages of the unfolding of the law', and he claims elsewhere that this practice did prevail amongst Pharisees, apparently in, or close to, Jesus' time. He writes, 'What was the dominant trait of Pharisaism before 70 CE? It was, as depicted both in the rabbinic traditions about the Pharisees and in the gospels, concern for matters of rite, in particular, eating one's meals in a state of ritual purity as if one were a temple priest . . . '.[118]

To summarize, it seems probable that there were conflicting views from early days concerning the scope of the purity rules; but it is sufficient to render the Pharisaic question at v. 5 credible if *some* Pharisees could, consistently with *their* views on purity, have asked it. Since both conflicting traditions acknowledged the need of purity for Temple-connected purposes, we propose to test the legal credibility of the question, first, according to the restrictive view that the Temple was the sole raison d'être of the purity rules. If the question is not intelligible on this basis, that it was legally necessary to handwash before eating in order to avoid ultimate defilement to 'Temple persons or food', we will, secondly, examine whether it is credible on the basis that the questioning Pharisees were among those who either handwashed as a work of supererogation, or held the expansive view that ritual purity should be maintained in some circumstances, and in particular when eating ordinary food, even when the purity of the Temple was not threatened.[119]

Chapter 4

THE HISTORY OF PURITY IN EATING

According to Mark 6.53 Jesus and the disciples were at Gennesaret in Galilee when the discussion in our passage with the Pharisees took place, and even if that verse is not historical,[1] it is accepted that Jesus and his disciples were Galileans, and that much of his ministry was exercised there. What consequence, therefore, could the need for purity in the Temple possess, according to the restrictive tradition, for the washing habits of Galileans, many miles away?[2] However, although the Temple was far away, Temple persons and food were not. The priests[3] in Galilee would officiate in the Temple according to their course (Sukkah 5.6-8), and some of the local people would accompany them (Bikkurim 3.2); further, many Galileans probably made the pilgrimage to Jerusalem for the three Feasts (Exod. 23.17; Josephus, *Bellum* 6.423f.).[4] However, there would be no need to wash hands to avoid the passage of impurity to such Temple persons, since persons are only susceptible to a Biblical source of impurity,[5] and even if they were defiled, they would probably bathe in any case at the end of their pilgrimage, in one of the many *miqvaoth* near Jerusalem.[6]

If the impurity of the hands was transmissible to the extent necessary, it is more likely that hands were washed for fear of ultimate defilement of the holy food in Galilee. For the priest was authorized by Num. 18.11 to eat his share of the sacrificial offerings at home, both himself and any other clean person in his house, and by 18.12-13 to eat his *terumah gedolah*[7] at home with other clean persons. Thus, the holy food in the priest's house was theoretically liable to defilement by a visiting unclean layman, since foodstuffs can be defiled by an offspring of impurity.[8] Since the priest naturally received *terumah* from sacrifices only during his course's brief period of service in the Temple,[9] the *terumah* in Galilee which was most liable to be defiled in practice was the *terumah gedolah* in the possession of the farmer or fisherman[10] from the time of its separation from other produce (when it became susceptible as *terumah*)[11] until its delivery to the local priest (Betzah 1.6; Terumoth 2.4).[12] It is very probable that a large proportion of the Galileans were farmers[13] or fishermen. Josephus (*Bellum* 3.42) notes the richness of the soil, and that every inch is cultivated, and both the NT (e.g. Mark 1.16-20 and John 21.3-14) and Josephus (*Vita* 163-65) testify to the fishing[14] in Galilee. Josephus (*Bellum* 3.516-20) praises the region around Lake Gennesaret for its production of every species of plant to be harvested in the various seasons.[15] *Terumah* had to be separated from these various crops at their respective harvests (Num. 18.12; Terumoth 2.4), and the farmer needed to be pure while he separated and delivered it to the priest.[16] It is thus arguable that, even according to the restrictive tradition, there was cause for hands to be washed in Galilee, in order to preserve the purity of *terumah gedolah* there.

However, the Pharisaic question asks why the disciples do not wash before *eating*, which presumably implies that the defilement to be avoided is the defilement of the eater; such an assumption is supported by Jesus' logion at v. 15 (which in Part I we concluded to be the reply to the Pharisaic question), for it also treats the impurity of the eater as the issue.

Thus, the route to be taken by the impurity, in order to render the question credible, is from hands to *hullin*, thence to the eater, and thence to *terumah*. We will now consider whether this transmission is possible according to such rules of purity as are indicated by the sources to have been observed by Pharisees generally in Jesus' time.

a. *Are hands susceptible to impurity separately from the body?*

1. *The Pentateuch*

Many provisions of the Priestly Code (e.g. Lev. 11 and 15 passim) decreed that the body could become impure through contact with an impure thing. The contact could be by touch of the unclean thing with the hands (e.g. Lev. 15.5) or with another part of the body, as in the case of sitting or lying upon it (e.g. Lev. 15.6). But could the hands alone become unclean? Washing of the hands and feet by priests before entering the tent of meeting, or approaching the altar to minister, is required by Exod. 30.17ff.[17] Indeed, Finkelstein[18] notes that the early scribes, disturbed by the prolixity of that passage compared to the conciseness of most Pentateuchal legislation, and seeing that washing was commanded in it three times, ordained three ablutions: the priest must bathe on entering the Temple, and must wash his hands and feet on both approaching and leaving the altar. The relevance of this Exodus requirement is that it may have been by analogy to these priestly washings of the hands and feet that lay washing of the hands arose.

Finkelstein[19] mentions that according to rabbinic tradition the priests regarded the eating of *terumah* as a divine service. He cites Pes. 72b, where R. Tarfon, a priest, explains to R. Gamaliel II that he has been engaged in 'priestly worship'. Gamaliel asks how there can be a ministry for priests when the Temple is in ruins. Tarfon replies that he was eating the heave-offering which is considered by priests to be like the Temple service itself. Finkelstein claims that the priests transferred to the eating of their priestly food outside the Temple the ablutions required for their duties at the altar (which included eating there some of the priestly dues), and that the custom passed from the priests to the more rigorously observant laymen 'who liked to believe that any table can become like the table of the Lord'. This Talmudic pericope need not put a post-70 date on the priestly practice and the subsequent lay practice, for Gamaliel's ignorance may only have been that Tarfon treated the eating of *terumah* as priestly worship; the eating of it only after washing may have been a long-established practice. However, it may not be justifiable to deduce priestly washings outside the Temple from this pericope, since its context at 72b is that of explanation that the eating of *terumah* is a religious duty which continued notwithstanding the destruction of the Temple.[20]

The only reference in the Pentateuch[21] both to the washing of hands by a layman and to the washing of hands separately from any other part of the body (even feet) is at Lev. 15.11, which concerns a *zab* (a man with a bodily discharge), and provides, 'Anyone whom he that has the discharge touches, without having rinsed (שטף) his hands in water, shall wash his clothes, and bathe himself in water, and be unclean until the evening'. Finkelstein[22] cites R. Eleazar ben Arak (c. AD 80-120 according to Danby's Appendix) as authority for a view that the scribes relied upon this verse in ordaining the washing of hands by laymen before eating *hullin* (Sifra, Mezora, perek 4, end, 77a; Hullin 106a). This origin seems at first sight less likely, for the

analogy is so remote; the fact that a *zab* contaminates by touch
unless he has washed his hands is not closely related to the fact that a
person *without* a discharge automatically needs to wash his hands
before eating![23] It could be deduced from that scripture that a person
who *knows* he is unclean, either because he is a *zab*, or otherwise, will
defile by touch unless he washes his hands, but that would justify
washing only on that occasion, not the routine washing indicated by
our passage.

Some commentators[24] mention that the Rabbis based lay handwashing before meals on Lev. 11.44, 'Sanctify yourselves' (התקדשתם),
and even on 11.43, 'ye shall not make yourselves abominable', but the
generalized nature of these injunctions tends to support the view that
the Rabbis were there making post hoc rationalizations in an attempt
to find scriptural basis for the practice.

The derivation of the practice of handwashing by laymen from the
Exodus imposition on priests doing Temple service and their later
eating outside the Temple in similar purity seems a more likely origin
of the practice. The Pentateuchal evidence itself, however, contains
no authority for handwashing by laymen before eating. Neusner
(*Purities*, XXII, p. 26) notes that while the law on *sources* of uncleanness rises 'in easy stages on an elevator of exegesis' from Scripture to
Mishnah, this is not so in the case of loci of uncleanness (times,
places or activities to be kept clean) and modes of purification. In
addition to the handbreadth passage of corpse uncleanness, he cites
purification by natural water and the meal outside the cult as
concepts wholly outside the framework of Scripture.

However, we have so far only considered the Pentateuch, so we
turn to the other relevant literature for evidence of a scriptural or
other origin for a rule decreeing the separate impurity of hands.

2. *The Prophetic and Inter-testamental Literature*
There are references in the prophetic books to the washing of hands,
but the washing seems to symbolize a moral cleansing. At Isaiah
1.15-16a Yahweh says, 'When you spread forth your hands, I will
hide my eyes from you ... your hands are full of blood. Wash
yourselves; make yourselves clean.' In the Psalms also, there is
symbolical use of handwashing.[25] Sometimes the speaker is a priest,
though. Thus at Ps. 26.6 we read, 'I will wash my hands in innocence,
and go about thy altar, O Lord'. Symbolical, surely, is 24.3-4, 'Who
shall ascend the hill of the Lord? And who shall stand in his holy
place? He who has clean hands and a pure heart ... '

Admittedly, the essence of a symbol or metaphor is that words are transferred from a situation where they have a literal meaning to another situation where they are understood not literally but according to the *kind* of meaning which they originally possessed. Thus, for handwashing to have a symbolic meaning of moral purification or reform, hands must literally have been washed in the original situation. We incline to think, however, that the original situation was the washing of hands by the priest in connection with service at the altar, following the Exodus provision, rather than a practice of handwashing by laymen. At 1 Sam. 20.26 David, a layman, is thought by Saul to have stayed away from the new-moon meal through impurity, but bodily impurity is presumably meant.

Nor is there any clear evidence from the inter-testamental literature of laymen handwashing before eating. Grundmann[26] comments in reference to 'all the Jews' washing their hands in v. 3 of our passage that the statement may have related to the situation in the Diaspora, and he cites Judith 12.7 and the Sybilline Oracles 3.591f. Büchler,[27] also, has suggested, partly on the strength of Judith 12.7-9, that some lay Jews practised handwashing there before the first century AD, even if it was not required of Jews in Palestine; being constantly surrounded by Gentile impurity, they may have had strict rules about handwashing earlier than the Jews of Palestine. We wonder if this suggestion is based on a correct estimate of the legal position. It is recorded that Jose b. Joezer and Jose b. Johanan decreed uncleanness upon the land of the Gentiles in pre-Tannaitic times (Shab. 14b), but contact with this uncleanness would more likely require purification by bodily immersion than by washing of the hands.[28] Before AD 70 halakhoth affecting the Diaspora could probably issue only from the Sages or Sanhedrin of Jerusalem,[29] and we have no record in Mishnah or *baraithoth* of a provision requiring *handwashing* after Gentile contact.

Further we are not convinced that the Judith passage supports stricter handwashing customs in the Diaspora. It is recited in this passage that Holofernes, chief captain of Nebuchadnezzar, was sent against Syria and Egypt, and on his way there went to Esdraelon and near to Bethulia (7.1-3) where Judith, a widow of Bethulia, went to him (10.6, 17). As Cowley[30] points out, the geography in the book is not very clear, but Torrey[31] has shown that, on taking Bethulia to be Shechem, the other place-names can be identified. Thus, Esdraelon is then the Greek form of Jezreel, which covers lowlands between Galilee and Mount Gilboa. It may, therefore, be incorrect to suggest that either Judith's normal residence or the camp of Holofernes was in the Diaspora. The washing habits described may be those of a non-Diaspora Jewess whilst among Gentiles temporarily.

However, the practice there described is more likely to be immersion than handwashing. The passage reads, ' . . . and she abode in the camp three days, and went out every night into the valley of Bethulia, and washed herself at the fountain of water in the camp. And when she came up, she besought the Lord God of Israel to direct her way to the raising up of the children of his people. And she came in clean, and remained in the tent, until she took her meat towards evening.' Cowley points out that the Greek reads literally in the first-quoted sentence, 'she used to go out [of her tent] by night and bath in the camp at the spring'.[32] Both the reference there to bathing and the reference in the next sentence to coming up, indicate immersion rather than hand-washing,[33] and do not appear to support the alleged Diaspora practice.

Lanchester[34] translates the Sybilline sentence mentioned by Grundmann as, 'But they instead raise heavenwards holy arms, rising early from their bed and ever cleansing their *flesh* with water, and they honour Him alone . . . ' Unfortunately, there is textual doubt concerning what is cleansed, for Rzach[35] gives the variants as χέρας, which he adopts, χεῖρας, a much supported reading, and χρόα, attested by Clement and Gfroer. Lanchester has adopted χρόα while Grundmann has preferred χέρας or χεῖρας. The reference at 4.165-66 to washing in rivers and raising hands to heaven seems to support Lanchester's reading of χρόα (from χροία or χρώς, the surface of the body). In any case, these Sybilline sentences speak of washing before prayer, not food. Lanchester sees Essene influence on them.

In the Letter of Aristeas, lines 305-306, it is related concerning the translators of the Hebrew Bible into Greek that in the morning they washed their hands in the sea and prayed to God, and then read and translated the text. The washing before prayer is there explained as a token that they had done no evil. A handwashing in these circumstances does not appear to be related to washing before eating, or to ritual purity, and so does not assist our enquiry.

It is appropriate that we should next discuss the Qumran sect and the Essenes with regard to lustration. A strong school of thought regards the two groups as identical; Vermes, after a review of the reasons, concludes that the identification 'possesses a high degree of intrinsic probability. The only remaining alternative is that the archaeologists have uncovered relics of a hitherto totally unknown Jewish sect almost identical to the Essenes.'[36]

However, we cannot explain the question in our passage by assuming that the Pharisees were influenced by Essene practice, since the evidence (infra) in the Qumran documents of purificatory rites relates to bodily immersion rather than handwashing. Nor (infra) does Josephus refer to them washing their hands only. As the Pharisees generally lived in the towns, we would expect them to be more influenced by those Essenes who also lived in the towns, rather than by the Community at Qumran, but with regard to purifications there may well have been some uniformity of practice. We therefore consider evidence from the Community Rule, which applies primarily to the desert Community, as well as evidence from the Damascus Document, which applies primarily to the devotees in the towns.

In the Community Rule V (Vermes, p. 79) we read that the 'men of falsehood . . . are not reckoned in His Covenant . . . they shall not enter the water to partake of the pure Meal of the Saints, for they shall not be cleansed until they turn from their wickedness'. Also respecting washing before eating, Josephus writes that the Essenes are employed strenuously until the fifth hour when they assemble together and 'after girding their loins with linen cloths, bathe their bodies in cold water . . . pure now themselves, they repair to the refectory, as to some sacred shrine'.[37] This treatment of the refectory as a holy shrine[38] and the preceding immersion may have influenced the probably Ushan treatment of the domestic table as a shrine,[39] preceded by handwashing. It is stated in the Damascus Document V (Vermes, p. 113) that no man shall enter the house of worship unclean and in need of washing, but there is no provision there about washing before eating.

All the indications are that total immersion rather than hand-washing[40] is involved in these purifications, and this is supported by a specific provision in the Damascus Document X (Vermes, p. 111) that no man shall bathe in dirty water or in amount too shallow to cover a man. It is pertinent to our enquiry, however, that in the Essenes we learn of a body of laymen who preserved as high a standard of purity as the priests,[41] doubtless because they considered that, until the legitimate priesthood was restored in Jerusalem, they *were* the true priests of the true Temple, their assembly.

3. *The Rabbinic Literature*

As we find no support for the susceptibility of hands alone to

uncleanness, in the case of laymen, from the prophetic or inter-
testamental literature, we next look at the Talmud for early[42]
Rabbinic evidence. A decree imputing impurity to the hands is there
attributed to the Houses.

At Zab. 5.12 the hands are included in a list of ten things which are
all stated to invalidate *terumah*. Although these rulings are there
expressed anonymously, there is evidence elsewhere of their authors.

At Shab. 1.4 it is stated that 'these' (ואלו) are among the rulings
which the Sages mentioned[43] in the upper room of Hananiah b.
Hezekiah b. Gorion; they voted and the Shammaites outnumbered
the Hillelites, and they decreed 18 things. We must enquire whether
the rulings made then included the *terumah* rulings,[44] for if they did,
we may have the identity of their authors.

Although Jastrow defines אלו as 'these, the following', which would
then refer to certain rulings about the Sabbath at Shab. 1.5f., the
Sages at Shab. 13b identify 'these' of Shab. 1.4 as two Sabbath
lemmas at Shab. 1.3. However, according to those Sages, those two
Sabbath lemmas are apparently not among the 18 decrees. For at
Shab. 13b-17b in response to the question, 'What are the 18
measures?', 18 other decrees are recalled, starting with a *baraitha* of
terumah rulings in the same terms as at Zab. 5.12. Earlier evidence
placing the *terumah* rulings among the Hananiah decrees is contained
in the P.T. gemara on Shab. 1.4 where it is stated,

תני שמונה עשר דבר גזרו ובשמונה עשרה רבו: ובשמונה עשרה נחלקו:

The gemara adds, ואילו הן שגזרו and then sets out 8 prohibitions on
Gentile food, etc., and then the 10 things which invalidate *terumah*[45]
as at Zab. 5.12. We interpret this *baraitha* as meaning that 18 things
were decreed (גזרו) implying unanimously, through the contrast with
the following רבו), 18 things were passed by a majority (רבו), and 18
things were disputed (i.e. no solution was reached);[46] on this
construction of גזרו the additional gemara indicates that the *terumah*
decrees were unanimous. Schwab[47] translates to this effect, but
Zeitlin[48] interprets the *baraitha* as saying that these 8 Gentile
prohibitions and 9 (he counts) *terumah* rulings were passed by a
majority.

The P.T. gemara next records a statement of the Rabbis of
Caesarea that

אלו שגזרו ממה שרבו שובעה אינון:
ואילין אינין חורנייתא:

The meaning of this is not entirely clear;[49] our interpretation is that the Caesarean Rabbis said that, of the things which they decreed (the above allegedly unanimous 18), in fact, seven were by a majority, and these are the others (i.e. majority decrees). Of the 11 decrees then mentioned, 6 require the burning of *terumah* where it is of doubtful purity, and all the remaining 5, plus a 19th attributed to R. Jose b. Aboun,[50] are included in the 18 decrees in the B.T.

The P.T. rather cryptically continues,

אלו הן שגזרו אילין עשרתי קדמיית:
והשא מן מה דתני ר״ש בן יוחי בו ביום גזרו

We interpret this to mean, as a statement by the editor countering that of the Caesareans, 'These are they which they decreed by a majority—those last-mentioned Caesarean ones are the first ten, and the rest are among those which R. Simon b. Yohai taught—on that day they decreed . . . ' Then follow 18 decrees against the Gentiles, their food, offerings, etc.

Zeitlin[51] rightly observes, 'On voit que le Yerouschalmi présente aussi[52] de la confusion au sujet des dix-huit mesures', and as regards what was unanimous or not, ambiguity is created by the imprecise use of גזרו and רבו. Moreover, we cannot know to what extent the statements in the Tosephta and Talmuds concerning the content of the decrees represent independent oral tradition and to what extent the Tosephta repeats the Mishnah, the P.T. the Tosephta, and the B.T. the P.T. However, there is, in our view, sufficient discrepancy between all four documents to suggest little mere copying, but rather some fairly homogeneous strands of tradition. Thus, we cannot agree with Neusner (*Purities*, XII, p. 206) that it is untenable to assume that the story of Hananiah's upper room speaks of an historical event. We attach a chart which we think illustrates the comparative homogeneity of the tradition.

Zeitlin[53] accepts the P.T.'s evidence that they enacted 18 decrees unanimously, and 18 by a majority, and Hengel[54] thinks the P.T.'s account of the surrounding violence at Hananiah's is more historical.[55] Zeitlin[56] argues that of the 18 decrees passed by the Shammaite majority, 15 were forbidding the food of, social relations with, and Temple offerings of, Gentiles, and in fact were intended 'd'établir une séparation tranchée entre Juifs et Romains'; the other 3 concerned purity matters disputed between the Houses. The purpose of the 18 unanimous decrees, he claims,[57] was to prevent the Sadducean priests from being able to eat their *terumah*, because they decreed

Summary of traditions concerning subject-matter of decrees passed in upper room of Hananiah

Mishnah	*Tosephta*	*P.T.*	*B.T.*
Shab. 1.3 states towards end:	Shab. 1.16: Repeats Shab. 1.4.	Gemara on Shab. 1.4 states *18 DECREES PASSED UNANIMOUSLY, 18 BY MAJORITY, AND 18 MATTERS UNRESOLVED.* 18 unanimous are:	Gemara on Shab. 1.4 states that they ENACTED *18 MEASURES AND DIFFERED ON 18 MEASURES.*
1. Don't search clothes near Sabbath. 2. Nor read by lamplight. 3. *Zab may not eat with zabah.*	Shab. 1.18 and 19 state 2 rulings by Shammaite majority:	8 RULINGS AGAINST FOOD, DAUGHTERS, SONS ETC. OF GENTILES.	18 majority decrees are (Shab. 13b-17b): 1-10, 10 rulings re TERUMAH AS AT ZAB. 5.12.
Shab. 1.4: 'These' are among halakhoth mentioned by Sages in Han's room. THEY *VOTED, AND SHAMMAITES OUTNUMBERED HILLEL-ITES, AND 18 THINGS THEY DECREED ON THAT DAY.*	1. MOVABLES THICK AS GOAD DEFILE by over-shadowing. 2. UTENSILS LEFT UNDER SPOUT DEFILE MIQVEH.	10 rulings re TERUMAH AS ZAB. 5.12. Caesarean Rabbis say 18 majority decrees are: 1-7, unspecified 7 of above unanimous 18.	11. UTENSILS LEFT UNDER SPOUT. 12. MOVABLES THICK AS GOAD. 13. *Vintage grapes in purity.* 14. *Produce of terumah is ter.*
Shab. 1.5: *Shammaites say, ink, dye-stuffs or vetches may not be soaked on Fri.* unless time to be wholly soaked then. *Hillelites permit it.*	Shab. 1.20-21 state *1 UNRESOLVED MATTER*: Hillelites claim but Shammaites deny that dyes and vetches may be soaked on a Friday even if there is not time for them to be wholly soaked that day.	8. *Confide purse to Gentile Fri. eve.* 9. *Zab not to eat with zabah.* 10. MOVABLES THICK AS GOAD. 11. *Vintage grapes in purity.* 12. UTENSILS LEFT UNDER SPOUT.	15. *Confide purse to Gentile Fri. eve.* 16-18 or 19. 4 or 5 rulings against FOOD, DAUGHTERS, SONS ETC. OF GENTILES.
Zab. 5.12: List of 10 things (including hands) which INVALI-DATE TERUMAH. Anon.		13-18, 6 doubtful cases where terumah to be burnt. 19. *Produce of terumah is ter.* Editor says maj. decrees are 10 of above Caesarean ones and 7 from 18 ANTI-GENTILE DECREES report-ed by R. Simon b. Yohai.	

Key: Material in small capitals (roman) represents traditions attested in three documents, or in the case of the anti-Gentile decrees three potentially independent traditions. Material in small italic capitals represents tradition partially attested in three documents. Material in italic represents traditions attested in two documents.

that nearly anything rendered it impure; thus, this 18 included the 10 *terumah* rulings at Zab. 5.10 (and Shab. 13b and P.T.) and the 6 cases of doubtful *terumah* at Shab. 15b and P.T. The reason for these 18, he writes, was the brutal action of the high priests in sending their servants to collect by force the tithes which would otherwise have been received by the local priests[58] and the Levites (Josephus, *Ant.* 20.181, 206-207; cf. Pes. 57a). We are disinclined to accept this motivation for the unanimous decrees, however, since התרומה of which the Mishnah and Talmuds speak, is almost certainly the first portion of the harvest[59] (Num. 18.8f.) and not the priest's portion of the Levitical tithes which Josephus's δεκάτας indicated, nor the priests' portions of the sacrifices indicated by 'the skins of sacrifices' at Pes. 57a.[60] We do, however, with Zeitlin, accept the evidence of P.T. that there were two sets of Hananiah decrees, and the evidence of both Talmuds that the Zab. 5.12 *terumah* decrees were among them; since we have no evidence of disputes between the Houses about the invalidation of *terumah*, it seems more likely that they were some of the unanimous decrees.

Date of the Hananiah decrees

Since the decrees on the impurity of hands, and on the eater of unclean food (another of the *terumah* rulings), bear so directly upon the v. 5 question, their date is important for our enquiry. Two guides to their date are their content and the identity of Hananiah.

It seems very probable that the decrees included decrees against Gentiles, their food, marriage with their children, etc. Both Talmuds testify to this. Partly for this reason Graetz,[61] followed by Hengel,[62] dates the decrees at the outbreak of the revolution against Rome in AD 66. Such a conclusion receives support from Josephus who relates that at the time of the capture of Masada by the Jews (AD 66), Eleazar, captain of the Temple and son of Ananias, the high-priest, persuaded the priests to accept no gift or sacrifice from a foreigner. Since the sacrifice for Rome and the emperor were thus rejected, Josephus declares (*Bellum* 2.409), τοῦτο δ᾽ ἦν τοῦ πρὸς Ῥωμαίους πολέμου καταβολή. Only in the P.T. is the prohibition of gifts from Gentiles mentioned, and there it is in the list of 18 anti-Gentilic decrees attributed to R. Simon b. Yohai, but Simon's is early evidence, for, according to Danby's Appendix, he flourished c. AD 140-165, although at Berakoth 28a he participates in an incident also involving Joshua b. Hananiah; Zeitlin[63] mentions that he was a disciple of Akiba.

The identity of Hananiah has also given rise to difficulty. Two other facts about this Hananiah are mentioned at Shab. 13b. It is recorded there that Hananiah b. Hezekiah and his companions wrote the Scroll of Fasts, and that he reconciled contradictions between the Book of Ezekiel and the Torah, and thus prevented Ezekiel from being excluded from the Canon. This story is also told at Menahoth 45a, but he is there called Hanina b. Hezekiah. At Hagigah 13a, Hananiah b. Hezekiah's work on Ezekiel is again recounted, but is followed by another story of Hananiah b. Hezekiah defending Ezekiel from being suppressed when a child understanding the meaning of חשמל (1.27) was consumed by fire. The composing of the Scroll of Fasts and the reconciling of Ezekiel with Torah indicates to us the skill of the scribe, and the enthusiasm to rescue Ezekiel when it conflicted with written Torah indicates a Pharisee rather than a Sadducee.[64] But Zeitlin[65] identifies this Hananiah with Hananiah the father of Eleazar, who refused Gentile sacrifices. Eleazar's father, called Ἀνανίας by Josephus, is described by Josephus as the High Priest (ἀρχιερεύς, *Bellum* 2.409, 426, 441) and his murder by rebels, about AD 66, is recorded by Josephus (2.441). Even if this Ananias is not the Ἄνανος noted to be a Sadducee by Josephus at *Ant.* 20.199,[66] it seems unlikely that a Pharisee should have been High Priest in the generation before the destruction.[67] Graetz,[68] however, thinks that the decrees were made in the upper room of Hananiah's said *son*, *Eleazar*. He notes that the scholion (appendix) to the Scroll of Fasts mentions Eleazar b. *Hananiah* and his group as its authors, and this is supported by the Seder ha-Doroth quoting the Yukasin (c. 12th cent.). But, as Weiss[69] declares, this is little evidence that the Mishnah wrongly names *Hananiah* at Shab. 1.4! Graetz[70] cites other early texts mentioning Eleazar b. *Hananiah* (e.g. Mekhilta, *Bahodesh*, 7.66) but they have no connection with the 18 decrees, so Weiss well asks what reason this is for altering all other Hananiah references to Eleazar. Admittedly, it appears that Eleazar was a Shammaite,[71] and the Shammaites, according to Weiss,[72] were sympathizers with the Zealots, but we cannot equate an audacious rebel who defied the remonstrances of τοῖς τῶν Φαρισαίων γνωρίμοις (*Bellum* 2.411) and τοὺς ἐμπείρους τῶν πατρίων ἱερεῖς (2.417), and refused the sacrifices of foreigners, and attacked Menahem even in the Temple (2.445), with the devoted scribe who used 300 barrels of oil during his labours proving the consistency of Ezekiel with the law (Hagigah 13a).

The anti-Gentilic content of the decrees passed by the Shammaites certainly indicates a period of oppression under Roman rule but it need not be as late as the outbreak of war. Weiss[73] writes that the relations between the two Houses were amicable at first, but that hostility was caused by their different attitudes towards the power of Rome after Judea was made a Roman province on the banishment of Archelaus in AD 6 (Josephus, *Bellum* 2.111, 117). For, while both Houses disliked Roman rule, the Hillelites quietly awaited divine intervention, while the Shammaites, says Weiss, openly supported the Zealots. Weiss[74] claims that the decrees were passed in Hananiah's room not long after the death of Agrippa I who, according to Josephus's evidence, died in AD 44 (*Bellum* 2.219-20). We think it more likely that decrees designed to prevent association between Jews and Gentiles were passed at a time when relations with the occupying power were worsening, rather than at a time when revolution was breaking out; for Graetz[75] dates the decrees after the Jews' defeat of Cestius Gallus in AD 67, while Zeitlin[76] dates them in 66 after Gessius Florus's massacre of Jews in Jerusalem. At such a time, there was probably little danger of association between Jews and Romans, so decrees aimed at building a wall between the two were unnecessary. We prefer Weiss's dating, for after the death of Agrippa Rome was again placed under Roman procurators, and while Josephus tells us (2.220) that the first two kept the nation at peace through non-interference with its customs, the third, Cumanus, enraged the Jews by his failure to punish a soldier who insulted them by indecency on the Temple roof at Passover, and by his apparent reluctance to punish a soldier who burnt the Scripture (2.223-31). Also at this time a Galilean pilgrim to Jerusalem was murdered in Samaria; the Jews avenged themselves on Samaritan villages, but were then set upon by Cumanus's forces (2.232-36). The Samaritans went to the governor of Syria who executed many Jews involved, and then transferred the dispute to the emperor, Claudius, who condemned the Samaritans, and banished Cumanus (2.239-45). A time of such provocation of the Jews by Romans and by Samaritans would seem appropriate for the passing of anti-Gentilic decrees, and in ritual and cultic matter Samaritans were treated as Gentiles (Shab. 16b includes in the 18 decrees one which, in effect, prohibits marriage with the daughters of 'Cutheans' i.e. Samaritans). Cumanus was procurator from AD 48-52, and as the Samaritan dispute ended his rule we suggest c. AD 51 as the date of the Hananiah decrees. We do not identify Hananiah with Ἀνανίας the ἀρχιερεύς of whom Josephus speaks, but think it likely that he was a leader of Shammaites at this time. The suggested date can only be made tentatively in view of the imprecise nature of the evidence; as regards the anti-Roman content of the decrees, anti-Roman feeling must have persisted from Pompey's invasion till after the Bar-Kochba war, and Hananiah's work on the Scroll and Ezekiel does not permit precise dating.

We can now consider whether this suggested date for the Hananiah decrees is supported by the history of the law of hands.

We think that the *terumah* rulings probably show that hands are *assumed* to be impure in the second degree since, like a Scroll of Scripture (והספר), they are not referred to as defiled in the ruling. Büchler,[77] however, claims that the ruling relates to hands *actually* defiled, and points to the fact that in eight of the ten things mentioned at Shab. 13b as invalidating *terumah*, the persons or objects concerned are affected by impurity from outside. This argument does not persuade: the expression of those eight defilers as defiled from outside supports an argument that defilers not so expressed, but stated simply as a Book or one's hands, defile per se. Büchler also refers to the discussion of R. Joshua, R. Akiba and the Sages about the impurity of hands at Yad. 3.1-2, and notices that in all the cases mentioned by them, the hands are defiled by an impurity from outside. Moreover, he says, in the whole Tractate (Yadaim) there is no mention of a grade of impurity for hands generally, without impurity being transferred to them. We must grant these facts, but if caution required hands to be washed for fear that they might have been actually defiled, would not the resultant custom of washing them produce an *assumption* that they were unclean? Nor can we ignore the evidence of v. 3, and of the v. 5 question, in our passage, which imply a routine washing. It is, however, the unqualified reference to hands in the Hananiah decrees which persuades us that an assumed impurity of hands is intended.

A further question is whether the hands mentioned in the decree are intended as priest's hands or all hands including laymen's. Büchler[78] argues that the decree only applies to priests' hands since 1. only priests deal with *terumah*, the subject of the decrees, 2. much more frequently than the holiest laity, priests had occasion to immerse (inter alia, before eating *terumah*), and, as *tebulei yom*, by touching the *terumah* before sunset, they would defile it with their hands unless washed immediately beforehand, and 3. the decree that a Book (of Scripture) defiled *terumah* would be unintelligible unless the decrees related to priests only. We agree that, regarding the *terumah* which was formerly stored near the Scroll of the Law in the Temple, as explained at Shab. 14a, the particular danger to *terumah* only concerned the priests, but we think that the decrees were intended to state comprehensively the circumstances in which *terumah* could be defiled. The fact that one cause of defilement could only affect priests, and that the hands of a priest more frequently touched *terumah*, does not preclude an intent that the decrees should apply to laymen where appropriate. Thus, produce became *terumah* from the moment of separation by the farmer from other produce,[79] so that it was liable to be defiled during storage until delivery to the priest, and particularly by handling.

Two of the eighteen decrees at Shab. 13b which we did not mention above are that *terumah* is also invalidated by one who enters with head and the greater part of his body into drawn water (i.e. one who immerses in water which has been carried in a vessel, rather than immersing in rain water in a well, or river water), and by a clean person upon whose head and the greater part of his body there fell three 'logs' of drawn water. Although priests had to immerse regularly, before *terumah*, laypeople also had frequent occasion,[80] and three logs of drawn water might be dropped upon anybody. We are reinforced in our view that the decrees applied both to priests and laymen by the absence of any reference to priests either in the decrees themselves or in the gemara thereon.

We accordingly interpret the decree to mean that the hands of a priest or a layman are assumed to be separately impure in that they invalidate *terumah* by touching it.

A decree of Shammai and Hillel

However, the Hananiah decree may not have been the earliest enactment of the Sages concerning the separate impurity of hands. For at Shab. 14b we read in the gemara on Shab. 1.4, 'and the hands'. Did then the disciples of Shammai and Hillel decree this: (surely) Shammai and Hillel decreed it! For it was taught, Jose b. Joezer of Zeredah and Jose b. Johanan of Jerusalem decreed uncleanness in respect of the country of the heathens and glassware. Simeon b. Shetah instituted the woman's marriage settlement and imposed uncleanness upon metal utensils. Shammai and Hillel decreed uncleanness for hands.' The gemara in the Palestinian Talmud on Ket. 8.11, Shab. 1.4 and Pes. 1.6 contains the similar *baraitha*, 'Hillel and Shammai decreed concerning the cleanness of hands'.

The problem thus arising in the history of hands is whether Hillel/Shammai and the Houses made separate decrees affecting hands or whether the disparate accounts record different versions of

the same single decree. One explanation proposed at Shab. 14b is
that Shammai/Hillel decreed that the *terumah* touched by hands
should be suspended, i.e. neither eaten as clean nor burnt as invalid
(since the hands were only to be *suspected* of uncleanness), while
their disciples decreed that it be burnt, i.e. as unclean (since the
hands were *definitely* unclean). An earlier authority, however, had
stated that the *original* decree was for burning the *terumah*. Another
explanation then put forward is that Hillel and Shammai made a
decree about hands, which was not accepted, but that the disciples
later made the same decree which was then accepted.

Neusner thinks that this explanation was a reasonable construction
to have put upon the evidence, but he believes that only one decree
was made. He writes (*Traditions*, I, p. 317), 'The *baraitha* which
places the decree in the list of eighteen measures need not be
regarded as a contrary tradition. It has provided a more accurate
picture of events. The Houses made the decree,[81] but then, in
making up a list of the master's [sic] decrees, assigned it to Shammai-
Hillel.' We do not find this convincing, for while we acknowledge the
respect accorded to the rulings of early Masters, why should the
Houses have made eighteen decrees and only, according to the
records, have attributed one of them to Shammai/Hillel?

Alon,[82] when studying the anti-Gentilic decrees which he accepts
were included in the Hananiah decrees,[83] notes that the prohibition
of the oil and bread of Gentiles is shown by Josephus (*Bellum* 2.591;
Ant. 12.120; *Vita* 14) to have been in force many generations before
AD 70; he concludes that some of the Hananiah decrees were
intended to reinforce laws previously disputed.

The Talmudic evidence of separate decrees is, however, supported
by the following aspects of the development of the law:

1. The decrees at 14b which imposed uncleanness on glassware,
metal untensils and hands probably ordained only that these things
are susceptible to uncleanness, i.e. capable of suffering uncleanness.
In the case of glass objects such a decree was, perhaps, necessary to
remove doubt because Lev. 11.32-33 specifically mentions that certain
objects, e.g. earthenware and wooden ones, are defiled by certain
dead creeping things, but does not specifically mention glassware.[84]
But regarding metal objects Baumgarten[85] asks what need there was
for Simeon's decree in view of Num. 31.22, which assumes metal
objects to be susceptible, by providing that gold, silver, etc., shall be
cleansed by being passed through the fire; at Shab. 16b that decree is
interpreted as perpetuating the susceptibility of unclean metal utensils

even after they have been melted down and made into new utensils. The decree attributed to Shammai and Hillel and providing for the susceptibility[86] of hands to uncleanness separately from the body was occasioned, we suggest, through the Priestly Code speaking of the person becoming unclean, but not of the layman's hands separately from the body, except in the one situation at Lev. 15.11. The decree on hands attributed to the Houses seems to be a distinct lemma, yet supplemental to that of Shammai/Hillel, for it *assumes* that hands can be separately impure, and develops the law by adding that they invalidate *terumah*. It thus establishes that the hands are of second degree impurity.

2. We suggest that the decree of Shammai/Hillel related to the susceptibility of hands to *actual* defilement by a first-degree *offspring* of impurity; by an offspring, since it is clear in the Priestly Code that if any part of the body is touched by a source of impurity mentioned by the Code (a father), then the whole body becomes unclean (e.g. Lev. 15.5-7). We think their decree related to actual defilement because it seems likely that the first development regarding hands would be their rating as separately susceptible to impurity by *actual* defilement; only after the vulnerability of hands to actual defilement had been experienced for some years, would caution, we think, have instigated a *presumption* that they are defiled. To such a presumption after a lapse of time, the Houses' ruling ('the Hananiah decree') testifies, in that וחידים without mention of any manner of defilement, are said to invalidate *terumah*.

The Talmuds do not give a reason why Shammai and Hillel imposed uncleanness on hands, but for the Hananiah decree the gemara at Shab. 14a anonymously states the reason that the hands are fidgety, clearly meaning that they are liable to touch unclean things among the many things which they are continually touching. This reason supports an imputation of assumed impurity to the hands mentioned in the Hananiah decree.

3. At Shab. 15a it is said that Solomon decreed in respect of sacrificial food, while Shammai/Hillel decreed in respect of *terumah*. In view of the probably mythical nature of the ascription to Solomon, we would suggest that it was Shammai/Hillel whose declaration of the susceptibility of hands related to their power to defile *kodashim* while the Hananiah decree confirmed their power to invalidate *terumah*, i.e. we would accept hands' historical increase in defiling power, as stated in the Talmud, but would bring forward in time the two stages.

Evidence *against* the Talmudic statement that Shammai and Hillel decreed the separate impurity of hands may be constituted by Judith 11.13 on which Alon[87] relies in arguing that the washing of hands for holy things was practised before the Masters' time. Judith is usually dated about the middle of the second century BC,[88] and this verse states, according to Charles,[89] that the people 'are resolved to spend the firstfruits of the corn and the tenth of the wine and the oil which they had sanctified and reserved for the priests that stand before the face of our God in Jerusalem; the which things it is not fitting for any of the people so much as to touch with their hands'. In our view, the verse does not demand Alon's interpretation, since the reason for not touching the holy things with the hands could be due to the *whole* body being unclean—the verse does not postulate the separate impurity of the hands. Also, the verse need not be understood with particular regard to the transfer of impurity to the holy things— Judith is anxious to describe the great sinfulness of mis-use of the first-fruits and tithes, and does so by explaining that these things are so holy that non-priests should not even touch them, let alone consume them. Καθῆκεν has an ethical connotation ('it is proper, it is fitting'; Bauer, *s.v.*) rather than one of ritual error. Büchler[90] casts doubt on the authenticity of the verse. We would not thus reject it, but do not think it strong evidence for the separate impurity of hands.

The Talmudic evidence that Shammai/Hillel and the Houses made separate decrees about hands thus seems supported by the likely course of development of the law, and we consider that cumulative evidence to outweigh the evidence from Judith. Nor is the Talmudic evidence opposed by evidence of an anachronism between the dates of the respective activity of the Masters and the Houses, and the stages in the development of the law.[91] It is likely that Hillel's activity took place from about 10 BC to about AD 10,[92] and as Hillel is thought to have died first, their joint decree was made not later than about AD 10. We tentatively placed the date of the Hananiah decrees at about AD 51, and a period of forty or more years between the Masters decreeing the hands to be susceptible to impurity, separately from the body, in relation to *kodashim*, and the Houses decreeing the hands to possess an assumed impurity capable of invalidating *terumah*, does not seem anachronistic. For it seems likely that the impurity of hands would first be feared and guarded against in connection with the holiest food, the sacrificial food which the priest was allowed to eat in his home, and that hands would only after a lapse of time be considered as liable to invalidate the less holy food which the priest ate. It also seems feasible that a fear that hands actually defiled would defile holy food should have matured after forty or more years into a belief that hands, unless recently washed, are always unclean; people must surely experience for some years the danger of hands becoming actually defiled, before anxiety that their hands may have been defiled without them knowing leads people to purify them 'just in case'. Our hypothesis is that this attitude can gradually lead to the assumption that the hands *are* defiled.

We conclude that our tentative proposal of about AD 51 as the date of the Hananiah decrees is not opposed by contrary evidence from legal history, and that the hands were first decreed susceptible, apart from the body, by Shammai and Hillel not later than about AD 10.

b. *Is hullin susceptible to impurity from hands?*

The next link to be tested in the chain of logic required to give credibility to the Pharisaic question, is whether the ordinary, non-holy, food which the disciples were presumably eating, can receive impurity from hands. For if it can, and if the ordinary food thus defiled is itself capable of defiling holy food or holy persons (priests or intending worshippers), the Pharisaic concern that the disciples should handwash before food is credible.

The answer to this question depends on two connected issues: the intensity of impurity to which ordinary food is susceptible, and the intensity of the defiling power of hands.

1. *The susceptibility of ordinary food to impurity*

The Pentateuch
It is clear from the Priestly Code that sacrificial food is susceptible to impurity. At Lev. 7.19f. which concerns peace offerings, we read, 'Flesh that touches any unclean thing shall not be eaten: it shall be burned with fire. All who are clean may eat flesh, but the person who eats of the flesh of the sacrifice of the Lord's peace offerings while an uncleanness is on him, that person shall be cut off from his people. And if anyone touches an unclean thing . . . and then eats of the flesh of the sacrifice of the Lord's peace offerings, that person shall be cut off from his people.'[93] Since knives and forks were not used,[94] the uncleanness of the eater would be transmitted to the flesh by his touching it.

But ordinary food, unaffected by water, is not stated to be susceptible.[95] Indeed, at Deut. 12.15 and 20-21 permission is given for non-sacrificial meat to be slaughtered away from the sanctuary, in the towns, and vv. 15 and 22[96] expressly provide that the unclean and the clean may eat it. An illustration of this difference in susceptibility between sacrificial food and ordinary food is at 1 Sam. 21.4 where in response to David's demand for bread, the priest replies, 'I have no common bread (אֵין־לֶחֶם חֹל[97]) at hand, but there is holy bread; if only the young men have kept themselves from women'. Gray[98] comments that the need for purity when eating sacred food was thus an ancient regulation.

However, at Lev. 11.33-34 and 37-38 it is indicated that ordinary food is susceptible to defilement by an unclean creeping thing if the food has first been affected by water. The difficulty in eliciting the meaning of vv. 33-34 as they were originally interpreted lies in doubt as to whether v. 33 should be read as qualifying v. 34. Verse 33 provides that if a dead creeping thing falls into an earthen vessel, everything in it is unclean, and it shall be broken. Verse 34, according to the RSV, states, 'Any food *in it* which may be eaten, upon which water may come, shall be unclean; and all drink which may be drunk from every *such* vessel shall be unclean'. The italicized words, which link 34 with 33, do not appear in the Hebrew. If the Hebrew verses are construed independently, then food, being comprised within 'everything' in v. 33 is defiled by the carcass *without* prior contact with water, and v. 34 means that *any* food affected by water is unclean, and liquid drunk from *any* vessel is unclean. Snaith[99] and Noth[100] consider that the food said by these verses to be defiled is food generally, not simply food *in* the earthen vessel. Snaith writes that the reference is to food onto which water *from* the unclean pot is poured, and Noth writes that food and drink prepared *with* water *from* an unclean vessel before the vessel's uncleanness had been noticed should no longer be consumed. But the unlikelihood of v. 34b meaning that all drink drunk from *any* vessel is unclean is the strongest argument in favour of linking the two verses; that limb must surely mean that drink from a vessel into which the dead creeping thing has fallen is unclean. Once we allow v. 33 thus to qualify v. 34,[101] it is hard to deny that v. 34 qualifies v. 33, so that everything in the vessel is, per 33, unclean, but in the case of food it is only unclean if water comes first upon it, per 34. We accordingly think that the RSV interpolations are justified, and that, notwithstanding the generality of v. 33, food is only defiled by the creeping thing, if it is first affected by water.

Verse 37 provides that if any part of the dead creeping thing falls on any seed that is to be sown, it is clean. Noth[102] remarks that the indispensable cultivation of the field could not be endangered by any declaration of uncleanness here. But at v. 38 it is decreed that if water is put on the seed, and a part of the carcass falls on it, it is unclean.

Thus, according to the Pentateuch, food in general is only susceptible to impurity in one circumscribed situation. Water must have come upon it, and a dead creeping thing, or part, must have fallen upon it in an earthen vessel. Containment in an earthen vessel is not, however, necessary in the case of a wetted *seed*, upon which part of a creeping thing falls.

The Rabbinic Literature
In view of the limitation of susceptible food in vv. 33 and 34 to food, according to our view, in an earthenware vessel, it is not surprising that the Rabbis based their extension of the susceptibility of ordinary food (*hullin*) on v. 38. They developed the law by widening the susceptibility of 'seed' to include any *hullin*, and by expanding the potential defilers beyond a dead creeping thing.

Much of the Mishnaic tractate Makshirin is devoted to discussion of what is meant in that verse by, 'if water is *put on* the seed', וכי יתן־מים על־זרע. The principle derivable from the many circumstances considered there is that for *hullin* to be rendered susceptible (predisposed) to uncleanness by liquid, the liquid must be applied intentionally, or, if not, the presence of the liquid must be acceptable to the possessor of the *hullin*.

Early attributed evidence that *hullin*, and not just seed, was considered susceptible to impurity, if affected by water, is recorded at T. Maksh. 3.4: 'Joshua b. Perahiah says, "Wheat that comes from Alexandria is (capable of becoming) unclean on account of its baling machine (which sprinkles water on the wheat)". The Sages said, "If so, let it be unclean for Joshua b. Perahiah, and clean for all Israel".' Both views here apparently take as a datum that *hullin* can be rendered susceptible to uncleanness by liquid, but differ over whether water from a baling machine can thus predispose wheat. Following our method described in ch. 3.f we take as evidence the Mishnaic editor's implicit statement that in the time of Joshua wheat, and, since it is not seed, ordinary food in general, could be rendered susceptible by liquid being put on. We next consider other evidence including evidence from legal history. Neusner (*Traditions*, I, p. 82) notes that this pericope is in good Mishnaic Hebrew, and thinks that if Joshua's own words had been preserved, they would have been Aramaic. We cannot treat this argument as evidence against the truth of the editor's statement, since its Hebraic form may be the editor's work.

Looking at the evidence of legal history, we note that in the chain of tradition at Aboth 1.6 Joshua and Nittai the Arbelite come immediately before Judah and Simeon b. Shetah, said to be the brother of Queen Alexandra who favoured the Pharisees.[103] She reigned from 76 to 67 BC so that Joshua's alleged saying can be dated around 150-100 BC. In that the evidence of Lev. 11.38, dated around 400 BC, is that a seed could be predisposed by water at that time, it does not seem an inconsistent development that about 250 years later wheat (and thus probably ordinary food generally) could be rendered susceptible in the same way. We accordingly consider the statement about wheat's susceptibility not to be opposed by the other evidence, and we accept it.

There is a saying of Shammai indicating that Second Tithe vetches are susceptible (MS 2.4), and a discussion of Shammai and Hillel indicating that grapes are susceptible (Shab. 17a), so that, even if these sayings should be rather later than attributed, it seems likely that *hullin* generally was rendered susceptible by liquid in the time of Jesus.

But what intensity of uncleanness was *hullin*, thus predisposed, capable of receiving in the time of Jesus? We note from Lev. 11.38 that a seed, when water is put on, can be defiled by a dead creeping thing. According to the Mishnaic classification of impurity described at ch. 3.d the dead creeping thing, being a Scriptural source, was a 'father' of impurity, while the seed defiled by it became an 'offspring' of impuriy of the first degree. Following the expansion from merely seed at or before the time of Joshua, ordinary food generally was presumably liable to be defiled in the first degree. Can we go a step further, and say that *hullin*, when rendered susceptible, was liable to be defiled *by* an offspring of impurity so as to become unclean in the *second* degree? If Snaith and Noth's interpretation of v. 34, that food defiled by water, itself made unclean by the dead creeping thing, is rendered unclean, were correct, it would be early authority for food being unclean in the second degree, i.e. at second remove from the Scriptural cause. We have, however, rejected this interpretation on the ground that the food must be contained in the earthen vessel of v. 33. However, one of the Hananiah decrees provides that the eater of food of the second degree, אוכל שני, renders *terumah* invalid. Here we have a datum that food can be impure of the second degree.

Admittedly, אוכל rather than חולין is mentioned, but Jastrow defines it as 'food, edible', and refers to Betzah 1.8 where the word is used to mean the edible part of pulse. It thus appears sufficiently comprehensive to include *hullin*. We estimated above (pp. 167, 173) that the Hananiah decrees were made about AD 51, but since it is *assumed* therein that food can be impure of the second degree, it seems probable that *hullin* could sustain that intensity of impurity in the time of Jesus.

The evidence concerning the capacity of *hullin* to suffer *third-degree* uncleanness is conflicting. At Sotah 5.2 R. Akiba interprets Lev. 11.33 to mean that a loaf unclean in the second degree can defile another loaf in the third degree. To this R. Joshua replies, 'Who will take away the dust from off thine eyes, O Rabban Johanan ben Zakkai!—for thou didst say that another generation would declare the third loaf clean, for there is no verse in the Law to prove that it is unclean'. It can be inferred from ben Zakkai's words that in his time *hullin* could suffer third-degree impurity, for he expected *another* generation to prove from the law that it could not. Ben Zakkai was active both pre-70 and immediately afterwards when he established the Rabbis at Yavneh.[104] Yet at T.Y. 4.2-3 which contain lemmas concerning the Dough offering, and may therefore relate to Temple times, we read in each pericope, 'third-grade uncleanness counts as clean in common food'. Also, in the Hananiah decrees various defilers, all of second-degree impurity, are expressed only to *invalidate terumah* which is a holy food and thus presumably more susceptible to uncleanness than common food; it would accordingly be surprising if before c. AD 51 a second-degree subject could *defile common food*. We conclude that *solid hullin* was not susceptible to third-degree impurity in the time of Jesus according to the balance of Mishnaic evidence of Pharisaism, and there is no evidence of a contrary view at Qumran.

As we shall see, *liquid hullin* was probably defilable by second degree impurity, but we decided that the Pharisaic question concerned the eating of solid food.

Susceptibility to impurity possessed by the kind of hullin probably consumed by Jesus and his disciples
We are primarily concerned not so much with whether *hullin* in general was susceptible to impurity as with whether the kind of food which formed the diet of Jesus and his disciples was so susceptible. It seems likely that fruit,[105] fish,[106] bread,[106] eggs and vegetables

would form the basic diet[107] of the Galileans, so we must consider whether it was necessary for water to be 'put on' these foods before they became susceptible to impurity.

According to Makshirin 6.4 juice of fruit was not one of the seven liquids which operated as predisposers, and in any case juice exuding from the fruit would presumably not be there with the intent of the eater. Other liquid must be put on the fruit with intent or approval of the owner if it is to be predisposed (i.e. rendered susceptible to impurity). The same applies to vegetables. Maksh. 6.2 states, 'If a man took up to the roof bundles of vegetables or blocks of figs or garlic to keep them fresh, the law, If water be put on, does not apply (if dew fell on them)'. T. Maksh. 3.1, 2 show the same need for intent that water be applied in the case of fruit generally. It is difficult to date these anonymous lemmas, but as they follow the Levitical requirement that water 'be put on', the principle involved may be ancient.

Regarding fish, the Shammaites say at Uktzin 3.8 that they are susceptible when they are caught, but the Hillelites say when they are dead. Either way, they are susceptible before they are handled when eaten.

Bread is rendered susceptible to uncleanness by the application of water in its baking.[108] Eggs are not susceptible till water is applied, in accordance with the basic principle; indeed, they are normally presumed not susceptible (Maksh. 6.3).

Because their susceptibility accords with the basic Levitical principle, the liability of fish and bread to be defiled immediately by the eater, and the immunity of fruit, eggs and vegetables until water is put on, are likely to have been the position in the time of Jesus. Any wine, water or other liquid drunk by the disciples was, of course, immediately susceptible, but the Pharisaic question related to eating food.

Summary regarding the susceptibility of hullin to impurity
It seems probable that solid *hullin*, if rendered susceptible by water being put on, was capable of suffering first- or second-degree impurity in the time of Jesus, but not third-degree. Of the disciples' likely diet, the fish and bread were so susceptible without further water being 'put on', but the fruit, eggs and vegetables would not be susceptible, unless water were intentionally, or with consent, 'put on'.

2. *The defiling power possessed by hands*

The second factor on which the susceptibility of *hullin* to receiving impurity from hands depends is the intensity of the defiling power possessed by hands. We again attempt to assess the position in the time of Jesus by charting the historical growth of the law.

The Pentateuch

The only provision ascribing defiling power to the hands of a layman is Lev. 15.11 whereby if a *zab* (a man who has suffered an abnormal bodily discharge) touches a person without having washed his hands, that person shall wash his clothes, bathe himself, and be unclean till evening. It is hard to believe that a provision that the hands of an unclean person, unless washed, defiled, did not have *any* influence on the subsequent development of the law, but, notwithstanding the view of R. Eleazar ben Arak, it was not, according to the Talmudic evidence, an apparent source of development. Indeed, in Sifra the reference in this provision to handwashing is interpreted as meaning immersion of the whole body, the 'hands' just indicating that the hidden parts of the body do not require water upon them.

The Rabbinic Literature

We decided above that Shammai/Hillel and the Houses made separate decrees concerning hands, and that the decree of the former imposed on hands alone susceptibility to *actual* defilement by a first-degree offspring of impurity. This defilement would result in the hands becoming unclean in the second degree. We interpreted the decree of the Houses that hands invalidate *terumah*, as confirming that by that time (about AD 51) hands were *assumed* to be impure of the second degree. For, as the Houses only decreed that hands so assumed rendered terumah *invalid* (פסול), it is clear that, according to the Mishnaic system of declining impurity on transmission, such hands were only second degree, for if first degree, they would have rendered the terumah *unclean* (טמא). Did the degree intensify, after the Shammai/Hillel decree, in the case of hands *actually* defiled? It was argued by Akiba at Yadaim 3.1 that hands could become unclean in the *first* degree, and the examples he gave were of hands actually defiled. He asserted there that if a man put his hands alone into a house afflicted with leprosy, his hands would suffer first-degree impurity, but the Sages (החכמים) said only second-degree. Akiba also claimed that whoever imparts impurity to clothes when he touches them, conveys first-degree impurity to the hands,[109] but the Sages

say only second-degree. Akiba here refers to a man who has contact
with a *zab*, a *zabah* (a woman with an abnormal discharge), a
menstruant or a woman after childbirth or with a bed or chair made
unclean by them; during such contact that man conveys impurity to
clothes which he touches, i.e. is a father of impurity.

The Sages then ask Akiba what authority there is for the hands
suffering first-degree impurity under *any* circumstances. Akiba's
reply is difficult to interpret for it does not seem to 'connect' in the
sense of agreeing or disagreeing with the Sages' question. He asks
how then is it possible, except in this case (חוץ מזה), by which he
intends to refer, we think, to the *two* cases[110] he has cited above, for
the hands to suffer first-degree uncleanness without the whole body
also becoming unclean? This answer does not give the Sages an
authority, or reason, for the hands suffering first degree but merely
appears to limit the argument for that degree to these two cases. We
wonder if Akiba's reply has been redacted to bring it closer to
orthodoxy. The difficulty impeding Akiba's argument is that it was
settled law, that if the hands contact a father of uncleanness, the
whole body, not just the hands, becomes unclean of the first degree.
The importance of this debate for us is its evidence that in the time of
Akiba, who flourished c. AD 120-140 hands were *still* incapable of
becoming separately unclean in the first degree except, according to a
minority view, in those two limited situations.

The Mishnaic editor's evidence that Akiba took part in this debate
is not opposed by the evidence provided by the course of the law's
development. We decided earlier that the Shammai/Hillel decree
that hands were separately susceptible to actual defilement by a first-
degree offspring, and thus became second degree, was made not later
than AD 10; we also decided then that the Hananiah decree whereby
hands assumed defiled were adjudicated second degree was made c.
AD 51, but due to preceding custom they were probably considered
second degree for some years before then. It is not inconsistent with
this history that c. AD 120-140 the hands were still not generally
considered to be susceptible separately to first degree. This history
also shows that the defiling power of hands actually or presumptively
defiled was probably second-degree in the time of Jesus also, since the
period of his ministry lay between the dates of the Shammai/Hillel
decree and the Hananiah decree.

Transmissibility from Hands to Hullin
Since we have already concluded that solid *hullin* was probably only

susceptible to defilement by a father or first-degree offspring in Jesus' time, it follows, prima facie, that hands, being second degree, could not directly defile it. It is stated by the Sages at Yad. 3.1 in debate with R. Joshua that something suffering second degree cannot convey second-degree impurity to anything else. However, the *main* activity of Joshua (probably Joshua b. Hananiah) was post AD 70, and it is mooted by Hübner that the defilement of food by unclean hands was accepted in basically undifferentiated form in Jesus' time. We must, therefore, examine a story at Yad. 3.1 which indicates that in the time of one of the Gamaliels, whether hands were defiled depended on whether the defiler was a father or an offspring of impurity.

'Rabban Simeon b. Gamaliel' recounts there that a woman came before his father, and told him that her hands had entered the airspace of an earthenware vessel. His father asked her from what was its uncleanness, but he did not hear her reply. Now the question shows, we think, that whether or not the hands were defiled depended on that occasion on the intensity of the impurity contacting them, and that there was not an undifferentiated transmission of uncleanness. Certainly, the Sages there construe the story as showing that if the airspace was defiled by a father of impurity, it can defile the hands, but if only by an offspring, it cannot. Consequently, the date of the Gamaliel question greatly interests us. It is difficult to identify the Gamaliel whose father asked the question, due to the ambiguity of the textual evidence and 'the failure of the tradents everywhere to distinguish carefully among the Gamaliel's'.[111]

Neusner (*Purities*, XIX, p. 138) notes that some texts read simply 'Gamaliel', while others read 'Simeon b. Gamaliel'. Danby and Neusner read 'Rabban Simeon b. Gamaliel', but Neusner puts brackets round 'Simeon b.'. Blackman[112] also reads שמעון בן גמליאל, but he notes that some consider בן גמליאל to be redundant.

Nor do the chains of tradition assist greatly. In the chain of tradition at Aboth 1.16 it is implied, we think, from the place of 'Rabban Gamaliel' after Hillel and Shammai, that he received the law from them.[113] At 1.17 a saying of 'Simeon his son' follows, and that is followed at 1.18 by a saying of 'Rabban Simeon b. Gamaliel'. There is thus ambiguity in two Sages both apparently called 'Simeon b. Gamaliel'. Clarity is not aided by the claim in the *baraitha* at Shab. 15a that Hillel and Simeon Gamaliel and Simeon wielded their Patriarchate during one hundred years of the Temple's existence, for, however punctuated,[114] this conflicts with the Aboth chain.

Dating of the Gamaliel question may, though, be possible, if the discussion between Gamaliel and the Sages about the story is part of the same debate as the discussion between Joshua and the Sages, and Akiba and the Sages, which are all at Yad. 3.1. Pursuant to the method we adopted earlier, we treat the Mishnaic editor's assembly of the discussions in one debate as evidence of the unitary nature of the discussions. The content of the debate at Yad. 3.1-2 concerns the extent of the susceptibility of the hands to uncleanness, and discussion with Joshua immediately both precedes and follows the discussion with Gamaliel. In both places Joshua is arguing, against the Sages, that a thing suffering second degree *can* convey second degree to something else, so the Gamaliel story, as interpreted by the Sages, is integral to that debate. There is evidence of redaction, in that a reply in the same words is given by the Sages both to Joshua's preceding argument and to Gamaliel's story, except for the initial comment to Gamaliel, 'The matter is manifest'; but this conforming of the replies is hardly evidence of a composite content. We do detect some disruption of content between the Akiba discussion and the first Joshua discussion, since Akiba argues that hands can in two cases become *first* degree, while Joshua next argues that something of *second* degree can defile the hands.

To date the Gamaliel story, however, we can rely on its being unitary with the Joshua discussions. The Mishnaic editor's evidence to this effect is not opposed by the evidence of legal history. For Joshua argues in similar vein with R. Eliezer at Toh. 8.7 so it is very likely that he is Joshua ben Hananiah who, with Eliezer, smuggled b. Zakkai out of Jerusalem c. AD 70.[115] Rabban Simeon b. Gamaliel II who succeeded b. Zakkai as *nasi* at Yavneh[116] was a contemporary of Joshua,[117] so that Gamaliel's father would be a pre-70 Sage. It seems likely that his father was the Simeon b. Gamaliel to whom Josephus refers (*Vita* 190f.), in connection with the Galilean campaign of AD 66-67, as a leader of the people and of the Pharisees.[118]

That the Sages should, in the time of Joshua, interpret the story as confirming that a thing of second degree cannot convey that impurity to something else susceptible in the second degree (in the story, the hands), is also consistent with legal history, since the Hananiah decrees of c. AD 51 confirm that hands are second degree, for they only *invalidate terumah.*

The Mishnaic evidence that Gamaliel, Joshua and the Sages debated together is thus not opposed by any evidence of inconsistency with legal history, and the evidence of Joshua's participation enables us to identify the Gamaliel's father as being a Sage, who was active in and before the war, and as probably being the Simeon b. Gamaliel mentioned by Josephus. We accordingly have evidence that probably some years before the start of the war, and possibly in Jesus' time (on the basis that custom precedes judicial application), the transmission of impurity *to* the hands was not undifferentiated, but was limited by its remoteness from the source. This would suggest that transmission of impurity *from* the hands to food was affected at that time by like considerations, particularly since sacrificial food was from early times differentiated from ordinary food as more susceptible to impurity.

The Interposition of Liquid

An analysis of the defiling power of hands would not be complete without an examination of their enhanced power when liquid is interposed between them and whatever they touch.

We have noted above, from Baumgarten's translation of Damascus Document XII, the probably early recognition of oil at Qumran as an agent of contamination. This may indicate a pre-70 date for the Rabbinic ruling at Parah 8.7 that liquids, when contaminated by something of only first or second degree, themselves become unclean of the first degree. Such a date is supported by the Hananiah decrees which we have placed at c. AD 51. For included in them is a decree that foodstuffs and vessels defiled by liquids invalidate *terumah*. Pursuant to the Mishnaic 'mechanics' of impurity (see ch. 3.d), to do this, the foodstuffs and vessels must be second degree, and the liquids, to defile them, must be first degree. The decree does not state the intensity of the defiler of the liquid, but it seems reasonable to assume that it could be a thing of first *or second* degree. This assumption is supported by the interpretation of the decree by the Sages at Shab. 14b, where they conclude that 'liquid' means liquid defiled by the hands (which are, per the Hananiah decrees, second degree). 'Foodstuffs' in the decree clearly includes *hullin* for the Hebrew is והאוכלים which literally is 'things eaten'. An early application, perhaps, of the custom confirmed by this decree is at Berakoth 8.2, where the Shammaites say 'they wash the hands and then mix the cup', and the Hillelites claim the reverse order; the gemara on this (Ber. 52a) states, 'Our Rabbis taught that if the cup were filled with wine . . . before the hands were washed, the liquid on the back of the cup might be rendered unclean through the unwashed hands of the filler, and that liquid (being first class unclean) would defile the cup'. This, however, may only be ex post facto rationalization of what was a hygienic dining procedure.

Nevertheless, it does seem likely that in the time of Jesus, if water was interposed between hands and solid *hullin*, its agency would render the *hullin* defilable by the hands: the hands, assumed second degree unless recently washed, would render the liquid first degree which, in turn, would render the *hullin* second degree. Unclean liquid, thus interposed, at the same time as defiling predisposes *hullin* that needs water 'put on', irrespective of intent (Maksh. 1.1).

But was it sufficiently likely that water would come between the disciples' hands and food, to necessitate routine washing before meals? The hands could probably defile *hullin* at a Passover or other formal meal where the guests dipped their hands in a communal dish (as at Matt. 26.23), for if the dish contained cooking oil or gravy, that liquid, defiled by the hand, would then defile the meat or vegetables taken from the dish. At John 13.26 Jesus says βάψω τὸ ψωμίον, and in the dipping of a small piece of bread, it is hard to prevent the fingers contacting the liquid. But any meal, however informal, usually comprises not only eating, but drinking, and it must rarely happen that in the course of a meal, drops of water do not fall from the beaker, or the mouth of the drinker.

We accordingly conclude that, in practice, hands were very likely to defile *hullin* at a meal, through the medium of liquid.

c. *Is the eater of defiled hullin rendered so impure as to be liable to defile or invalidate holy food?*

Although it is provided at Lev. 17.15 that the eater of an animal which dies of itself (*nebelah*) or is torn by beasts (*terefah*) is unclean (cf. 11.40), the Priestly Code does not state that the eater of *contaminated* food (i.e. food suffering a derived uncleanness) is unclean. Hosea at 9.4 prophesies, 'Their bread shall be like mourners' bread; all who eat of it shall be defiled'; but it would be rash to presume from this isolated reference in a prophetic context a general rule that in Hosea's day the eater of unclean food was defiled thereby.[119]

However, one of the Hananiah decrees provides that the eater of food suffering second-degree uncleanness renders *terumah* invalid. This entails that the eater has been defiled in the second degree, like the food, for *terumah* is not susceptible to less than third-degree unfitness (see ch. 3.d).

Earlier, we dated the Hananiah decrees at c. 51 AD. But, pursuant to our view of the rôle of custom in law's development, we think that second degree impurity was *customarily* assigned to the eater of second-degree *hullin* before the Hananiah decree adjudicated it to be so.

We accordingly deem it possible that in Jesus' time the eater of second degree *hullin* was considered to invalidate *terumah*.

d. *Does the washing of hands remove their impurity?*

Regarding the purification of hands defiled by a Biblical source of impurity, the Priestly Code implicitly states at Lev. 15.11 that the hands of the *zab* can be purified by rinsing them (שטף) in water.

Neusner notes (*Purities*, XIX, p. 103) that washing hands before eating is first attested in any literature at Mark 7.1-5, and we are justified in translating the root νίπτ- in vv. 2 and 3 as 'rinse', since it is used in the LXX to translate the root שטף at Lev. 15.11. Indeed, it seems natural that, from not later than AD 10, when Hillel and Shammai decreed the separate susceptibility of hands, the method of their purification should have been rinsing. The early use of this remedy receives some support from the story of the wedding at Cana at John 2.1-10, for we read at v. 6, ἦσαν δὲ ἐκεῖ λίθιναι ὑδρίαι ἕξ κατὰ τὸν καθαρισμὸν τῶν Ἰουδαίων κείμεναι, χωροῦσαι ἀνὰ μετρητὰς δύο ἢ τρεῖς. Now the water in these very large stone jars (each holding 20 or 30 gallons) must have been used for *hand*washing, since the *miqveh* in which *persons* and *vessels* were purified was required to be a natural pool, and this rule probably developed before Jesus' time (Eduyoth I.3). We accordingly treat this verse as evidence that not later than the time of John's writing, hands were washed to remove impurity. John's Gospel was probably written between 90 and 100 AD,[120] but the story about Cana comes from John's Signs source (v. 11), and probably contained much earlier tradition.[121]

The Mishnaic evidence at Yadaim 1.1 (probably post AD 70 at Yavneh) mentions pouring water over the hands, and at Hagigah 2.5, rinsing them (נוטלין לידים). There is thus a remarkable uniformity of evidence both before and after Jesus' time, that hands were rinsed to remove impurity.

However, we are confronted now by a fundamental point. While rinsing of the hands removes *their* impurity, it does not purify the unclean *body*. Until he purified his body by immersion in a *miqveh*, a male Jew would routinely be impure in body by reason of sexual emission (Lev. 15.16, 18), but he would not normally immerse unless he intended to visit the Temple or a priest, or separate[122] *terumah*. These occasions would not, we think, be sufficient, even in Galilee with its many crops, to found a practice of daily immersion in a *miqveh*. Thus, a question to an ordinary lay Jew as to whether he had washed his hands before eating would probably have amazed him: when his whole body (including his hands) was a father, or first-degree offspring, of impurity, what was achieved by removing the slight (second-degree) impurity of his hands only?

It might be thought that it would be unnecessary for a person who that day had taken a *miqveh* (a *tebul yom*) to wash his hands, on the basis that the greater purification supersedes the lesser. But a Hananiah decree provided that a *tebul yom* invalidates *terumah* (i.e. is second degree), and Tebul Yom 2.2 provides that although a *tebul yom* does not defile liquid *hullin* (even though he is second degree), his hands defile it. So until sunset, unless the lay *tebul yom* washed his hands before eating, he was liable to defile solid *hullin* through the medium of liquid. However, we have no cause to think, either from the terms of our passage or from the purificatory practices of non-priests, that the questioning Pharisees believed the disciples to have immersed that day.[123]

e. *Conclusions to Chapter 4*

We now summarize our conclusions in this chapter concerning whether the Pharisaic question was credible according to the *restrictive tradition* in that impurity could pass from hands to *hullin*, thence to the eater, and thence to *terumah*, and be removed by washing the hands.

To avoid repetitive qualification, we state the results of our enquiry in absolute terms, but we cannot claim that those results show more than the possible position in the time of Jesus. Although we have considered OT and inter-testamental evidence as well, the Talmudic evidence (particularly the Hananiah decrees) has played a conspicuous part in our charting of the law's development. The possibility that this evidence may represent only the Pharisaic views which survived through their dominance, or through their conformity with later orthodoxy, obstructs a more confident claim.

I.   Hands could not *directly* defile solid *hullin*, even if rendered susceptible, on the following reasoning:

a. *Hullin* was capable of suffering only first- or second-degree impurity.

b. Hands, separately from the body, suffered assumed impurity in the second degree.

c. A thing unclean in the second degree could not defile another thing which could suffer only first or second degree impurity.

II. Hands could directly defile liquid *hullin*, but the Pharisaic question concerns washing before *eating*.

III. Hands could defile solid *hullin indirectly* if the hands contacted liquid which then contacted the *hullin*, and this would happen sufficiently frequently for it to be considered that hands *did* defile *hullin* when eating.

IV. The eater of defiled *hullin* invalidates *terumah*.

V. The rinsing of the hands removes their impurity when they alone are unclean, but if the whole body is unclean, rinsing of the hands has no effect, because the hands, together with the rest of the body, are a father or first-degree offspring of impurity, and are only purified by immersion in a *miqveh*.

VI. Since the body of the ordinary lay Jew would usually be thus unclean, it is unrealistic to suppose that the Pharisees would have asked the disciples about the uncleanness of their hands which was irrelevant in the circumstances.

Thus, the result of the first test of legal credibility proposed at the end of ch. 3, is that, although according to the restrictive tradition and the laws thought to be applicable to the Pharisees generally, impurity might pass from hands to holy food (per III and IV above), yet the Pharisaic question urging handwashing is not credible on this basis, because there was no reason to wash the hands when the whole body was presumptively defiled with a more serious impurity (per V and VI above).

We must accordingly apply the second test of legal credibility proposed at the end of ch. 3, and investigate whether the exhorted purification of the hands is intelligible as a work of supererogation, or according to the expansive view of purity.

Chapter 5

SUPEREROGATORY HANDWASHING

We discovered in the last Chapter that there was no reason,
according to the restrictive tradition, why lay Jews should wash their
hands before *hullin* since their whole bodies usually suffered from a
degree of impurity which could not be so removed. We will now
enquire whether any Jews, as a work of supererogation, or pursuant
to the expansive tradition, washed their hands.

Since the washing of hands before eating *hullin* might be explained
through the assignment to hullin of a sanctity denied to it by the laws
which we have hitherto studied, and which were generally applicable,
the most appropriate place to search for such a practice of washing
seems to lie in the area of supererogatory behaviour.

Such behaviour has historically been a common feature in the
religious life of the pious,[1] and we would point to the life-style of the
Rechabites[2] and the Nazirites[3] as early Biblical examples. We must
accordingly consider whether the Pharisees regularly washed their
hands before eating *hullin* at a time when it was not required by the
law applying to all.

We have no evidence of other sects practising handwashing before
ordinary food prior to Jesus' time. Rabin,[4] writing on the Community
Rule V, 'They shall not enter the water to partake of the pure
Meal . . .',[5] notes that the Qumran sectarians were men who ate
ordinary food with all the ritual precautions which priests had to
employ when eating *terumah*. But at Qumran they immersed their
bodies before eating. However, Schiffman, writing on the Damascus
Doc. XI, 'On the road, if he goes down to wash let him drink where
he stands . . .'[6] interprets לרחוץ there as referring to 'the ritual
cleansing of the hands (and feet?) performed upon rising and before

eating'. Vermes[7] and Dupont-Sommer[8] translate רחוץ as 'bathe'. While we agree with Schiffman that ritual immersion of the body is not intended in view of the requirement to drink 'where he stands', we think that the washing referred to is not ritual handwashing, but a washing caused by the heat and dust of the Sabbath journey.[9]

However, we do know that at some stage in their history the persons referred to in the Mishnah as *haberim*, began to wash their hands before eating *hullin*.[10] We must therefore look at the relationship between the *haberim* and the Pharisees and scribes of our passage.

a. *The Scribes*

There is no great difficulty over the origin of the scribes (οἱ γραμματεῖς) mentioned by Mark. Ezra, who came from Babylon to Palestine c. 457 BC, is described as 'the scribe' (הספר). The scribes copied the scrolls of the law, and by doing this, acquired a detailed knowledge of it. Consequently, people asked them about the application of the law to new situations, and by their decisions they created the traditional law. Finkelstein,[11] who stresses their plebeian origin as opposed to the patrician priest, appears to treat them as identifiable in their later history as the Sages (חכמים) of the Mishnah.[12] Bowker,[13] however, distinguishes them. He argues that the Sages gradually displaced the scribes as interpreters of written Torah because the scribes conservatively referred each question to written Torah for solution, while the Sages were prepared to build on the precedents created by previous decisions, if they were satisfied that the previous decisions were reliably transmitted by the chain of tradition. While the scribes remained copyists, they could, of course, join the Hakamic movement, and become Sages (as R. Meir).[14] The reading οἱ γραμματεῖς τῶν Φαρισαίων at Mark 2.16 indicates this scribal membership of the Pharisaic movement, and supports the presence of scribes from Jerusalem in our passage. We have, however, no evidence that the scribes, as such, tended towards extra-ordinary piety, and it is in relation to the Pharisees that the position of the *haberim* must be defined.

b. *The Pharisees*

In studying the Pharisees, we embark upon deeper waters. A serious danger lies in the terminology employed. All the Gospel writers use the term Φαρισαῖοι when referring to those who are hostile to Jesus on account of his neglect of the Jewish law. Josephus,[15] also, writes of Φαρισαῖοι and while he mentions their belief in fate and the immortality of the soul, he sees as distinctive their rôle as interpreters of the law, and explains that they passed to the people regulations handed down by the Fathers and not written in the Mosaic law. He adds that these regulations are rejected by the Sadducees who hold valid only the written law.

Now in the Mishnah at Yadim 4.6-7 the Sadducees dispute several points with פרושים, which is usually translated 'Pharisees'. The *perushim* here do seem to be the same party as the Houses of Shammai and Hillel, for the complaint of the Sadducees is the view of the *perushim* that the Holy Scriptures render the hands unclean, which view is probably connected with the Hananiah decree that a Scroll defiles *terumah*.[16] Yet Johanan b. Zakkai, who was the pupil of Hillel and the leader at Yavneh, replies to the Sadducees as if he was not a *perush*.[17] The text of the debate at Yad. 4.6 is rather ambiguous, however, and it may be that Johanan is being ironic. Both the Jerusalem Talmud (Berakoth 14b) and the Babylonian Talmud (Sotah 22b) contain lists of types of hypocritical or exhibitionist *perushim*, which recall the woes on the *Pharisaioi* at Matt. 23.23-36, par. Luke 11.42-52. So what is the relationship between the *Pharisaioi* and *perushim* described by different authors, and to what extent do they overlap with the *haberim*? The answer may lie in the gradually heightened strictness of legal observance, particularly regarding purity, of those variously described as *Pharisaioi* and *perushim*.[18] They seem to have originated in the Hasideans (the faithful ones—ʾΑσιδαῖοι—of 1 Macc. 2.42) and continued as the Sages (חכמים, the wise ones mentioned in the Mishnah) who were the Masters of the traditional law. It appears to be the followers of these *Hakamim* that Josephus calls '*Pharisaioi*' and the Talmud '*perushim*' in their conflict with the Sadducees. At a later date some of their more extreme successors were castigated in the lists of types of *perushim* in the Talmuds.

Regarding the *Pharisaioi* in our passage, Bowker[19] thinks that the emphasis on the importance of tradition there indicates the attitude of the *Hakamim*, but that the attitude evinced towards handwashing is more severe than that of the *Hakamim*. Bowker accordingly thinks that our passage shows the *Pharisaioi* in transition from their position as described in Josephus to their later position as extremists for which they are attacked in the Talmud. But while he quotes Marcan instances where the attitude of the Pharisees equates with the *Hakamim* (e.g. the debate about divorce at 10.2-9 is similar to an issue discussed by Shammai and Hillel at Gittin 9.10), the only instance he cites where the *Pharisaioi* of Mark take a more severe attitude than the *Hakamim* is the handwashing in our passage. And may this severity reflect not the rigorous tendency of the Pharisaic movement but the independent viewpoint of some of its members?

c. *The Haberim*

This brings us to a consideration of the *haberim*. The formulators of the Mishnah seem to regard the *haberim* as voluntarily undertaking obligations not imposed by the general law. At Demai 2.2, 3 where rules to be observed regarding tithes and purity are set out, the person to observe them is called המקבל עליו להיות נאמן ('He that undertakes to be trustworthy') at 2.2 and is called המקבל עליו להיות חבר ('He that undertakes to be an Associate') at 2.3.[20] At Tosefta Demai 2.11 the language used relates to a person being accepted into a club: ומקבלין לכנפים ואחר כן מקבלין אתו לטהרות ('And he is accepted first with regard to 'wings' and is afterwards accepted for purities'). The solemnity associated with entry into a society is indicated at Bekhoroth 30b where a *baraitha* reads, 'One who desires to accept the obligations of a haber is required to do so in the presence of three haberim . . . ' It seems clear that the *haberim* were Pharisees, but how did they differ from other Pharisees, for we see in 'Q' at Matt. 23.23 (par. Luke 11.42) that the *Pharisaioi* there applied tithing to minutiae, and from Mark 2.16 and Matt. 23.25-26 (par. Luke 11.39) that the *Pharisaioi* were anxious concerning the purity of persons and things?

Finkelstein,[21] who identifies the scribes with the Pharisees, also identifies the *haberim* with them in the sense that all Pharisees were *haberim*. He points out that the purity law could only be observed on a co-operative basis. The *haber* could not be pure in his home, if the persons from whom he bought his food had defiled, or not tithed, it. He adds that the *haber* who was a trader would be limited in his dealings, unless he could establish a sufficiently wide clientele of those who observed the same standards of tithing and purity as himself. He writes, 'The members of the Society called one another haber, comrade. The expression "members of the Synagogue" . . . was sometimes used to distinguish the masses of the Order from their leaders, the scholars or Scribes (soferim). But the wall between them and the other Jews gained them, most commonly, the name of 'Separatists' (Hebrew, Perushim; . . . Grecized into Pharisaioi, whence the English, Pharisees) . . . it implied merely separation from impurity and defilement.'[22] Moore[23] even suggests that the Pharisees developed out of the *haberim* in that the name 'Pharisees' was first applied to the members of the *haburoth* formed for strict tithing and purity, and was subsequently applied to all who were similarly scrupulous. The difficulty about these views is that, as indicated, the Pharisees in the Mishnah refer to the *haberim* as if they are distinct from themselves.

In contrast to these views, Neusner[24] sees no indication that all Pharisees were members of a *haburah*, although all *haberim* were Pharisees, and accepted their views on Jewish law. Bowker, too, describes the *haberim* as a movement within a movement, 'a kind of extreme deduction, drawn from the basic Hakamic Vision'.[25]

Although the position is not clear, we believe that the ambiguities in the evidence, and the contrasting views of critics, are best reconciled in the conclusion that the terms *perushim* and *Pharisaioi* indicate a general class within which lie at least four species: those who joined *haburoth*, the better to observe the law; the extreme Pharisees, who are condemned in the Talmud and Gospels for their ostentation and hypocrisy; the 'ordinary' Pharisees who tried to observe the law binding upon all, but did not take upon themselves the additional legal obligations accepted by the *haberim*; and the *Hakamim*, or Sages who upheld the oral law against the Sadducees, and made both the laws which are generally applicable, and the laws applicable only to persons of particular status, such as priests, Nazirites or *haberim*; the hallmark of the *Hakamim* was not, however, the strict purity of the *haberim*, but devotion to the traditional law.[26]

Confusion is caused because the generic term is probably used to refer to the species, as at Hagigah 2.7 where the clothes of an *'am-ha'ares* are said to be *midras*—unclean to a *perush*, when a *haber* is intended.[27] In the Gospels also, including our passage, the *Pharisaioi* are mentioned in places where we believe the *haberim* are intended, and in other places, e.g. the woes in 'Q', where we believe the extremists are intended. Thus, Zeitlin[28] challenges Bowker's reference[29] to the scribes of the Pharisees as criticized at Mark 2.16 for condemning association with the *'am-ha'ares*: he claims that the *perushim* (= *Hakamim*) never opposed association with the *'am-ha'ares*, it was the *haberim* who would not dine with them, because they suspected them of not observing carefully the tithing and purity laws.

We accordingly identify the *haberim* as the Pharisaic group most zealous to avoid defilement, and will now examine whether they washed their hands before eating *hullin*.

d. *Handwashing and the Haberim*

We will consider, first, the earliest attributed evidence, and then, whether it casts light on the practice in Jesus' time.

a. *T. Demai 2. 11-12*

We noted above that at T. Demai 2.11 the novice member is said to be accepted first with regard to 'wings' and afterwards for purities.[30] The effect of accepting only one of these obligations is then stated (also anonymously), and then (v. 12) we read, 'Until when is a man accepted? The school of Shammai say, For liquids, thirty days; for clothing, twelve months. The school of Hillel say, For either, thirty days'.

The noun translated as 'wings' is כנפים which is construed by Lieberman[31] as referring to cleanness of hands, 'wings' being a theriomorphism. This meaning is supported by a *baraitha* at Bekhoroth 30b: 'Our Rabbis taught: we accept a haber if he promises to observe cleanness of hands and afterwards we accept him as one who will observe the other rules of levitical purity'. Miller and Simon[32] interpret the reference to cleanness of hands here as 'washing the hands before eating and before touching food of terumah'. This seems to construe the condition as relating only to priest-applicants since the layman does not eat *terumah*, although, if a farmer, he may touch it. However, as T. Demai 2.2 mentions eating even *hullin* in purity as a condition of membership, it seems more likely that in v. 11 and Bek. 30b the cleanness of hands for the purpose of contacting *hullin* (and, a fortiori, *terumah*) is intended.

1. *Do vv. 11 or 12 indicate handwashing in the Houses' time?*

Consequently, if vv. 11 and 12 were unitary so that the Houses were the authors of the anonymous lemmas about hands at v. 11, we would have explicit evidence (assuming the attribution to the Houses to be correct) that the *haberim* handwashed before *hullin* pre-AD 70.[33] Unfortunately, the balance of evidence favours the composite nature of the verses. Applying our forensic model, we doubt that the editor's juxtaposing of these verses is evidence that they are unitary, for they are able to stand independently of each other. And while there is an internal link between hands and purities[34] in v. 11 and liquids in v. 12, the Schools' reference to clothing in v. 12 is evidence of discreteness for v. 11 does not mention it. Rabin[35] accepts Luzzatto's suggestion that כנפים in v. 11 means clothing, which thus creates continuity with v. 12.[36] But even if כנפים does here mean clothing (and there is evidence against this),[37] it seems strange, if the verses are a unity, that a different word, כסות, should be used for garments in v. 12. We prefer the translation 'hands', and thus find the internal evidence, also, to deny unity. Further evidence indicating a composite nature is the formulation of the verses as separate *baraithoth* at Bek. 30b.

However, although not so explicit, there is some evidence *in v. 12 itself* that it comprehends purity of hands. For in that verse the Houses agree that a novice is to be tested for thirty days in respect of *liquids* (משקין). As discussed earlier, the significance of liquid in purity law was two-fold: it predisposed dry *hullin* to impurity, and through always being first degree when unclean, it was a sensitive conductor of impurity. Moreover, it could, when unclean, predispose and defile at the same time.[38] So Neusner[39] interprets 'liquids' here as meaning the obligations of the novice not to allow his liquids to predispose his *hullin* to impurity,[40] and to keep his liquids pure. Unclean liquid will defile any *hullin* it contacts.[41] Now, vessels, foodstuffs and hands can all defile liquids,[42] but the most likely defiler, in practice, must surely be the hands, which are described at Shab. 14a as 'fidgety'. Thus, in order to avoid any possible defilement to 'pure food' (טהרות),[43] the novice washed his hands to avoid defiling any *liquid*. This seems to be the interpretation which Alon[44] gives to this verse (which he calls v. 11) for he writes, 'The Halakha refers to eating common food in purity and to all Israelite Associates'.

Further, if the attribution to the Houses in v. 12 of opinions concerning the qualification periods for a novice *haber* in respect of *liquids and garments* is correct, it seems likely that the preservation of the purity of *hands also* was a requirement at the time of the Houses. For at v. 11 it is stated that if the *haber* accepts the obligation concerning 'wings' alone, he is accepted (into the haburah), but if he only accepts the obligation concerning purities, he is not accepted. Thus, the obligation concerning hands was apparently considered of more importance even than the obligation concerning pure foodstuffs. It accordingly seems to us unlikely that so primary a concern of the *haburah* was imposed at a later time than the duty of pure liquids and garments.

We accordingly conclude that if the attribution of v. 12 to the Houses is correct, then it was a legal requirement for novice *haberim* at the time of the Houses that they were to handwash before *hullin*.

2. *Attribution of T. Demai 2.12 to the Houses*

We now attempt to check whether this attribution is correct, for, if it is, we are able to place a date prior to AD 70[45] on a debate which implicitly acknowledged the legal obligation of *haberim* to wash their hands before *hullin*.

Pursuant to our forensic model, our first premise must be that the editor's statement that the Schools gave the opinion in v. 12 is evidence that they did so. Since it is not intrinsically improbable that they did so, we next consider whether the editor's statement is overborne or supported by other evidence. For we do not consider the fact mentioned by Neusner[46]—that this is the only Houses' pericope concerning the *haburah*—to be evidence of intrinsic improbability; this may be the only pericope of the Houses on the subject which survived, or this may, indeed, be the only *haburah* point which they pronounced upon.

We find evidence supporting the editor at Bekhoroth 30b, where v. 12 is repeated as a *baraitha*, except that Beth Hillel states the qualifying period for both liquids and clothing to be twelve months. It is then pointed out that this is a ruling where Beth Hillel (normally, the more lenient) is stricter than Beth Shammai. The Sages then say, 'Rather (read) Beth Hillel say: Both in the one case as well as in the other, the period is thirty days'. We think that this alteration[47] of the original tradition forms some evidence in support of the attribution to the Houses, since the Sages making the alteration were presumably convinced of the attribution in that they gave effect to the well-known leniency[48] of the House of Hillel.

Evidence tending against the accuracy of the attribution to the Houses of v. 12 is contained in M. Demai 2.2-3 where the Sages debate with R. Judah the obligations of the aspirant *haber* without mention of the Houses' debate. This is probably Judah b. Ilai who, according to Danby's Appendix, flourished c. AD 140-65, since R. Meir and R. Jose, also of that Generation according to Danby, debate at 2.5. It is arguable that the Sages would not, about a century later, discuss the novice's obligations without invoking the authority of the Houses' debate, if it had been attributed to the Houses. On the other hand, we are reluctant to place much weight on an argument from silence, and it is noticeable that earlier authorities are not referred to by Sages in the Mishnah as regularly as in the Talmud.

We next adduce the evidence afforded by legal history concerning the accuracy of the attribution to the Houses.

The question here is: is it likely, judging from the history of purity, that the Schools, whose recorded disputes date from about AD 20 to AD 70,[49] discussed the obligations of novice *haberim* regarding liquids and garments?

Early respect for the purity of liquids is shown by the Qumran sect, for the Community Rule VI[50] provides that the novice shall not touch the 'Drink of the Congregation' until he has lived for two years in the Community, even though he is allowed to partake of the 'pure Meal of the Congregation' after one year.[51]

Regarding garments, consciousness of the impurity arising from the clothes of persons observing a lower standard of purity seems to have prevailed within Pharisaism pre-70 AD. For at Hagigah 2.7 we read that Johanan b. Gudgada's apron was considered unclean by those dealing with the Sin-offering water, even though he maintained purity to the standard required for handling *kodashim*. Johanan is described at Arakhin 11b and T. Shekalim 2.14 as a Temple doorkeeper, and Neusner, *Traditions*, I, pp. 418f., does not doubt that both he and his sons lived in Temple times. Concern of the *haberim* over potential defilement of their garments by an '*am-ha'areṣ* or his garments may be connected with the lustration on return from market noted by Mark at 7.4, for we think that the Pharisees intended by Mark at vv. 3-4 were *haberim*; Mark was writing at AD 65-67, but the practice had probably not just begun.

It thus seems that the evidence of legal history is not clear: that relating to liquids is not of Pharisaic practice, and that about garments is rather peripheral.

However, we consider that the editor's attribution of v. 12 to the Houses is proved on a balance of evidence. His statement that the Houses debated the novice's obligations respecting liquids and garments is supported by the evidence of the Sages' alteration at Bekh. 30b, and is only opposed by the less cogent evidence of the non-mention of the v. 12 debate in the later debate at M. Demai 2.2-3. The other piece of early evidence connecting handwashing and the *haberim* is at Mark 7.3.

b. *Mark 7.3*

Here Mark states that the Pharisees and all the Jews do not eat unless they wash their hands, observing the tradition of the elders. The results of our enquiries in Chapter 4 indicated that the traditional

law applying to all did not demand washing before eating *hullin*, so
we are inclined to discount Mark's reference to 'all the Jews'.
However, Hart[52] inferred from a story in the gemara on Berakhoth
8.2 in the Palestinian Talmud, and at Numbers R. XX.21 that by the
time of Antiochus Epiphanes (175-163 BC) handwashing[53] before a
meal had come to be the characteristic mark of a devout Jew. In the
gemara a *baraitha* that to wash before meals is optional, but after
meals compulsory, is recorded. In Numbers R. this *baraitha* is
repeated, but the importance of washing before meals is illustrated by
the story of a Jewish shopkeeper who 'during the period of religious
persecution' used to sell clean meat and swine's flesh to avoid being
suspect as a Jew. If anybody came into his shop and did not wash his
hands, he assumed him to be a Gentile, and gave him swine's flesh.
But on one occasion a person did not wash his hands, and the
shopkeeper gave him pork, although he was, in fact, a Jew. We cannot
infer, with Hart, from this story that handwashing before *hullin* arose
in the persecution by Antiochus Epiphanes,[54] for there are no
references in the story pointing to that persecution, and we have no
other evidence of handwashing before *hullin* at so early a date. We
think it more likely that the Hadrianic persecution following the Bar-
Kochba revolt of AD 132-35 is intended.[55] We have evidence at
Erubin 21b of Akiba's concern about handwashing, while imprisoned
during that war.

We think that the *Pharisaioi* to whom Mark refers at v. 3 were
haberim. Of the four different species of *Pharisaioi* delineated above,
the washing of hands before *hullin* suggests those who joined
haburoth to observe standards of purity higher than the requirements
of the laws applying to all; we saw in Chapter 4 that the general law
did not demand such washing. Bowker[56] notes that by their handwashing at vv. 3 and 5 the *Pharisaoi* mentioned there express a
position more extreme than that of the *Hakamim*. This accords with
Rivkin's view[57] that, although the *Hakamim* legislated for the
haberim, their own hallmark was mastery of the law, not ritual
purity. Further, we know from T. Demai 2.2 that the *haberim* at *some
time* practised purity of hands. We therefore conclude that it was the
haberim who are stated by Mark to wash their hands before eating.
By inserting this parenthetical statement immediately after his
report that the Pharisees saw the disciples eating with unwashed
hands, Mark is clearly attesting that the *haberim* and all the Jews
washed their hands before eating, in Jesus' day. We judge that
evidence of date to be overborne, though, by the evidence of his

inaccuracy respecting 'all the Jews', but we accept his v. 3 statement as evidence of handwashing by *haberim* not later than AD 65-67, his time of writing.

c. *Did the haberim handwash before hullin in Jesus' time?*
We will try to answer this question by analysing the evidence set out above.

We accepted the evidence of T. Demai 2.12 that the Houses opined concerning the novice *haber's* obligations respecting the purity of liquids and garments. Since we deduced that the obligation to preserve the purity of liquids necessarily involved an obligation to wash the hands before *hullin*, we can state that not later than AD 70[58] the Sages had decreed that novice *haberim* were to wash their hands before *hullin*. But pursuant to our view of the relationship between custom and decree, we think that the *haberim* practised handwashing for a substantial period before novice handwashing became the subject of a Sages' decree. Alon rightly observes, ' . . . this religious observance [eating common food in purity] was firmly practised before the time of these disputants [the Houses], since they differ with respect to only one condition, the qualification period relating to it'.[59]

Evidence which at first sight opposes handwashing by the *haberim* in Jesus' time is constituted by the Hananiah decree of c. AD 51, that hands assumed impure invalidate *terumah*. Is it likely that some lay Jews practised handwashing for *ordinary* food, before the Houses had decreed that hands invalidate *priestly* food (*terumah*)? We do not think this is so unlikely as it first appears. The priests may have been following a custom of handwashing before *terumah* for some years before the Hananiah decree. More significantly, however, the *haber's* desire to preserve the purity of his *hullin* and his liquids, and consequently to handwash, may have been provoked by the priests' practice, not of handwashing before *terumah*, as confirmed by the Hananiah decree, but of handwashing to remove actual defilement before handling *kodashim* pursuant to the Shammai/Hillel decree of not later than c. AD 10. The *haber's* zeal to handwash might even have been fired by the priest's purification of hands and feet pursuant to Exod. 30.17ff.

The evidence at Mark 7.3 suggests that handwashing before *hullin* was practised before Mark's time, since although his claim that 'all the Jews' handwashed is an exaggeration, it is hardly likely that the practice had just arisen at the time of so wide a claim. We consequently judge the evidence of T. Demai 2.11-12, with limited support from Mark 7.3, to outweigh the contrary evidence of the possible anachronism with the Hananiah decree, and we conclude that it is possible that the *haberim* handwashed before *hullin* in the time of Jesus.[60]

e. *Handwashing and the Expansive Tradition*

We have discovered that a Pharisaic group, the *haberim*, washed their hands to avoid defiling liquid because liquid might predispose or defile *hullin*. But was this concern to avoid defilement to *hullin* an example of the expansive tradition, namely that some things unconnected with the Temple were to be protected from impurity? This, we think, depends on whether the *haberim* considered the domestic table to be a locus of purity or whether, following the restrictive tradition, they feared the defilement of Temple-connected things: this latter reason would involve the fear that their hands, through the agency of liquid, would defile their *hullin*, and that thence the impurity would pass to Temple-connected things.

Further, since the *haber* handwashed before *hullin*, it follows that he had previously immersed his body in a *miqveh* for he would be routinely impure in body by reason of sexual emission (Lev. 15.16, 18), and, without removal of the body's major impurity, an attempt to purify the hands of a lesser impurity would be nugatory. He would also consider his body presumptively impure after a visit to a market or other busy public place because of its possible defilement by accidental contact with, for example, the clothes of an *'am-ha'areṣ* (see Section d.(a) above; Hagigah 2.7) or a menstruous woman (Lev. 15.19f.). The *haber* probably routinely immersed every morning, and after passing through a crowded public place. Thus the interpretation at the start of Chapter 1 of ἐβαπτίσατο at Luke 11.38 as 'immersed himself' is credible on the basis that the host Pharisee (a *haber*) was expressing mock suprise (in an effort to recruit Jesus) that Jesus had not immersed himself in a *miqveh*, like a *haber*, after a journey to his host presumably through a public place where he might have been defiled. This practice of the *haberim* also supports the accuracy of Mark's reference at 7.4 to a custom of not eating on return from market unless βαπτίσωνται, although it did not extend to 'all the Jews'. Βαπτίσωνται (A D W O fi [f13] and most of the Latin tradition), is thus preferable to the variant ῥαντίσωνται (Codex Sinaiticus, B and some Sahidic codices) meaning 'sprinkle themselves'. 'Sprinkle' must connote the water of the ashes of the

Red Heifer, which was the only means of purification from corpse-uncleanness (Num. 19.17f.). But it hardly seems practicable that every time *haberim* returned from market they should so sprinkle themselves. The ashes with which water had to be mixed were inconveniently situated, being distributed between the Temple, the Mount of Olives and the divisions of the priests (Parah 3.11). Moreover, the sprinkling took place on the third day after defilement (Num. 19.12) which would have resulted in a *haber* thus defiled being unable to eat for two days! By contrast, immersion in a *miqveh*, which was the means of purification from other defilement of the whole body, could comparatively easily be effected at or near home. We are persuaded that the immersion and handwashing practices of the *haberim* lie in the expansive tradition, since Deuteronomy 12, 15 and 22 provide that both the clean and the unclean may eat non-sacrificial flesh (בשׂר). Such food has no connection with the Temple, and no Jew need worry about its possible defilement. Indeed, there is a widespread view that the *haberim*, exceeding Scriptural obligation but pursuant to the expansive tradition, sought to preserve the purity of *hullin* because they treated the domestic table as an altar.[61] Thus at Berakhoth 55a it is explained by R. Johanan (probably ben Zakkai) and R. Eleazar, '... as long as the Temple stood, the altar atoned for Israel, but now a man's table atones for him'. Neusner writes that the Pharisees maintained that 'Israelites can and should pretend to be priests by eating their ordinary food at home as if they were priests engaged in eating the priestly portions of Holy Things in the Temple'.[62] But if the *haberim* equated themselves with priests eating at the altar, they should strictly have washed their hands and feet (Exod. 30.21). It might be thought that, since the *haberim* only washed their hands, the standard of purity which they sought to achieve was that of the priest not eating at the altar, but eating his *terumah* at home (Hagigah 2.5). Hyam Maccoby has pointed out to us, however, that while both priests and *haberim* probably immersed daily, following Lev. 15.18, and were thus *tebulei yom* till sunset, the *haberim* probably did not wait until then before eating,[63] as the priests did; for a *tebul yom*, being second degree till sunset, invalidates *terumah*, the priestly food, but not *hullin* provided he has washed his hands (Zab. 5. 12; T.Y.2.2; and see Chapter 4.d). Thus, in that he ate before sunset, the *haber tebul yom* was not modelling his purity on that of the priest eating *terumah*. Similarly, although it is claimed at Hullin 106a that the washing of hands for *hullin* was only ordained in order that the habit might be acquired with regard to *terumah*, this does not explain why *non-priestly haberim* washed their hands for *hullin*.

However, as indicated above, there is evidence that other pious persons observed prior to AD 70 a standard of purity exceeding that required by the general law.[64] We noted the evidence that Johanan b. Gudgada treated *hullin* as if it were *kodashim*, and that he was a Temple doorkeeper. At T. Yad. 2.17 'those who immerse at dawn' (who might, of course, have been *haberim*) complain against the Pharisees, and it seems possible that they routinely immersed pre-AD 70, for that pericope follows a complaint by the pre-70 Boethusians (Sadducees) against the Pharisees. Perhaps the earliest example of voluntarily undertaken purity is the Nazirite who by his vows bound himself to avoid impurity from the corpse of even his closest relatives (Num. 6.6-7). In the same way, those who chose to join a *haburah* voluntarily undertook to keep their ordinary food ritually pure.[65]

Thus, we think the true position to be that from early times pious persons would seek, perhaps as a spiritual exercise, to achieve a higher standard of levitical purity than was demanded by either the written or traditional law applicable to all. It seems that a pious person would choose which standard of purity he would attempt to maintain in this supererogatory way: b. Gudgada aimed at the purity of the priest eating sacrificial food, while the *haber* aimed at a standard a little less than that of the priest eating terumah.[66] Thus, the handwashing of the *haberim* was supererogatory, and, in that it aimed to preserve the purity of food unconnected with the Temple, it arose from the expansive tradition.

f. *Conclusion to Chapter 5*

We conclude that the Pharisaic question is credible in the time of Jesus on the basis that the Pharisees concerned were *haberim*[67] who did handwash before *hullin*, and were urging Jesus and his disciples to adopt the supererogatory handwashing which they themselves practised, i.e. to become *haberim*. It was an exhortation to undertake a higher standard of piety, addressed to Jesus as a religious leader. In this sense, the question could be elaborated—'Why do your disciples (since you, their Teacher, 'are true, and teach the way of God truthfully')[68] not wash their hands before they eat and observe the same standard of purity as we pietists do'? In this form the question still intersects well in debate with the reply at v. 15.

Our qualified acceptance of the authenticity of the Pharisaic question in Part I on traditio-historical grounds is thus rendered unconditional by historico-legal criticism, which also confirms the exclusion in Part I of the breach of the παράδοσις alleged in that question. For, not being *haberim*, the disciples were not breaking the traditional law or, more likely, custom which, in Jesus' time, only imposed handwashing, we think, on those who joined *haburoth*.

Chapter 6

THE SOURCES OF IMPURITY

We have now determined the authenticity of our form of the
Pharisaic question at v. 5 which we assessed in Part I by traditio-
historical criticism, to be supported by historico-legal criticism. We
also decided in Part I that the purity logion of Jesus in v. 15 was the
authentic reply to that question. We next investigate whether the
authenticity of that logion is supported by the evidence of legal
history concerning the law prevailing in the time of Jesus. But since
we are examining the genuineness of the logion as a reply, we have
also to investigate whether the law express or implicit in it credibly
connects with (or 'intersects with' as Neusner puts it), the express or
implicit law in the question. Thus, in examining the authenticity of
the reply from this standpoint, we test two things, (a) whether the
logion is authentic Jesus-material, and if so, (b) whether the logion
was the reply to the question at v. 5 or was spoken on some other
occasion. To decide (a), we must consider whether the logion is
credible in the mouth of Jesus in the light of his attitude towards, and
knowledge of, Jewish law of the time, while to decide (b), we must
consider whether the logion intersects on the level of Jewish purity
law with the v. 5 question, so as to constitute a credible reply to it. If
the logion is not credible in the mouth of Jesus, then its authenticity
is jeopardized, but if the logion does not intersect with the question,
then its authenticity is not jeopardized—it was simply not the reply
to the question at v. 5.

a. *The credibility of the logion according to Jewish law*

We concluded in Part I that the original form of the logion was:

οὐδέν ἐστιν ἔξω τοῦ ἀνθρώπου ὃ δύναται κοινῶσαι αὐτόν, ἀλλὰ τὰ ἐκ τοῦ ἀνθρώπου ἐκπορευόμενά ἐστιν τὰ κοινοῦντα τὸν ἄνθρωπον. We also decided that the logion should be interpreted in a relative sense—'There is nothing outside a man which can defile him *as much as* the things which come out from him'. In order to discover whether the authenticity of the logion can be checked by reference to its consistency with the law thought to prevail in the time of Jesus, we must ask whether the logion so formulated is to be understood in a legal (i.e. cultic) sense, or in an ethical sense.

Legal or Ethical Interpretation of the Logion

The *first limb* appears to require a legal interpretation. For although, according to Jewish concepts, things outside a man can ethically defile him (e.g. bad company, Prov. 7.25-27), it does not seem likely that Jesus would depreciate an ethical concept in the first limb in comparison to another ethical one (or, a minori, a cultic one) in the second limb. We therefore interpret the first limb in the sense of 'Things outside a man do not *cultically* defile him as much as . . .'.

In the *second limb* two aspects are susceptible to either a legal or an ethical interpretation. First by 'things coming out from a man' did Jesus mean bodily discharges or evil words? Secondly, does κοιν- in *this* limb mean defile cultically, or morally? It is theoretically possible for 'things coming out from a man' to mean things coming out from a man's *body* (bodily discharges) which defile cultically, or things coming out from a man's *mouth* (words) which defile ethically.

I. Bodily Discharges or Evil Words

A decision here may be aided by comparing the second limb with the first limb. Is the logion more credible as 'Nothing outside a man can cultically defile him as much as his (bodily discharges cultically defile him)', or as 'Nothing outside a man can cultically defile him [1] as much as his (evil words ethically defile him)'?

The credibility of the cultic version of the second limb will be affected by its legal accuracy. Do the bodily discharges cultically defile more than things outside man? The main cultic sources of impurity external to man comprise a dead creeping thing (שׁרץ, Lev. 11.29-31), carrion (נבלה), being corpses of clean animals, which die otherwise than by ritual slaughter (Lev. 11.39), of dead unclean animals (Lev. 11.26) and of dead clean birds (Lev. 17.15), the leprous garment (Lev. 13.51) and the leprous house (Lev. 14.46-47). There are several important sources of impurity which 'come out from a man'. At Lev. 12.1-5 a woman who has borne a child is stated to be unclean, and this impurity, perhaps, arises from the bodily discharge which follows the birth of the baby. According to Lev. 13.1-3, when a man has on the skin of his body שאת (literally, a rising) or ספחת (literally, an eruption or outpouring) or בהרת (literally, a bright spot), then, subject to diagnosis by the priest, he is unclean as a leper. Thus, the principal manifestation of this impurity is something protruding or 'coming out' from the skin of man. Similarly, the impurity decreed by Lev. 15 on the *zab*, the emitter of semen, the *niddah* and the *zabah*, arises in each case from a bodily discharge.[2]

The other main Biblical source of impurity is a human corpse, and it seems likely from Num. 19.11-16 that a discharge of uncleanness, like a vapour, was thought to flow from a corpse.[3] For it is not only decreed there that the toucher of a corpse is unclean, but also that every person in a tent where a man dies, and every open vessel without a cover, is unclean.

We do not perceive why Jesus should declare that the sources of impurity outside a man cultically defile less than those which come from within a man. If the impurity of a corpse can properly be classified as a source inside a man, then there is a partial justification in Pharaisaic law for the comparison, since a corpse is the only 'father of fathers', in that any person who touches it is himself a father of impurity. This rule is based, we think, on Num. 19.11 which provides that the toucher of a corpse is unclean for seven days, for the degree of defilement later termed 'a father' is often indicated in the Pentateuch by the consequence of seven days' impurity, while the 'offspring' is often indicated by impurity only till evening.[4] However, a corpse is generally classified as an external source, and was probably always considered so, for a dead body is not a man in the significant sense of personality.[5] There is thus no legal justification for the statement that things outside a man are less defiling than those coming from him, since the other external sources mentioned above are equally defiling as the bodily discharges, while the corpse is *more* defiling than them. This legal inaccuracy may not, though, render the statement incredible on the lips of Jesus; he may simply have been wrong. If Jesus was a charismatic *hasid*, as Vermes[6] avers, then, particularly as a Galilean, he may have been unversed in some aspects of purity law.[7]

Even if the suggested cultic comparison in the logion were legally correct, there seems to be no motivation for Jesus to make it. When applying the criterion of coherence in Part I, we determined that Jesus generally respected and observed the cultic written Torah, although he disregarded that law if moral claims demanded. But Jesus had no cause to contrast one Biblical source of impurity with another.

However, Jesus probably disapproved of some of the additions to the law made by the tradition (see, e.g., the Korban Unit),[8] and for this reason we think that the cultic interpretation of 'things coming out from a man' is more credible if we add back into the first limb Mark's phrase, εἰσπορευόμενον εἰς αὐτόν; we then translate the logion: 'Nothing *going into a man from* outside can defile him as much as the things which come out from a man'. This version sounds more credible on the lips of Jesus, for 'nothing going into a man from outside' probably means food, and the disliked *tradition* had added to the Biblical law concerning the kinds of unclean food which would defile the eater. To test the legal accuracy of this version, we must compare the defiling effect of the various unclean foods with that of bodily discharges.

There were three different kinds of unclean food. First, in Lev. 11 various creatures are declared to be unclean (טמא) to the people, and they are forbidden to eat such flesh; we will term this *prohibited food*. Secondly, at Lev. 17.14 the people are forbidden to eat the blood of any creature, and this is followed by the consequential provision (v. 15) that everyone who eats (flesh of) an animal which dies naturally (נבלה), or is torn by beasts (טרפה), shall be unclean (טמא) till evening. It is these provisions which gave rise to the practice of ritual slaughter (שחיטה) whereby all the blood is drained from the animal, and none of its prescribed organs is injured. This practice is not explained in the Pentateuch but, as part of the 'oral law received by Moses at Sinai', is contained in the Mishnaic and Talmudic tractates, Hullin, and its Sinai origin is presumed from the permission at Deut. 12.21, 'you may kill any of your herd or your flock *as I have commanded you*'.[9] Food not slaughtered according to the correct ritual is termed *non-kosher*. Thirdly, food which has been defiled by an unclean thing, usually by its touch, is unclean (טמא), and the law on this was developed from Lev. 11.38, as previously discussed. We will call this *contaminated food*.

The following consequences ensue from eating these three kinds of food. Regarding *prohibited diet*, although the toucher of the unclean creatures is stated at Lev. 11.24, 26, 27 to be unclean, there is strangely no provision that the eater of them is unclean: such a provision may be thought unnecessary since, without utensils, it is difficult to eat food without handling it. In construing the phrase 'nothing going into a man', however, we are surely concerned with the power of the food to defile the *eater*, not the toucher.

Regarding *non-kosher food*, Lev. 17.15 provides that the eater is unclean, and this is also stated respecting *nebelah* at 11.40. However, 17.15 is interpreted in Sifra as referring only to the eater of the carrion of a clean bird, which defiles only during the time it passes through the gullet. Lev. 22.8 relating to the priest is interpreted in the same way. Sifra also interprets 11.40 restrictively, as meaning that the toucher of carrion is only defiled if he touches an amount not less than the amount which can be eaten, i.e. a mouthful or olive's bulk. Hyam Maccoby has suggested to us that the arbitrary nature of these interpretations, which cannot naturally be deduced from the verses, argues for an ancient origin, but we are reluctant to accept that they prevailed in the time of Jesus, or of Mark or Matthew, since scholars date the material in Sifra to the second century or later, and stress the interpolations in it.[10]

Regarding *contaminated food*, the earliest authority for the defilement of its eater lies not in Scripture, but in the *tradition*, in the Hananiah decrees which we have dated c. AD 51, although we considered that the defilement thereby decreed may have been assigned to the eater by custom in the time of Jesus.

We accordingly think it was legally correct for Jesus to say that things going into man cultically defile less than things going out if, when uttering the logion, he was thinking primarily of *contaminated* food (to which the Pharisaic question related). For we have seen that the impurity of the bodily discharges from man is scripturally ordained, so that the sufferer is a father of impurity, while the severest degree of impurity assigned to the eater of contaminated food was, according to the generally accepted Pharisaic view, second degree.[11]

Thus, if we restore Mark's phrase εἰσπορευόμενον εἰς αὐτόν to the *first* limb of the logion, the phrase τὰ ἐκ τοῦ ἀνθρώπου ἐκπορευόμενα in the second limb can bear a cultic meaning as bodily discharges, since a depreciation of the defiling power of contaminated food, imposed by the tradition, in comparison with the Scriptural defiling power of bodily discharges, is legally justifiable, and perhaps acceptable as a statement of Jesus. There are, however, two objections to this course:

1. We excluded Mark's phrase from the first limb in Part I on traditio-historical grounds.

2. The second limb has been interpreted almost unanimously by critics in the ethical sense of evil words or thought.

Perhaps the uncertainty thus attending the meaning of 'things going out from a man', will be reduced if we turn now to the second question affecting this second limb—whether κοινοῦντα means defiling cultically or ethicallly. For if that verb is more likely to have one meaning than the other, then that consideration will influence the interpretation of 'things going out from a man'.

II. Κοινοῦντα—*cultic or ethical defilement*

Although κοιν- is used with a cultic sense in the first limb, there is no linguistic reason why it is unlikely to be used with a different meaning in the second limb. Riches[12] argues that if 'pollute' is used univocally in v. 15b, it would have to refer to man's own bodily emissions, e.g. semen, spittle and excrement, and that such interpretation of the second limb would make nonsense of the whole saying, since it would adopt the notion of pollution which the first limb has just rejected. This argument is vitiated, we think, by his identification of things entering a man in the first limb as unclean foods without differentiating between the several kinds of unclean food and the respective consequences of eating them. He accordingly does not consider the possibility that Jesus, instead of rejecting 'any notion of pollution', may only be depreciating the scribal decree that *contaminated* food defiles the eater, in favour of the Pentateuchal sources of defilement, roughly summarized as the things which come out of man. Nor does Riches consider the relative rather than the absolute interpretation of the οὐδέν . . . ἀλλά construction in the logion. His failure to discuss these possibilities, and his rash reliance on the relative infrequency of the term 'purity' in Jesus' sayings[13] give the impression that his certainty that Jesus shunned the conventional associations of ritual purity is constructed on shallow foundations.

There are, however, the following weightier points in favour of an ethical understanding of κοινοῦντα in the second limb:

1. Matthew[14] probably considered Mark to intend the verb ethically, for he alters 'coming out from *man*' (τοῦ ἀνθρώπου) to 'coming out from his *mouth*' (τοῦ στόματος). Thus, κοινοῖ must have an ethical meaning in *Matthew's* second limb, for we are aware of no authority in Biblical or Talmudic law for the proposition that evil

words defile in a *cultic* sense. We note our conclusion in Part I that the early church interpreted the second limb ethically (and κοινοῦντα as part of it) in vv. 21-23, and Mark saw no reason to alter that interpretation.

2. It does not seem linguistically objectionable that κοινοῦντα should be employed with a transferred meaning of ethical defilement. We have previously discussed how the root expanded from meaning 'common' or 'shared' to meaning also 'cultically impure', through its application to food eaten by the Gentile nations in common. In view of this flexibility of meaning it does not seem a difficult transition for the meaning of the verb to be stretched from 'cultically defile' to 'ethically defile', even though our passage and Matthew's parallel hold the only uses of the root in the Greek Bible with this sense. It is pertinent, however, that at Didache 14.2 κοινωθῇ is used in the metaphorical ethical sense with reference to the defilement of a spiritual sacrifice, since the Didache is thought to reflect the life of a Christian community towards the end of the first century.[15]

3. In favour of the ethical interpretation of both 'things coming out from a man' and 'defile' in the second limb is other teaching of Jesus which lays emphasis on inward purity. Examples of such teaching are Matt. 5.8 ('M'), μακάριοι οἱ καθαροὶ τῇ καρδίᾳ . . . , and 23.25 ('Q'), καθαρίζετε τὸ ἔξωθεν τοῦ ποτηρίου καὶ τῆς παροψίδος, ἔωθεν δὲ γέμουσιν ἐξ ἁρπαγῆς καὶ ἀκασίας.[16]

A Jesus-debate which, if authentic, strongly supports an ethical rather than a cultic meaning for the second limb is recorded at Papyrus Oxyrynchus 840, which, discovered in 1905, is thought to have been written about 400 AD.[17]

To summarize that Fragment, Jesus is asked by a Pharisaic High Priest why he and his disciples are walking in the Temple without having immersed, and changed their garments. The Pharisee, in response to Jesus' counter-question, asserts that *he* did immerse, and change his garments. Jesus retorts that the Pharisee has washed in water in which dogs and pigs have been cast, and prostitutes have washed, whereas Jesus and his disciples have immersed in the waters of eternal life.

Critics are divided concerning the historicity of the passage. James,[18] and Grenfell and Hunt,[19] think that the writer shows gross ignorance of Jewish matters, especially in regard to swine being near the Temple, but Jeremias[20] maintains that the writer is excellently informed, and that the story represents a valuable tradition. Büchler[21] even writes, 'We have here more original materials than are to be found in the Synoptics who transfer from Jerusalem to Galilee the dispute between Jesus and the Pharisees on the purity-laws of the Temple'. To assist a decision on these contrasting opinions, we must look at the detail of the passage:

(a) The Fragment states that Jesus led the disciples εἰς αὐτὸ τὸ ἁγνευτήριον, and walked ἐν τῷ ἱερῷ. ᾽Αγνευτήριον is defined by Bauer as 'lit. place of purification, perh. sanctuary of the part of the Temple precinct in which the ἅγια σκεύη were kept'. Stress is laid on its sanctity by the αὐτό το, so that it is 'the very' place. Probably, the area meant is that part of the Court of the Priests which is between the altar and the Priests' Steps,[22] for at the South side of this part was placed the huge brass laver in which the priests sanctified their hands and feet. Τῷ ἱερῷ probably means the Temple Mount or, as Bauer puts it, 'the whole Temple precinct with its buildings, courts etc.'. We wonder how the Pharisee could know that Jesus had not immersed elsewhere, for the laver in the Court of the Priests was for the *priests* to wash before entering the Sanctuary. But it seems unlikely that Jesus, as a generally observant Jew with great zeal for the Temple,[23] was in the Court of the Priests anyway, since Kelim 1.8 provides that no Israelite may enter therein except for the laying on of hands, and for slaughtering and waving in connection with sacrifice. Jeremias,[24] however, thinks the Court of the Israelites is intended, but the ἁγνευτήριον must surely be the place where the laver is situated, i.e. the Court of the Priests.

(b) The Pharisee claims that Jesus and the disciples gazed upon the ἅγια σκεύη. Bauer in defining σκεῦος refers to Heb. 9.21, τὰ σκεύη τῆς λειτουργίας, so we may expect our phrase to mean the holy vessels or equipment. Büchler[25] points out that it would be difficult for someone in either Court to see the candelabra, etc., in the Holy Place, but since the term connotes something *used*, the sacrificial equipment in the Court of Priests, i.e. the marble table for the flesh, and the table of silver, may be intended; these, of course, could be seen from the Court of the Israelites.

(c) The Pharisee concerned is said to be an ἀρχιερεύς and the name is fragmentary, only Λευ being visible. There is, however, no record of a High Priest with a name commencing thus in the first century AD to 70.[26] Indeed, it is unlikely that a Pharisee would have been High Priest in the time of Jesus. Although Bauer (*s.v.* ἀρχιερεύς) defines it as meaning High Priest in a Jewish context, he mentions that the plural is used in the NT and Josephus to describe male members of High Priestly families, and it is quite possible that such a person was a Pharisee.

(d) Grenfell and Hunt[27] consider that the mention of two stairways to the pool of David is detail invented for rhetorical effect. Büchler,[28] though, points out that a hyper-pious person might exit from the lustration by a different route from that which he entered when defiled. There is no record of a 'pool of David',[29] but it would not be surprising if there were a pool of that name.

(e) That a High Priest should wash in a pool into which dogs and swine were cast, is considered incredible by Grenfell and Hunt.[30] Büchler,[31] however, notes that the waters which supplied the Temple came from the pools of Solomon, south-west of Bethlehem, and thinks that Jesus, in referring to 'running' waters, meant that the waters in which the Pharisee had bathed, had, during their passage through the intermediate villages before the Temple, received dogs and swine which had been thrown in for a wash. But it is surely unlikely, in view of the Jews' abhorrence of the pig, that pigs were reared so close to Jerusalem. Further, the extraction from χεομένοις of a reference to the earlier course of the waters appears rather forced.

In view of the difficulties in this Fragment, and the surprising ferocity of Jesus' polemic against the cult, we are inclined, on balance, to regard the passage as the product of a Hellenistic, strongly anti-Jewish church, and we prefer not to rely on it for our present purpose.

Nevertheless, the preponderance of other evidence of Jesus' teaching does indicate that he gave priority to ethical rather than cultic purity.

Conclusion regarding the second limb

Notwithstanding the capability of both 'things coming out from a man' and κοινοῦντα to bear a cultic meaning, we are persuaded by the above cumulative considerations, but particularly by the church's ethical interpretation in vv. 21-23 and the ethical priority in Jesus' teaching, that the second limb should be understood in an *ethical* sense.

Conclusion on a., the credibility of the logion according to Jewish law

Since we have decided that the first limb of the logion is to be interpreted cultically, and the second ethically, the logion compares the severity of cultic defilement with that of ethical defilement. Although the degrees of cultic defilement conferred by things outside a man were regulated by the law, the severity of ethical defilement was not measured in this way, so that the authenticity of the comparison in the logion, produced by tradition criticism, is not susceptible to the test of legal criticism.

However, one point does remain for final consideration by legal criticism. We considered earlier that a *cultic* interpretation of τὰ ἐκ τοῦ ἀνθρώπου ἐκπορευόμενα in the second limb was more credible if εἰσπορευόμενον εἰς αὐτόν was added back into the first limb. But as we have now decided that the second limb is to be interpreted *ethically*, we must consider whether our deletion in Part I of the phrase in the first limb on tradition-critical grounds is supported by the test of legal history. For if we restored that phrase, the first limb would primarily refer to the Hananiah decree whereby the eater of contaminated food is defiled. However, we do not think that Jesus would have compared ethical defilement generally in the second limb with merely a rule of the tradition in the first limb, but rather with cultic defilement generally: that phrase would thus be omitted from the first limb.

Moreover, in view of Jesus' depreciatory attitude towards the tradition we doubt whether he would have given even relative weight to the Hananiah decree in comparison with *ethical* impurity—he would have denied the decree absolutely. Yet we do not think that this point outweighs the evidence in Part I in favour of interpreting οὐδέν . . . αλλά in a relative sense. We accordingly conclude that the deletion in Part I of εἰσπορευόμενον εἰς αὐτόν from the first limb is supported by legal criticism.

Our above enquiries into the law involved in the logion, and into Jesus' attitude towards that law, cause us to conclude that the logion is credible as a saying of Jesus in the form, 'There is nothing outside a man which *cultically* defiles him as much as the things coming from a man *ethically* defile him', although in the heat of dispute, it is unlikely that the logion would be uttered in that rather pedantic, precise way. Indeed, in debate, Jesus may not have weighed the literal and metaphorical connotations of defilement, but may have used 'defile' in both limbs in the looser sense of 'spoil the character' or simply 'harm'. This is particularly possible since the root κοιν- is probably translating an Aramaic[32] אמט which, if Palestinian Jews of Jesus' day considered impurity in Biblical categories (as they probably did), had a similar meaning to the Biblical אמט.[33] The majority of uses of אמט as verb or adjective in the OT are in a cultic sense, but religious and ethical uses are also cited by BDB, and occasionally in the Priestly Code it is difficult to gauge which meaning is intended.[34] Thus, the Aramaic מטא was probably used by Jesus in an over-riding sense of 'corrupt' or 'harm'.

b. *The correspondence of the logion to the question at v. 5*

We have decided that historico-legal examination confirms the logion as an authentic saying of Jesus, but was it uttered in reply to the Pharisaic question? For the logion could have travelled independently in the tradition, perhaps as the reply to a different question. Question and answer, as now understood, are: 'Why do your disciples eat food with unclean hands?' 'There is nothing outside a man which can cultically defile him as much as the things coming from him morally defile him.'

Although the logion would have achieved a closer correspondence with the v. 5 question about eating if εἰσπορευόμενον εἰς αὐτόν were included in the logion, the remaining ἔξω τοῦ ἀνθρώπου more than covers the issue raised in the question. Both hands and food are outside man, so that the response 'nothing outside man defiles . . . ' clearly intersects with the question. Indeed, we are inclined to think that a comprehensive contrast of things outside a man with things coming from inside him is a more likely thrust in debate than a contrast of the *particular* cultic point of contaminated food with the *general* ethical point. We accordingly view the logion at v. 15 as the reply to the question at v. 5.

c. *The Medical and Ethical Explanations*

Finally in this Chapter we must consider whether our attribution to the Hellenistic church of the Medical Explanation and the Ethical Explanation on traditio-historical grounds is supported by the standard of legal history. For, while the main point of the Medical Explanation is that food does not defile because it enters not the heart but the stomach, the reason why food entering the stomach does not defile is stated to be that it is excreted.

There is no authority in the OT for the legal proposition that a person defiled by the consumption of unclean food is purified by the excretion of it. Lev. 17.15 provides that the eater of *nebelah* or *terefah* shall wash his clothes, immerse, and be unclean until evening; Lev. 11.40 provides that the eater of *nebelah* shall simply wash his clothes and be unclean until evening. Indeed, the requirement at

Deut. 23. 12-13 that excrement must be covered up in a place outside the camp indicates that there is nothing purifying about the process. It is reported in the Rabbinic writings[35] that the ancient pious men suffered from diarrhoea for about twenty days before death in order that everything might be purged, but this can hardly be considered authority for the general purifying effect of excretion, and it is uncertain whether physical, moral or cultic purity was achieved by this purging.

As mentioned in Part I, we do not think that a Palestinian Jew, even possessing Jesus' qualified attitude towards the law, would have resorted to a biological argument to explain opposition to a lemma of cultic law; a denial of *cultic* defilement by eating is in too different a thought-world for a Jew to support it with *medical* argument. We acknowledge that there is some evidence for Jesus referring to the function of excretion in his teaching. In Qoheleth Rabbah on 1.8 (the story is also told at A.Z. 17a) it is related that Jesus had suggested that the hire of a harlot, which must not be brought into the Temple in payment of a vow (Deut. 23.18), should be used in constructing bath-houses and privies on the basis that the money came from filth, and should be expended on filth. (In the Talmudic version the suggestion is only related to the construction of a privy for the High Priest.) We do not need to investigate the authenticity of this story, for Jesus there treats the latrine as a suitable destination for a thing which is primarily *morally* unclean, and the story does not suggest that Jesus in any way connected excretion with *cultic* purification. Thus legal history supports the attribution in Part I of the Medical Explanation to the Hellenistic Church on the ground that a Jew, Palestinian or of the Dispersion, would not have created a biological explanation for a cultic lemma.

The Ethical Explanation which explains that things coming from man morally defile because they come from the heart, being an ethical proposition, is not susceptible to testing by its conformity with law.

Chapter 7

Conclusions

In the Introduction we stated that we aimed in this book to discover
the evidence which our passage affords of the attitudes of Jesus and of
the early Christians towards the Jewish law. We have attempted to
obtain that evidence by the use of traditio-historical criticism in Part
I, and of historico-legal criticism in Part II. Since this is, so far as we
know, the first application of the two disciplines in harness in this
way, it may be instructive concerning the future utility of the second
discipline as a check upon the results of the first if we now review the
inter-action of the two tools in determining the origin and history of
the Purity Dispute and its Explanations.

Legal criticism confirmed the results of tradition criticism in the
following respects:

1. 'All the Jews' in v. 3 is probably secondary since handwashing
before *hullin* was practised only by the *haberim* in the time of Jesus.[1]

2. 'According to the tradition of the elders' in vv. 3 and 5 is also
probably secondary since it is unlikely that in Jesus' day the custom
of the *haberim* to wash their hands had been incorporated into the
traditional law applying to *haberim* through adjudication by the
Sages upon the details of the practice.[2]

3. The form of the Question in v. 5 produced by tradition criticism
is credible on the basis that it was asked by the Pharisaic *haberim*
who were urging Jesus that his disciples, being religious people,
should observe their standards of purity.

4. The form of the Reply by Jesus in v. 15 produced by tradition
criticism is credible if it is interpreted as a relative depreciation of
external defilement generally in favour of ethical defilement.

5. 'Going into him' in the first limb of the Reply should be deleted
partly on the ground that in comparison with ethical purity Jesus

would probably have denied rather than merely depreciated the scribal decree imposing defilement on the eater.[3]

6. Ουδέν . . . ἀλλά in the logion should be interpreted relatively on the ground that an absolute statement by Jesus, that nothing outside man defiles, is unlikely in view of his usual respect for the Pentateuch and the pervasiveness there of the concept of cultic purity.[4]

7. The Medical Explanation should be attributed to the Hellenistic Gentile church since cultic defilement of the eater of unclean food was not removed by excretion of the food, and certainly no Palestinian Jew is likely thus to have confounded the cultic and the biological.[5]

8. Although not part of the Purity Dispute, legal criticism at Chapter 5.e showed that 'immersed himself' was probably the correct interpretation of ἐβαπτίσατο at Luke 11.38, and that Mark's βαπτίσωνται at 7.4 was similarly accurate if restricted to the *haberim*.

In no instance has the test of legal criticism invalidated the results of tradition criticism. It is, perhaps, only in rare cases that the conclusions of legal criticism should be preferred to those of tradition criticism, when they conflict. For the difficulty of asserting with confidence that Jesus or the Pharisees could *not* have said something because its content conflicts with the current law arises from the differing views within Judaism on legal issues, and from uncertainty as to when the various views prevailed. Another problem concerning Jesus-material is that effective legal criticism often depends not only on ascertaining the relevant law, but on assessing Jesus' probable attitude towards that law, which can be difficult to gauge; for his willingness to over-ride the law depended on the needs of his ministry.[6]

Although we found it convenient to apply tradition criticism to our passage and then, as a separate stage, apply legal criticism as a test of the results, the tools cannot be applied in entire isolation from each other. For, in Part I we occasionally found ourselves using the legal position to support an interpretation of ambiguous syntax,[7] or an identification of redaction,[8] and in Part II we applied redaction criticism to certain Rabbinic passages.[9] Moreover, in Chapter 6, we sought the aid of legal criticism, linguistics and redaction criticism to elucidate whether the second limb of the logion should be interpreted in a legal or ethical sense.

Finally, legal criticism can only serve as a test of the results of tradition criticism where the material is legally verifiable. We were thus unable to test by the standard of legal accuracy the logion's comparison involving the gravity of ethical defilement, since this is not a concern of the law; similarly the Ethical Explanation cannot be tested legally.

We will now assess the evidence which the Purity Dispute and its Explanations afford of the attitude of Jesus and of the early Christians towards the law. Tradition criticism and legal criticism reveal to us the respective attitudes of Jesus, the early churches, Mark and Matthew.

Jesus

Since we have attributed the Explanations to the early church, any evidence of Jesus' attitude towards the law must be gleaned from his reply in the purity logion to the Pharisaic question. But is the logion's interpretation to be restricted by the nature of that question, or is it to be given a wider meaning? Put briefly, the Pharisees ask, 'Why do your disciples eat with unclean hands?', to which Jesus responds, 'Nothing outside a man defiles him as much as the things coming from him'.

Although assessment of the breadth of meaning intended by a reply expressed in general terms to a question on a limited point is very difficult, we see in principle no cause to limit the depreciation in the logion to contaminated food, simply because the question involves the defilement of food by unclean hands. Nor, since we have determined that 'going into him' should be deleted, as secondary, from the first limb, need the depreciation in the logion be restricted to unclean food generally. We note from Jesus' replies at Mark 2.17 and 3.4 to other Pharisaic questions, that he sometimes stated a wide principle in response to a question on a narrow point. These factors incline us to the view that Jesus intended his logion to be understood in the widest sense, namely that cultic impurity *in toto* does not harm a man as much as moral impurity.

As Jesus, in our view, did not deny the fact of cultic impurity in the logion, but only treated it as of less gravity than moral impurity, it is not surprising that disputes arose in the early church over the application of dietary and other cultic laws to Gentile Christians.

The early Christians

The Gentile Christians of the early church demonstrate in the

Dispute and Explanations their concern to justify, by words of Jesus, their complete freedom from the Jewish food laws. They insert 'going into man' in the first limb of the logion, to emphasize that *food* does not defile, and they add, as words of the Lord, the Explanations, of which the Medical one interprets in an absolute sense the denial of the cultic defilement of the eater.

We think that these Gentiles also substituted the πᾶν construction in v. 18b to stress that *nothing*, neither prohibited, nor non-kosher, nor contaminated food defiled the eater. Strictly, prohibited diet did not defile the eater in any case (only the toucher), but the Gentiles may have been unaware of such a legal nicety, and since they were being pressed by Jewish Christians not to eat pork, etc., they wished to emphasize that *no* food harmed a man. But the most conspicuous pointer in the Explanations to the Gentiles' independence from the thought-forms of Jewish purity lies in their production of the excretory process as the reason why unclean food does not defile.

Mark

In eliciting Mark's attitude towards the law from the Purity Dispute we note (1) our conclusion that in the tradition received by Mark the first limb included 'going into man', and (2) that since the Medical Explanation received by Mark interprets that first limb of the logion as an absolute denial of defilement by things entering man, Mark, who probably did not attempt to distinguish between authentic words of Jesus and words added during transmission of the tradition, supposed Jesus to have uttered the denial in an absolute sense.

Mark's attitude to the law appears as free as that of the Gentiles except that, as a Jew,[10] he is more conscious of the distinctions between the traditional law and the written law, and between contaminated food, non-kosher food and prohibited food.

He shows himself strongly opposed to the traditional law, but this opposition may spring from a primary dislike of the Pharisees arising from the attempts of the Jewish Christians to impose the whole law onto Gentile converts.[11] He attacks the Pharisees 'and all the Jews' by alleging purificatory practices which, in reality, are only observed by the *haberim* (vv. 3 and 4). In v. 5 his 'according to the tradition of the elders' seems to imply that handwashing was a traditional rule applying to all, rather than a condition for those who joined *haburoth*.

At v. 19c Mark's καθαρίζων πάντα τὰ βρώματα may only be a

typical summary, but we think the clause is more precise than that. For he does not emphasize that the *eater* of any food is clean, he stresses that all *foods* are clean. This neatly includes prohibited food since Lev. 11 ordains that the forbidden creatures are unclean, but does not ordain that the eater of their flesh is thereby unclean. The use of καθαρίζειν in the NT in the sense of declaring meats to be permitted diet is supported at Acts 10.15 and 11.9 where God says to Peter regarding the prohibited animals which Peter refuses to kill and eat, ἃ ὁ Θεὸς ἐκαθάρισεν, σὺ μὴ κοίνου.

Thus, in our view, the Purity Dispute shows Mark as well versed in the basic principles of the purity laws, but as opposed to those laws in their entirety. It is certainly arguable that in our exposition of v. 19c we pay too little attention to our own earlier strictures, and credit Mark with sophisticated nuances of meaning which may never have crossed his mind! But since we believe that in Mark's day the continuing attempt of the Jewish Christians to impose the whole law on Gentile converts was still an issue, it seems to us that Mark, brought up as a Jew, but converted to a probably Pauline view of the cultic law,[12] would be particularly conscious of the consequences of Jewish claims about the status in purity of the different classes of food and their eater.

Matthew

In contrast to Mark, we see in Matthew's treatment of the Purity Dispute the 're-Qumranizing and re-Judaizing' of the Gospel tradition, to which Hübner refers (pp. 9f.). We think that Matthew noticed in Mark the danger that the logion *might* be understood not just as a denial that the eater is defiled by contaminated food, but in the wider sense as a denial of the cultic impurity of food in general. He also noticed in the Medical Explanation in Mark that Jesus explained his logion in a manner that extended its meaning from a denial that the eater is defiled by contaminated food, to a denial of the defilement of the eater of non-kosher food and of the impurity of prohibited food; as a Jewish Christian, Matthew may have noted the separate functions of vv. 18-19b and v. 19c in these denials, but even if he did not, he would appreciate their combined effect as a comprehensive denial of the food laws.

These wider interpretations, we suggest, were not acceptable to Matthew and his Jewish Christian church, so he revised Mark's version principally by restricting the logion to a denial of the eater's defilement by *contaminated* food. In his v. 11 he stresses that the denial of cultic impurity is limited to the food laws by stating that the thing entering *the mouth* (τὸ στόμα) does not defile. By substituting στόμα for Mark's αὐτόν in this limb of the logion, Matthew reduces the comprehensive nature of the denial, ties the reply more closely to the question's reference to contaminated food, and thus weakens any claim that the denial extends to the defiling effect of non-kosher food.

In the explanation of the first limb of the logion at v. 17 Matthew again inserts his limiting τὸ στόμα.[13] Also in v. 17, although he retains the comprehensive 'everything entering man' in Mark's v. 18, he omits the denial that it can defile, and only states that it passes into the stomach, and is thrown out into the latrine. Thus, the point in Mark's v. 18 that non-kosher food does not defile is blunted. And, by omitting Mark's v. 19c, Matthew refused to acknowledge that Jesus abrogated the impurity of prohibited food.

Matthew was also, we suggest, disturbed by the interpretation of the logion even in the narrower sense of a denial that the eater of *contaminated hullin* was defiled, for it was settled traditional law that he was (Hananiah decrees). He did, however, feel entitled to deny that the *hullin* was defiled in the first place since, as we determined in Chapter 4, hands are not first-degree unclean and are therefore unable (without the interposition of liquid) to defile *hullin*, unless the whole body has been defiled by a father of impurity. But the hands referred to in the Pharisaic question are not first degree, because Mark has, in v. 2, defined the κοιναῖς χερσίν of which the Pharisees speak in v. 5, as meaning unwashed hands, i.e. hands which are assumed to be impure, unless recently washed. If the hands (with the rest of the body) were first degree, *the whole body*, not just the hands, would require immersion in a *miqveh*. So Matthew could reasonably deny that hands assumed to be impure defiled *hullin*, and thence the eater, since only the traditional law applying to the *haberim* classed hands as impure regarding *hullin*, unless washed.[14]

Matthew, therefore, revises Mark's version further, and impresses on the passage, as its main point on purity, the theme that *unwashed hands* do not defile *hullin*. He does this, first, by altering the complaint of the Pharisees from the Marcan version that they eat with κοιναῖς χερσίν (which, unless explained, could mean hands first-degree unclean as part of the body defiled by a father), to his version (v. 2) that they do not wash their hands when they eat (which, being a routine practice, can only mean hands assumed separately defiled).[15] Secondly and more significantly, in his final summarizing sentence at v. 20 he adds to Mark's summary (v. 23) the words 'but to eat with unwashed hands does not defile a man'. Matthew thus attempts to avert attention from the absolute denial in the logion, as interpreted by the Medical Explanation, that the eater of contaminated food is defiled.

It may be asked why, if this interpretation which projects a Matthew who supports the traditional law applying to all, but attacks the practice of the *haberim*, is true, does Matthew gratuitously insert into his Marcan material the unit of vv. 12-14 which contains a vehement attack on the Pharisees? We would reply that the Pharisees who complained at the neglect of handwashing before *hullin* were *haberim*, and it is consistent with Matthew's attack on this practice that he should condemn in that unit those *haberim Pharisees* as plants not planted by God, i.e. not instruments of God's will, and blind leaders of the blind, i.e. false teachers drawing others into their misguided ways.

Matthew's attitude towards the law thus appears from our passage to be one of support for the traditional law applying to all (and probably, a fortiori, the written law), but one of condemnation of the *haberim* and the traditional laws which sanction their practices.

It is not possible for us, for reasons of space, to test the above evidence of Jesus' relative attitude to the cultic law against other Gospel evidence. But even though we recognize that we are opposed by the majority view represented by Käsemann and others, we are confident that the other Gospel evidence would not challenge our conclusion that Jesus did not deny the concept of cultic impurity.

In reaching this, our principal conclusion, we have learned that the use of legal criticism is not free from difficulty, but we do believe that it has a supportive rôle to the conventional tools of NT criticism, and that it may be applied, with benefit, to other Gospel passsages with a legal content.

The notion of cultic impurity may be considered obsolete and distasteful by many, yet an understanding of it illumines the interpretation of a passage such as our own. Indeed, we are confident that more light will be shed on the idea of impurity by anthropologists such as Mary Douglas,[16] who deny the customary divisions between the ethical, the hygienic and the cultic, and insist that the concept of pollution must be studied in relation to its *total* structure of thought.

NOTES

Notes to Introduction

1. The written law is contained in the Pentateuch. Instead of 'traditional law', we should strictly speak of the 'tradition of the elders', since this is Mark's term at 7.3, 5. We call these traditions 'law' because our definition of law (vide Chapter 3.f. infra) includes the customary behaviour of a group of people whatever be the sanction inducing that behaviour. Since those of Pharisaic persuasion customarily behaved in accordance with the rules (halakhoth) declared by early Sages, we call those traditional rules 'law'; cf. Josephus's νόμιμα at *Ant.* 13.297. J. Bowman, *Mark*, pp. 164-65, notes that Mark's description of the halakhah in 7.3 as a tradition of the elders, rather than oral law, argues for an early date for his Gospel, since it was probably around 90 AD that the traditions were clearly elevated to the status of oral law given to Moses at Sinai; cf. R. Eliezer at end of Yad. 4.3.

2. Vide e.g. Robertson Smith, *Religion*, pp. 446-54.

3. Much creativity of the early Church is generally credited to Christian prophets, but in his article 'On the Evidence for the Creative Role of Christian Prophets', *NTS* 20 (1974), pp. 262-74, D. Hill claims that the evidence that the sayings of early Christian prophets were accepted by the Gospel tradition as dominical utterances is feeble. He argues that since Bultmann and other protagonists of creative prophecy say that the words of the prophets only gradually were accepted as words of the historical Jesus, this assumes that the community could distinguish between the two: moreover, if the words of the risen Lord uttered by the prophets were equal to λόγια Ἰησοῦ there was no reason for the retrojection of the former into a pre-Easter setting. We agree with Hill that Bultmann has not taken seriously enough the part played by tradition in the early Christian community, and the importance of the Twelve as witnesses of the tradition of Jesus' words. In particular, Paul's thrice-expressed distinction between his own injunctions and those of Jesus (1 Cor. 7.10, 12, 25) argues against Bultmann.

4. Thus, at Mark 10.1-9, Jesus treats Mosaic permission to divorce as God's concession to human weakness, whereas the true law of God is that he has joined man and wife together, and they should not be separated.

5. For example, Jesus' allegation that the scribes would not permit

release from the Korban vow may be incorrect, according to the lemma of R. Eliezer and the Sages at Nedarim 9.1.

6. Josephus tells us that the Pharisees had passed on to the people regulations handed down by former generations and not recorded in the Laws of Moses, for which reason they are rejected by the Sadducees (*Ant.* 13.297). The legal content of our passage largely concerns this 'tradition of the elders' preserved by the Pharisees. The Sadducees also enacted purity regulations (e.g. Parah 3.7) but they are not in issue here, because it was the *Pharisees* who asked the v. 5 question.

7. G. Margoliouth, 'The Tradition of the Elders', *ExpT* 22 (1910-11), pp. 261-63 (262).

8. References to the Talmud intend reference to the Mishnah, the Tosephta, the Babylonian Talmud and the Jerusalem Talmud, unless the context otherwise requires.

9. See, for example, his uncritical treatment of Synoptic references to the Pharisees in *Traditions*, III, pp. 244-47.

10. A. Büchler, 'The Law of Purification in Mark vii.1-23', *ExpT* 21 (1909-10), pp. 34-40 (40).

11. We intend to apply to the charting of the growth of early Jewish law, perhaps for the first time in the case of a theocratic system, principles of the development of law which have been discerned by jurists in secular law.

12. Käsemann, 'The Problem of the Historical Jesus', p. 34.

13. The issue is expressed in forensic form by McArthur, 'The Burden of Proof in Historical Jesus Research', p. 116, where he asks, 'Is the tradition to be regarded as innocent, i.e. historical, until proved guilty; or, is it to be regarded as guilty, i.e. a community product, until proved innocent?' N. Perrin in *Rediscovering the Teaching of Jesus*, pp. 26-28, points out that factual accuracy was not considered as important by the writer of an ancient Near Eastern religious text as by a modern Western court of law; that 'eye-witness' was not so strictly defined (Luke considers Paul an eye-witness of the ministry of Jesus), and that changes were made in the Jesus-tradition under the influence of the risen Lord. These points, with which we do not argue, may cause us to accept less weighty opposing evidence to rebut the Gospel evidence. Cf. Cadbury, *Luke–Acts*, pp. 319-20.

14. 'The Burden', p. 118.

15. Cf. N.J. McEleney, 'Authenticating Criteria and Mark 7.1-23', pp. 446-47.

16. A relaxation which is necessary in order to adapt English forensic rules of evidence involves the waiver of the hearsay rule. This rule prevents a witness in most cases from giving evidence of what another person has said or written, and even the exception in favour of 'first hand' hearsay contained in the Civil Evidence Act, 1968, s. 2, would not enable many Gospel statements to be admitted as evidence, since in the oral tradition the reports of what Jesus said and did have passed through several tradents, and are at least 'second hand' except where the report of a deed (not words) of Jesus is received by the Evangelist direct from an 'eye-witness', e.g. by Mark from

Peter. The weight of most Gospel statements as evidence is thus reduced, but they should still, we submit, be treated as evidence to be weighed in the balance against the opposing evidence. It is not suggested that lawyers' rules of evidence are the product of unusual insight or expertise. They are only the application to disputes of the wish of the sensible man to hear all relevant information before reaching a decision. Cf. Pollock, *Jurisprudence*, p. 82.

17. For example, at Matt. 26.1-2, Jesus says that the Passover is coming in two days, while at Mark 14.1 this is an editorial note.

18. See e.g. Branscomb, *Mark*, p. 155.

19. See e.g. Chapter 1.c.

20. 'The New Approach to the Synoptic Problem', pp. 42-43.

21. *Ibid.*, p. 43.

22. See 1 Cor. 11.1 and 1 Thess. 1.6. W.D. Davies in *Paul and Rabbinic Judaism*, writes, '. . . when Paul calls himself a μιμητὴς τοῦ Χριστοῦ and urges others to follow him in so far as he follows Christ we cannot fail to realize that for him every Christian is pledged to an attempted ethical conformity to Christ' (p. 147).

23. J. Jeremias, *The Parables of Jesus*, pp. 25-26.

24. Cf. G. Vermes, 'Jewish Literature and NT Exegesis', pp. 368-69.

Notes to Chapter 1

1. Generally concerning immersion and this verb, see Flemington, *Baptism*, pp. 15-23 and Jones, *Baptism*, pp. 18-29.

2. Cf. B-D, p. 317.

3. J.M. Creed, *St. Luke*, p. 166, mentions Wellhausen's view that δότε ἐλεημοσύνην is due to a mistaking of an Aramaic *dakki* (purify) for *zakki* (give alms). Similarly, G.B. Caird, *St. Luke*, p. 158, would translate, 'Cleanse the inside and behold all is clean for you'. Thus v. 41 would then have the same sense as Mt. 23.26, and perhaps form 'Q' material, although the structure and wording are so different in the two versions that Matthew and Luke may have been following separate traditions or a common Aramaic source (which could, indeed, be 'Q'). We are not persuaded, however, that δότε ἐλεημοσύνην is wrong, for the purifying effect of alms is attested elsewhere (e.g. Tob. 12.8; Sir. 3.30).

4. Of less importance to our enquiry is Saying 14 in the Gospel of Thomas which contains the purity logion in the form of Mt. 15.11. It is almost certainly a quotation from Matthew rather than a separate tradition. Its setting at the end of a missionary charge in which it is closely preceded by an injunction to 'eat what is set before you' indicates the dietary interpretation given there to the logion, which further supports the connection with Matthew, despite his stress on the washing.

5. Redaction criticism can then assist in stripping away amendments and additions made during the oral tradition, but we are concerned here only

with its function in removing written accretions.

6. *The Theology of St. Luke*, p. 12.
7. *A Study of St. Mark*, p. 23.
8. *The Theology of the Gospels*, p. 21.
9. *Die Schriften des Neuen Testaments*, I, p. 62.
10. *Mark the Evangelist*, p. 20.
11. 'What is Redaktionsgeschichte?', p. 56.
12. Although occasionally it is usefully applied; see section e on vv. 8 and 9.
13. *Der Rahmen der Geschichte Jesu*, 1919.
14. *Die evangelische Geschichte*, 1838.
15. *Die synoptischen Evangelien*, 1863.
16. Since, if it is historical, any other influence by Mark on the material would render it unhistorical.
17. *The Gospel History*, p. 103.
18. *Das Messiasgeheimnis*, 1913.
19. *The Quest*, p. 330.
20. *Das Evangelium des Markus*, p. 162.
21. *Mark*, pp. 93-94.
22. *The Mind of Mark*, pp. 221-29.
23. Lohmeyer, *Das Evangelium*, pp. 121f. also perceives a longer-sustained theme; he sees 7.27 as central to the whole section, 6.30–8.26, the over-all subject being 'The Bread Miracle', with ἄρτος as the binding catchword.
24. Admittedly, sociological critics doubt Paul's accuracy here, but *some* early Christians were probably unsophisticated, like the fishermen-Apostles, and the writer of Good News might well pitch its intelligibility at the level of the lowest common denominator.
25. Luke, the educated physician, who omits Mark's 6.45–8.26, either does not discern, or is not impressed by, the sustained themes, for he includes the first Feeding (Quesnell's offer of salvation to the Jews, and Paschen's first summons of the crowd), and omits the rest of Quesnell's theme, and nearly all the rest of Paschen's!
26. *Markus*, p. 146.
27. *Rahmen*, p. 198. Cf. Pesch, *Markusevangelium*, p. 384.
28. *Rahmen*, p. 195.
29. *Rahmen*, p. 196.
30. Vide J. Schneider, *TDNT*, III, p. 904.
31. Vide Bultmann, *Synoptic Tradition*, p. 18.
32. Grundmann, *Evangelium*, p. 46, suggests that the scribal commission had come to ascertain the general attitude of Jesus to the tradition, the washing being merely an example, and that the reply of Jesus in general terms to a question which, at first sight, appears to be phrased in the particular, would be expected. Cf. Rawlinson, *Mark*, p. 43.
33. *Ibid.*
34. We discuss these usages in Chapter 3. b.
35. *Markus*, p. 139.

36. *Die Funktion der alttestamentlichen Zitate*, p. 80.
37. *Evangelium*, p. 146.
38. Bruder, *Concordance*, pp. 26-27.
39. Translated by Stenning, *The Targum of Isaiah*, pp. 93-94.
40. The words in brackets are omitted by Rahlfs, but appear in Codex Vaticanus and Lucian's recension.
41. *New Testament Apologetic*, p. 165.
42. *Funktion*, pp. 80-81.
43. *According to the Scriptures*, p. 84.
44. Enunciated in *Testimonies*.
45. *According to the Scriptures*, p. 126 *et passim*.
46. See Chapter 2.B.c.
47. We also retain ὡς γέγραπται [ὅτι] although it is a Marcan phrase, since some such phrase probably prefaced the quotation in the tradition.
48. *Die Zusammensetzung*, pp. 5-6.
49. Applying our principles of evidence, we determine that Mark's evidence that Jesus spoke v. 8, is overborne mainly by the unlikelihood of Jesus uttering both vv. 8 and 9, due to their similarity, and by Mark's predilection for a summarizing sentence.
50. Pryke sometimes seems over-enthusiastic in his assignment of Markan text to redaction. Moody Smith writes in 'John and the Synoptics', p. 437 n. 30, 'I am not, in fact, always convinced by Pryke's apparent reasons or evidence for assigning material to redaction rather than tradition. Moreover, in the case of the Feeding of the Five Thousand . . . it is difficult to see how there could be a story at all, granted Pryke's far-reaching identification of redactional material . . . '
51. See B-D, §452.
52. 'ὅτι recitative', pp. 9-15.
53. *Zusammensetzung*, p. 8.
54. *Untersuchungen zum Markus-Stil*, pp. 4f., 45.
55. *Untersuchungen*, p. 25.
56. *Messiasgeheimnis*, p. 59.
57. 'Markus 7.15', pp. 353-54.
58. *Ibid.*
59. Bauer, *s.v.*
60. *Idiom-Book*, pp. 179-80.
61. *Textual Commentary*, pp. 94-95.
62. But note Micaiah at 1 Kings 22.28.
63. *Verstockung Israels*, pp. 58f.
64. *Duality in Mark*, pp. 54-63 and 125-26.
65. *From Tradition to Gospel*, pp. 229f.
66. Metzger, *Textual*, p. 95.
67. *Mark*, p. 241.
68. *Untersuchungen*, p. 135.
69. *Some Hellenistic Elements*, p. 5.

70. *Mark*, p. 242.
71. *L'Évangile selon S. Marc*, p. 192.

Notes to Chapter 2

1. But note Dibelius's views at *Tradition*, pp. 220-21.
2. *Memory and Manuscript, passim* but especially ch. 9.
3. *Memory*, pp. 328-29.
4. *Memory*, p. 333.
5. Edersheim, *Life*, I, pp. 230f.
6. Some Rabbis also did, e.g. Joshua ben Hananiah.
7. It is unlikely that the Passion Narrative, which was probably used at an early date, was standardized by a collegium, in view of the variations in the Gospel versions.
8. *The Sources of the Synoptic Gospels*, I, pp. 3f.
9. *Die synoptischen Streitgespräche*, p. 105.
10. This text is from the edition of *The Apologies* by A.W.F. Blunt, Cambridge, 1911.
11. Unless he dictated his material, like Paul (Rom. 16.22), but even then he would probably need to use written notes of oral tradition.
12. *Memory*, p. 335. A written parables collection and passion narrative are often posited. See e.g. Menzies, *Gospel*, pp. 21-23 and Perrin, *NT*, pp. 145-46.
13. *Tradition, passim*.
14. *Tradition*, p. 219, where he instances the interweaving of the story of Jairus with the healing of the woman with an issue (Mark 5.22-43).
15. *Tradition*, pp. 220-21.
16. *Synoptic Tradition*, pp. 329-30.
17. *Ibid.*, p. 322.
18. Dialectic analysis or criticism may appropriately be considered a branch of form criticism, for we use the term to signify the study of the most probable original form of a Gospel dispute by attention to logic, the correspondence of claim, defence and counterclaim, and other features of debate. We distinguish our use of this term from the dialectically critical method of Talmudic study, which is 'vertically oriented, looking for meaning below the textual surface' (Halivni, 'Methods of Study of the Talmud', p. 199).
19. *The Root*, pp. 66-67; cf. Hiers, 'Eschatology', pp. 174-84.
20. Neirynck, *Duality in Mark*, pp. 90-94, notes 89 instances of the use by Mark of this and allied constructions.
21. Neirynck, *Duality*, pp. 54-63, considers double questions and antithetic parallelism in Mark, but does not treat v. 5; this is suprising since our verse is the only case where οὐ . . . ἀλλά (which is, at least potentially, a double question) is used in a question.

22. We doubt that Mark created the whole question, for if he did, he wrote all vv. 3-5, and would probably have avoided the disjointing effect of the parenthetical vv. 3-4.

23. 'Jesus und der Traditionsgedanke', in *Heilsgeschehen*, p. 29.

24. But this more personalized description of the tradition could be Mark's work.

25. *Synoptic Tradition*, pp. 17-18.

26. Which verse we have deleted on redactional grounds, and see no cause to re-instate.

27. See section B.b. below.

28. Ellis, 'How the New Testament uses the Old', p. 202, cites Paul's alteration of Isa. 28.16 to serve his argument at Rom. 10.11.

29. See Chapter 4.c below.

30. Thus, Merkel, 'Markus, 7,15', pp. 352-60.

31. Indeed, p[45] reads ἔξω instead of ἔξωθεν in v. 15.

32. *Duality*, pp. 62-63.

33. The antithesis in our logion is οὐδέν... ἀλλά but it is an allied construction; see Neirynck, *ibid.*, pp. 90f.

34. 'Die Sprache des Christus', p. 103.

35. 'Dialektische Negationen', p. 390.

36. *Grammar*, pp. 517-20.

37. *Ibid.*

38. H.A.W. Meyer and B. Weiss as cited by Neirynck, *ibid.*

39. *Marc*, p. 246.

40. *Jesus*, pp. 83 and 147 n. 118.

41. *Mark*, p. 96.

42. See Chapter 4.d.

43. *Duality*, pp. 62-63.

44. It is structurally possible for the Explanation originally to have finished with ἐκπορεύονται in v. 21a, but in view of the wide meaning attaching to διαλογισμοί in the sense of 'thoughts, machinations', we think that the clarifying list which follows was probably part of the original Explanation.

45. *Synoptic Tradition*, pp. 52-54.

46. *Synoptic Tradition*, p. 17.

47. *Synoptic Tradition*, pp. 39f. (Subsequent page references to this work in the Excursus are in the text).

48. Although, on Bultmann's thesis, it could be argued that the church also disputed with the Sadducees, in view of the controversy dialogue with them at Mark 12.18. Cf. Maccoby, *Revolution*, pp. 82 and 296 n. 12.

49. Cf. Cullmann, *Christology*, pp. 124-25: 'The principle of form criticism... should not be so exaggerated that the question is no longer even asked whether this or that theme appearing in the Gospels... cannot actually be founded on *history*. After all, history should not simply be dissolved into apologetic "theories" of the early church.'

50. Ph.D. thesis on Mark 2.18-22, pp. 160-63.

51. *Tradition*, pp. 143-44.

52. *Die synoptischen Streitgespräche*, *passim*.

53. *Jesus and his Adversaries*, *passim*.

54. *The New Testament and Rabbinic Judaism*, pp. 141-50.

55. 'The Written Tradition in the Pre-Rabbinic Period', pp. 56-65.

56. Cf. the incident of Hillel's whole offering at y.Hag. 2.3, translated in Neusner, *Traditions*, I, pp. 313-14, and the debate concerning the purity of grapes vintaged for the vat at Shab. 17a.

57. 'Mark', p. 161.

58. 'Tradition History', pp. 172-74.

59. Owing to syntactical ambiguity, it is uncertain whether the reference is to one synagogue attended by several groups, or to several synagogues.

60. *Op. cit.*, p. 173.

61. *Mark—Traditions in Conflict*, pp. 159-63.

62. *St. Mark's Gospel. Two Stages*, pp. 1-3.

63. *Frühgeschichte I*, pp. 190-206.

64. See Betz, *Galatians*, pp. 259-60. Cf. Burton, *Galatians*, p. 275.

65. 'Quellenanalyse', pp. 160-62.

66. *Studies*, pp. 98-100.

67. *Type and History*, pp. 198-202.

68. *Op. cit.*, p. 99.

69. 'Paul, James', p. 442.

70. Jewish ritual slaughter of animals (*shechitah*), which are then 'kosher' meat, would secure observance of the Decree's prohibition of blood and things strangled.

71. Cf. Phil. 3.2. Both Philippians and Colossians are dated by Kümmel, *Introduction*, pp. 235, 245, at AD 56/58 (Caesarea) or 58/60 (Rome).

72. Barrett, *Pastoral Epistles*, p. 18 diffidently dates the Pastorals between AD 90 and 125.

73. We doubt that the insertion was aimed against Levitically prohibited food (pig, rabbit, etc.) since, although it is sacrilegious to eat it, Leviticus does not state that it defiles the eater. But the meat of clean animals, not ritually slaughtered, does defile the eater according to Lev. 17.15. See however Chapter 6.a re. Rabbinical interpretation of the verse.

74. The Greek text and translation of Philo's works are taken from the edition in the Loeb Classical Library.

75. At *De Spec. Leg.* 3.63 Philo *aggravates* the cultic strictness of Lev. 15.18 by deducing that after intercourse spouses must not touch anything before bathing.

76. In that Philo lived from c. 20 BC to c. AD 50 it is uncertain whether there was sufficient time for his writings to have influenced Hellenistic Jews of the early church; they may well have been affected, though, by earlier allegorical exponents (cf. Sandmel, *Philo*, pp. 23-24).

77. *The Sentences of Pseudo-Phocylides*, p. 258.

78. *Spruchbuch*, p. 23.
79. *Sentences*, pp. 82-83.
80. *Reinheitvorschriften*, pp. 1-2.
81. Charles, *Pseudepigrapha*, p. 115.
82. *Introduction*, p. 74.
83. *The Setting*, p. 147.
84. The translation of the Dead Sea Scrolls is taken from G. Vermes, *The Dead Sea Scrolls in English*.
85. Cf. *Ant.* 18.117 concerning the baptism of John the Baptist.
86. But see Chapter 5.d re. handwashing as later symbolic of the whole law.
87. The text of Egerton 2 is taken from *Fragments*, edited by Bell and Skeat, pp. 11 and 13.
88. Bell and Skeat, p. 2, consider it 'extremely improbable' that the papyrus can be dated later than AD 150. Jeremias, *Unknown Sayings of Jesus*, p. 41, adopts the majority view that the papyrus is dependent on the Four Gospels.
89. 'Tradition', pp. 173-74.
90. See n. 27 to Chapter 6, and Chilton, *Galilean Rabbi*, *passim*.
91. *Scriptures*, pp. 83-84.
92. *Scriptures*, pp. 61f., 126.
93. *New Testament Apologetic*, pp. 17f.
94. *Apologetic*, p. 166.
95. Vide Hübner, pp. 147f.; Nedarim 3.2. Contra Haenchen, *Der Weg Jesu*, p. 263 n. 2.
96. 'Authenticating Criteria and Mark 7.1-23', pp. 431-60.
97. *Agnostos Theos*, p. 365.
98. *The Poetry of our Lord*, p. 83.
99. *New Testament Theology*, I, pp. 14-18.
100. 'Criteria', p. 445.
101. *History*, p. 147. McArthur, 'Basic Issues', p. 18, commends this as the most objective criterion, and the only subjective element, we think, is the judgment on whether the independent sources do attest to the same saying, but this will generally be clear.
102. 'Criteria', p. 436.
103. 'The "Criteria" for Authenticity', p. 231.
104. 'Basic Issues', p. 48.
105. *Christology*, p. 18.
106. *Ant.* 13.297.
107. 'Criteria', p. 457.
108. 'Criteria', pp. 242-44.
109. 'On Using the Wrong Tool', p. 575. At p. 574 Hooker also points out that this criterion can only give us what is 'distinctive' of Jesus' teaching in the sense of unique, not in the sense of chracteristic.
110. *Markus*, p. 142.

234   *Jesus and the Laws of Purity*

111. Matthew's softening modification is valuable, however, for it increases the authentication provided by this criterion. Perrin, *Rediscovering*, p. 39, writes, '... the earliest form of a saying we can reach may be regarded as authentic if it can be shown to be dissimilar to characteristic emphases both of ancient Judaism and of the early Church, and this will particularly be the case where Christian tradition oriented towards Judaism can be shown to have modified the saying away from its original emphasis'. Matthew's Gospel would generally be regarded as affected by such a Judaizing influence.
112. *Markus*, p. 79.
113. And see section e following.
114. *Apostelgeschichte*, p. 43.
115. *Jesus and the Law of Moses*, pp. 175-82.
116. *Jesus and the Law*, pp. 139-41.
117. *Christus*, p. 85.
118. *De Legatione ad Gaium*, 1.1.
119. *Jesus*, pp. 181-82.
120. Midrash R. III, p. 758 (ed. Slotki, Soncino edition).
121. For example, Jubilees 23.21 and Assumption of Moses 7.6-10.
122. The importance at Qumran of ethical righteousness is also shown at Community Rule IX, 'They [the members] shall atone for guilty rebellion ... that they may obtain loving kindness for the Land without the flesh of holocausts and the fat of sacrifice' (Vermes, p. 87).
123. 'An Examination of the Criteria', pp. 214-15.
124. 'Criteria', p. 245.
125. *Rediscovering*, p. 43.
126. 'A Positive Criterion', p. 34.
127. Cf. Moo, 'Jesus', pp. 5-6.
128. Branscomb, *Jesus*, pp. 126-28.
129. *Judaism*, I, pp. 251-54.
130. The allegations of particular instances of neglect of the law (Why do you eat with publicans, not fast, not wash your hands?) may indicate that Jesus and his disciples were expected to, and generally did, observe the law.
131. It is probably true that, after examination by the priest, this sacrifice only signified (εἰς μαρτύριον αὐτοῖς) the return of the leper to normal life, but Jesus' endorsement of this procedure shows him as recognizing at least some utility in the cultic system.
132. Bauer, *s.v.*, states that κράσπεδον can mean simply the border or hem of a garment, and not necessarily the tassel which Jews were obliged to wear by Num. 15.38; we think the Mosaic tassel is intended, because of Mark's strategic placing of κράσπεδον, and because of Matthew's use (9.20, par. Luke 8.44, but not Mark) of κράσπεδον in the story of the healing of the woman with an issue. Cf. *TDNT*, III, p. 904.
133. Cf. R. Eliezer's satisfaction at a teaching of Jesus, Tos. Shehitah Hullin 2.24.

134. Alon, 'Gentiles', pp. 147-48. See also John 18.28.
135. *Ibid.*
136. Vide Taylor, p. 205. Cf. *TDNT*, I, p. 328(b).
137. Cf. Branscomb, *Jesus*, pp. 133-35.
138. Vide e.g. Hagigah 2.7. It is arguable that to become unclean involved no breach of the Mosaic law—it was only a breach for an unclean person to enter the Temple or touch holy food. Cf. Maccoby, 'Washing', p. 13 n. 6.
139. *Mark*, p. 51. Cf. Jesus' apparent disregard of the blood as 'life' in his command at the Last Supper to drink the wine as his blood (Higgins, *The Lord's Supper*, pp. 29-30).
140. But Maccoby, *Revolution*, pp. 269-71, argues that only the use of medicines for a slight ailment was forbidden on the Sabbath.
141. Perrin, *The New Testament: An Introduction*, p. 285.
142. *St. Luke*, p. 85.
143. Jesus' prophetic priorities are shown at Mt. 12.6-7, '... something greater than the Temple is here. And if you had known what this means, "I desire mercy and not sacrifice", you would not have condemned the guiltless'.
144. See Lev. 13.46.

Notes to Chapter 3

1. Our reference to 'the Pharisees' will hereafter include the scribes, unless the context otherwise demands, since they are here identified by Mark or the tradition as having the same view of the law. We discuss their inter-relationship at Chapter 5.a.
2. But 2 Kgs 3.1 refers to Elisha pouring water on the hands of Elijah (presumably for hygiene).
3. Vide Zebahim 19b; Yoma 32b. Cf. Yoma 3.2-3, 6.
4. 'The Bounds of the Laws of Levitical Cleanness', pp. 201-205.
5. 'The Washing of Cups' at p. 7.
6. *Ancient Law*, pp. 19-20.
7. *Encyclopaedia Judaica*, II, p. 85.
8. *Markus*, p. 139 n. 1.
9. E.g. 1 Sam. 20.26-27; 21.3-6; Hag. 2.10-13; Ps. 24.3-4; 73.13.
10. E.g. the rules in tractate M. Makshirin are built upon the circumstance that 'water is put on' at Lev. 11.38.
11. In Haggai, which Pfeiffer, *Introduction*, p. 602, dates at *520 BC*, the priests rule at 2.13 that a person defiled by a dead body himself defiles *ordinary food*. Thus, at this early date corpse-uncleanness appears to be transmitted twice, and even to ordinary food. Cf. Num. 19.22.
12. Cf. Westerholm, *Jesus*, pp. 145-46 n. 63.
13. Neusner agrees the inter-relationship between removes of uncleanness and levels of sanctification, and discusses it at *Purities*, XXII, pp. 160-64, but

he claims that the two concepts were evolved at Yavneh.

14. This distinction between the original source and the derived impurity, in respect to the duration of impurity, is not preserved in every case. Thus, at Lev. 15.16 and 18, a man's emission of semen produces uncleanness till the evening only, but to have decreed seven days' uncleanness would have presumably interfered with normal marital life.

15. *Qumran*, p. 91.

16. With Rost (*Die Damaskusschrift, ad loc.*) and Dupont-Sommer (*Essene Writings*, p. 155), Baumgarten (*Qumran*, p. 88) reads שמן rather than שמו, and he reads בהם rather than כהם. Cf. Dupont-Sommer, *ibid.*, n. 4.

17. *Controversies*, pp. 163-64.

18. Comment XI (p. 21) on 'Redaction, Formulation, and Form: The Case of Mishnah' by J. Neusner.

19. 'The Bounds', pp. 1-2.

20. *Ibid.* p. 1 n. 3.

21. Sometimes, as at Eduyoth 1.1, two views conflicting with the dominant one are preserved. Cf. Danby, preface, p. xxii.

22. Dated c. AD 51 at Chapter 4.a.

23. Vide Moore, *Judaism*, I, p. 287.

24. *Cairo Genizah*, pp. 205-208.

25. 'Early Halakhah in the Palestinian Targumim', *JJS* 25 (1974), pp. 114-22 at p. 117.

26. 'The Fence-Breaker and the actio de pastu pecoris in Early Jewish Law', *JJS* 25 (1974), pp. 123-36 at pp. 128-29.

27. *Ibid.* pp. 119-21.

28. 'The Dating of Targumic Literature', *JSJ* 5 (1974), pp. 49-62 at p. 52, where he quotes A. Diez Macho to this effect.

29. There are variations in the detail of purity law. For example, Hyam Maccoby has mentioned to us that whereas the Palestinian Targum on Lev. 11.32 states that the defiled utensil shall 'be unclean for use until evening' (Etheridge, II, p. 178), Tebul Yom 4. 3-4, specifies uses to which a kneading-trough and flagon may be put, *although immersed the same day*.

30. We discuss Mark's date of writing at section g below.

31. The principal sources for this and the following section, except where the OT and the Mishnah are specifically cited, are Danby's notes to his Mishnah translation, and the *Encyclopaedia Judaica*.

32. E.g. the corpse, the leper, persons suffering from a bodily discharge.

33. *Terumah* is the foodstuff most frequently mentioned in the Mishnah as rendered invalid, but *kodashim* and *hullin* could also be invalid (Toh. 2.7; Maimonides, *Cleanness*, p. 291).

34. It is this kind of *terumah* which is generally intended when the Mishnah mentions '*terumah*'. Vide Danby, p. 797 *s.v.*

35. 'Unwritten Law', p. 17.

36. 'The Written Traditions', p. 58.

37. 'Unwritten Law', p. 7.
38. E.g. The Damascus Document.
39. At least, in Jerusalem (Ezr. 7.10; cf. 7.25).
40. Bowker, *The Targums*, p. 61.
41. Cited by Stemberger, 'La Recherche', p. 556.
42. *Mishnah and Tosefta: a comparative study*, I. *Shabbat*.
43. *Études sur la littérature talmudique*, cited by Stemberger, *ibid.*, p. 558.
44. 'Review', p. 124. This view is supported by the fact that an express alteration of a tradition by the Sages at Bekh. 30b is followed by all texts of the Tosephta.
45. M.D. Herr, *Encyclopaedia Judaica*, XV, p. 1284.
46. Vide Stemberger, *op. cit.*, p. 566.
47. Strack, *Introduction*, p. 71.
48. 'The Dating of Aggadic Materials', pp. 116f.
49. Exceptionally, later teaching cancelled earlier law, as Hillel's invention of the *prozbul* defeated the law requiring the release of debts in the seventh year (Deuteronomy 15.1-3).
50. *Ibid.* p. 116.
51. *Introduction to the Talmud*, p. 229.
52. *Ibid.*, pp. 117-20.
53. *Ibid.*, p. 121.
54. *Ibid.*
55. 'Parallelomania', pp. 1-13.
56. 'The Use', pp. 110-22.
57. *Ibid.*, pp. 112-13. For example, Sifre on Numbers, Huqqat §123.5-7 (41b-42a) attributed the same saying to both Hillel and Johanan ben Zakkai. Cf. also n. 83 below.
58. *The New Testament and the Palestinian Targum*, p. 27.
59. *Ibid.*, p. 113.
60. 'The Rabbinic "Enumeration of Scriptural Examples"'.
61. *Ibid.*, p. 115.
62. *Ibid.* Cf. Montefiore and Loewe, *Anthology*, pp. 711-13.
63. *Ibid.*, pp. 115-16.
64. *St. Matthew*, p. 136.
65. 'The Formation of Rabbinic Judaism', pp. 11f. At 'History', p. 219 n. 7, he praises the historical approach shown by R. Yaron's *Gifts*, and B.S. Jackson's *Theft* is to be similarly commended.
66. *Ibid.*, pp. 113-14.
67. 'The History of Earlier Rabbinic Judaism', p. 230 n. 26.
68. *Ibid.*, pp. 232-33.
69. There is not much objective criticism of Neusner's methods. On the whole, they find no favour with traditional Jewish scholars (e.g. Zeitlin, Wacholder), while most other scholars fully approve. But see n. 75 infra on Neusner's conclusions.
70. '"Form Criticism" of Rabbinic Literature', pp. 262f.

71. *Ibid.*, p. 264.
72. *Introduction*, ch. 13.
73. 'The Use of the Later Rabbinic Evidence', pp. 222-23.
74. 'Form Criticism', p. 34.
75. Maccoby, 'Authenticating', has argued that Neusner's severe criteria for authenticity have produced scant data on which he has based unfounded speculation.
76. *Ibid.*, p. 266 n. 30.
77. *Ibid.*
78. *Ibid.*
79. *Ibid.*, pp. 273-74.
80. This was a second edition. In the first edition published in 1962, he had not employed form-critical methods.
81. *Philo.*
82. 'The History', p. 230.
83. There are sometimes different reports in the Talmud of the saying of a Sage. At B.B. 11a it is said, 'Two tannaim have reported the dictum of Rabbi Gamaliel differently'.
84. Our approach is thus similar to Neusner's amended position, just quoted in the main text.
85. Vide Haran, 'The Date of the Priestly Source', pp. 322-23 and n. 3. Scholars are generally agreed that the Priestly source (P) was included in the 'Book of the Law of Moses' read out by Ezra to the people (Neh. 8.1-8), and the date generally ascribed to this reading is 444 BC (but contra, Pfeiffer, *Introduction*, pp. 256, 827f.). Scholars differ, however, over whether P was composed before or after the Deuteronomic source. Haran (pp. 324-33) seeks to solve the conflict between the 'signs of antiquity' in P, and its apparent first publication and effect on religious practice in Ezra's time. He suggests that it was composed during Hezekiah's reign, and influenced that king's reforms (2 Kgs 18.4, 22); it was then obliterated from memory by Manasseh's apostasy (2 Kgs 21.3) and remained within the closed priestly circle without affecting again religious life, until promulgated by Ezra.
86. See section g below.
87. 'The Tradition', p. 262.
88. 'The History', p. 230.
89. *The Common Law*, p. 1.
90. 'The Logic of the Reasonable', pp. 195-96. Neusner (*Purities*, XXII, p. 268) claims that the Mishnaic system of purity did not impinge on the way in which ordinary people lived. He writes there, 'The Mishnaic system of uncleanness is an intellectual construction located at the fringes of the villages where people lived, but isolated from what happened therein'. But he mentions (pp. 267-68) four unassigned instances where ordinary people consulted Sages about the cleanness of food. Cf. the wives of the Sadducees (Niddah 33b).
91. *Sociology*, the foreword. Cf. Danby, preface, p. xvii.

92. Thus, it is recorded at Sotah 9.9 that when adulterers became many, Johanan b. Zakkai terminated the use of the rite of the bitter waters.

93. Cf. Kohler, *Hebrew Man*, p. 141. For a comparison of the views of Summer and Ehrlich on the status of the folkways, see Sawer, *Society*, pp. 171-77.

94. *Folkways*, p. 62. Cf. Neill, *Christian Faith To-day*, p. 202.

95. Vermes, *Cambridge History*, I, p. 221, writes of the Scribes, 'The point of departure for exegesis was no longer the Torah itself, but contemporary customs and beliefs which the interpreter attempted to connect with scripture and to justify'. He cites earlier the prohibition on making images at Lev. 26.1 and the exception made for pavement images in the Palestinian Targum *ad loc.* (pp. 217-18).

96. As interpreted by the Sages, vide Cohn, 'Prolegomena', pp. 51-52.

97. Vide Cohn, *ibid.*, pp. 48-53.

98. 'Prolegomena', p. 51.

99. We are not suggesting that there was uniformity of customs amongst all Israelites; the Essenes/Qumranians, the *haberim* Pharisees (see Chapter 5), the 'mainstream' Pharisees, the *'am-ha'areṣ*, each pursued the customs of their group. But what the group *did*, e.g. their purity practices, was the material of which the rules applied to the groups by the traditional law were made. Cf. Robertson Smith, *The OT*, pp. 45-46.

100. Cf. e.g. Hillel watching people's practice at T. Pisha, 4.13.

101. *The Pharisees*, II, p. 780f.

102. Cf. Introduction, n. 1; also, Wheeler Robinson, *Religious Ideas*, p. 38.

103. 'The Tradition', p. 262. Many practices of conveyancers of English land ('what they actually do') have subsequently been confirmed by judicial decision or statute. For example, the period for which a seller must show that he or his predecessors have duly owned the land was regulated by the custom of conveyancers, and their practice 'became the law for open contracts by receiving judicial recognition' (Farrand, *Conveyance*, p. 92). We think that the period was law *before* judicial recognition because it was the length of proved title which buyers and sellers, through their lawyers, actually required and supplied. Heath J. in Barnwell v. Harris (1809) 1 Taunt. 430 at p. 432 declared, 'It is a technical *rule* [our italics] among conveyancers to approve a possession of sixty years as a good title to a fee simple'. Similarly, a transferor's convenants for title and a mortgagee's power of sale which conveyancers used to specify in detail in the deed, have since the Conveyancing Act, 1881, been implied in the absence of contrary intent. See generally on the influence of conveyancers' practices Holdsworth, *Land Law*, pp. 261-64 and 299-300. Denning, L.J., although admittedly overruled, said in Re Downshire Settled Estates (1953) 1 Ch. 218, a case concerning the variation of trusts, at p. 279, 'The practice of the profession in these cases is the best evidence of what the law is—indeed it makes law'.

104. We think this book may be the first attempt to use this procedure, although we have very recently noticed a similar approach advocated by Vermes, 'Jewish Literature' at pp. 374-75.

105. Irenaeus, *Adv. Haer.* 3.1.2 and the *Anti-Marcionite Prologue.*

106. Robinson in *Redating the NT* at p. 116 argues that Mark began
writing shortly after AD 45, and that the Synoptics were completed by the
early 60s, but this is generally doubted.

107. 'Dead Sea Scrolls', p. 233.

108. Noth, *Leviticus*, pp. 159-60, suggests that the verse was originally
addressed to Israelites generally.

109. Snaith, *Leviticus*, p. 109, notes that the use of the verb נזר here means
that the people should observe strict rules of ritual cleanness.

110. *Jesus*, p. 64.

111. Deut. 12.15 and 22; 15.21-22.

112. E.g. 14.2.

113. At Tobit 2.5 Tobit washes himself after carrying a corpse, and he is in
Nineveh, far from the Temple, but his washing may have been for hygiene.
In 2.9 Codices Vaticanus and Alexandrian and Syriac versions have
μεμιαμμένος, implying that he may have slept by the courtyard wall because
he was unclean (a non-Temple sanction) but the causation is ambiguous.
Num. 5.2-3 indicates that defilement of any part of the camp was to be
avoided, not just the tabernacle. Cf. 11QT 47.3-5 and Janowski-Lichtenberger,
'Enderwartung', pp. 37f.

114. 'The Bounds', p. 190 and n. 3.

115. *Ibid.*, pp. 232-34.

116. I.e. the Sadducees held that purity was necessary only for the purpose
of the Temple cult, while the Essenes held that purity should be maintained
irrespective of the cult. Cf. Baumgarten, 'Controversies', p. 157.

117. *Ibid.*, p. 221.

118. 'Judaism', p. 670. See also Neusner, 'Scripture', p. 190. Regarding
the ubiquity of the 'as if' fiction, see Derrett, *Audience*, pp. 101-106.

119. The supererogatory and the expansive views may coincide to some
extent, but the divisive feature must be that the latter view regards the
preservation of purity in some situations to be unconnected with the
Temple, and *even in those situations* to be a matter of *legal* obligation.

Notes to Chapter 4

1. We have noted earlier Mark's lack of interest in geographical data.

2. Vide Büchler, *Piety*, p. 143: 'Not even if the High Priest accidentally
contracted the gravest defilement from a human corpse, did he incur the
slightest sin, unless he, in his defiled state, entered the Temple or handled
holy things'.

3. It seems unlikely that Jesus or the disciples were priests. Büchler, 'The
Law of Purification', p. 40 n. 2, argues that if Jesus had been a priest, the
Pharisees would have blamed him for touching a dead body or entering a
house where one lay.

4. Vide Freyne, *Galilee*, pp. 287-88, 293-94.

5. See Chapter 3.d. Such a source defiles the whole body, not just the hands.

6. Mikvaoth 8.1. Cf. Josephus, *Ant.* 12.145.

7. The difficulty of distinction between first fruits and heave offerings in the various OT texts is illustrated by Danby (p. 55 n. 5) in reference to Terumoth 3.7.

8. See Chapter 3.d.

9. Except as at Sukkah 5.6-8.

10. The fish harvest was also liable to *terumah gedolah* (Ter. 10.8).

11. See Chapter 3.e.

12. See Edersheim, *Temple*, p. 337.

13. See Freyne, *ibid.*, p. 166.

14. See Freyne, *ibid.*, pp. 173-74.

15. Cf. as to Galilee generally, Freyne, *ibid.*, pp. 171-73.

16. Cf. the declaration at Deut. 26.14, 'I have not . . . removed any of (the tithe) while I was unclean'.

17. It seems reasonable to infer that if washing of the hands is directed, the impurity of the hands, *apart from the body*, is assumed.

18. *Pharisees*, II, pp. 273-74.

19. *Ibid.*, p. 278.

20. Cf. J. Gereboff, *Rabbi Tarfon*, pp. 248-50.

21. Apart from the Deut. 21.6 reference to the elders washing their hands over unsolved murder, which seems to have no cultic element.

22. *Ibid.*, p. 719.

23. But also in Sifra, this reference to the washing of the hands is interpreted to mean that, although the whole body must be immersed, only the visible parts, such as the hands, need be made wet. Regarding the difficulty of dating the material in Sifra, see Chapter 6, n. 10. The literal interpretation of 15.11 rather than this abstruse one was surely the original meaning.

24. E.g. Hertz, *The Pentateuch*, III, p. 107.

25. E.g. 73.13; 18.20, 24. See, regarding the metaphorical use of defilement, Derrett, *Audience*, pp. 132-33.

26. *Markus*, p. 149.

27. As reported by Montefiore, *Synoptic Gospels*, I, p. 141.

28. Washing of the hands only cured a slight (second-degree) impurity, to which alone they were separately susceptible, while the impurity of Gentiles was of a serious nature (see Alon, 'Levitical Uncleanness', pp. 166f.).

29. Makkoth 1.10 provides that the Sanhedrin could exercise its office within or outside the Land (of Israel). There were lesser sanhedrins in the Diaspora (vide *TDNT*, VII, p. 866), but it seems doubtful whether they could create halakhoth.

30. Charles, *Apocrypha*, p. 246.

31. Cited in Charles, *ibid.*

32. *Ibid.*, p. 262.

33. Alon, 'Bounds', p. 202, and 'Gentiles', p. 154, also considers that she immersed bodily.

34. Charles, *Pseudepigrapha*, p. 389.

35. *Oracula*, p. 79.

36. *Perspective*, p. 130.

37. *Bellum Judaicum* 2.129.

38. Schiffman, 'Communal Meals', p. 55, argues that the Common Meals were not cultic, but were related to the Messianic banquet. The lustration required for these meals seems an obstacle to this.

39. Ber. 55a where a saying of Rabbis Johanan and Eleazar (both Palestinian Amoraim according to the Soncino Rabbinical Index) is quoted to this effect.

40. 'Cleanness of his hands' at Community Rule IX (Vermes p. 88) clearly has an ethical meaning.

41. By immersing before eating their Common Meal of ordinary food. Cf. Vermes, *Perspective*, p. 94. Not *all* meals eaten at Qumran were Common Meals, since the first-year novice and the backslider could not participate; see Rabin, *Qumran*, pp. 8, 29-30.

42. The evidence with the earliest attribution is the *baraitha* at Shab. 14b that Shammai and Hillel decreed uncleanness for the hands. But since it is cited there against the accuracy of the Hananiah decree which imposes this uncleanness, it seems best to discuss it in the context of the 18 decrees.

43. Danby *ad loc.*, translates שאמרו as 'enjoined', but literally it means 'said', and we think 'these' are to be contrasted with the 18 things they are stated in the last sentence of Shab. 1.4 to have 'decreed' (גזרו). Cf. the Sages at Shab. 13b.

44. There is very little modern scholarly literature on the agenda or date of this conference.

45. There is an ambiguity at the start of the *baraitha* listing the *terumah* decrees; it starts, תמן תנינן אילו פוסלין את התרומה. Does תמן mean in the previous *baraitha* stating that there were 3 sets of 18 things, or does it mean somewhere else? We think the former, but generally it is dangerous to place too much emphasis on single words in this Talmud, since 'the existing text is hopelessly corrupt' (L.I. Rabinowitz, *Encyclopaedia Judaica*, XV, p. 777).

46. So, Guttmann, *Judaism*, p. 104.

47. *Le Talmud*, III, p. 18.

48. 'Les "Dix-huit Mesures"', p. 24.

49. This may well be due to a corrupt text; see n. 45 above.

50. 4th cent. Palestinian Amora, according to the Soncino Rabbinical Index.

51. *Ibid.*, p. 24.

52. He has previously claimed on p. 24 that the Babylonian Amoraim did not remember any longer the detail of the 18 decrees.

53. *Ibid.*, pp. 27-35.

54. *Die Zeloten*, pp. 206-207.

55. Than the milder version in the B.T.
56. *Ibid.*, p. 27.
57. *Ibid.*, p. 32.
58. Betzah 1.6; Sotah 48a; Freyne, *Galilee*, p. 284.
59. See Chapter 3.e.
60. Also, if the purpose and effect of the decrees had been to render it impossible for the priests to eat *terumah*, the local priests would still have starved, together with the Sadducean ones.
61. *Geschichte*, III, p. 809.
62. *Die Zeloten*, pp. 210-11.
63. 'Les "dix-huit mesures"', p. 25.
64. Since the Sadducees only held valid the written laws of Moses (Josephus, *Ant.* 13.297), it is unlikely that a Sadducee would have strained to reconcile Ezekiel with the written law, although they probably would not have denied the sacredness of the Prophets and Writings (cf. Russell, *The Jews*, p. 159).
65. 'Measures', p. 36.
66. Cf. *Ant.* 20.203, 205, 208.
67. See Jeremias, *Jerusalem*, pp. 229, 378.
68. *Geschichte*, III, n. 26.
69. *Dor Dor*, I, p. 176.
70. *Ibid.*
71. So Zeitlin, 'Measures', p. 25; Shab. 130b.
72. *Ibid.*, p. 175.
73. *Ibid.*
74. *Ibid.*
75. *Geschichte*, III, p. 810.
76. *Ibid.*, p. 36.
77. *Der Galiläische 'Am-ha'Areṣ*, pp. 98f.
78. *Ibid.*
79. See Chapter 3.e.
80. After any defilement such as sexual intercourse (Lev. 15.18), or menstruation (Lev. 15.19).
81. Contrast Neusner's denial of the historicity of the Houses' decrees at *Purities*, XIII, p. 206.
82. 'Gentiles', pp. 156-57 and 158 n. 21.
83. So also Guttmann, *Judaism*, p. 104.
84. It may be that glass only came into common use at a later date. Freyne, *Galilee*, p. 174, cites Pliny's attribution of the art of glass blowing to the Phoenicians in the first century BC.
85. 'Controversies', p. 166.
86. We think this the correct interpretation of the words גזרו טומאה על הידים at Shab. 14b; they can hardly mean that they decreed uncleanness on hands at this early stage of the law, whether they had been actually defiled or not.
87. 'Bounds', p. 222 n. 85.

88. Charles, *Apocrypha*, p. 245.

89. *Ibid.* p. 261.

90. *Galiläische*, p. 68 n. 1.

91. As discussed, it is claimed by Neusner and others that the notion of degrees of uncleanness was not developed until after 70 AD, but for the reasons mentioned, we are disinclined to accept those views as evidence of such non-development.

92. This is the likely period of his activity according to *Encyclopaedia Judaica*, VIII, col. 481, although Shab. 15a indicates that he was appointed *nasi* in 30 BC; Sifra on Deuteronomy, 357, states that he held office for 40 years (and lived for 120!). Cf. Danby, p. 447 n. 3; Jeremias, *Jerusalem*, pp. 242 and 379; Strack, *Introduction*, p. 108

93. Noth, *Leviticus*, p. 63, thinks that the sacrificial meal enjoyed by the offerer and his family after the peace offering might have taken place 'at home', since no unclean food or person was allowed in the Temple: this seems unduly optimistic—laws are often broken!

94. See e.g. Matt. 26.23.

95. Hos. 9.4 mentions defilement by mourners' bread, but bread has had water 'put on', and is susceptible to defilement.

96. This is a good example of the Pentateuchal tradition which restricts the purpose of purity to the Temple.

97. The general obligation to distinguish between things particularly appropriated to Yahweh and things not so, is expressed at Lev. 10.10. Hence, the Sages called non-sacrificial food חולין. Cf. Snaith, *Leviticus*, p. 78.

98. *Numbers*, p. 224.

99. *Leviticus*, p. 87 n. 34.

100. *Leviticus*, p. 95.

101. The Rabbis qualified v. 33 by v. 34 to the extent of ruling that only food (not utensils) was defiled through being in the earthen vessel (Pesahim 20a-b).

102. *Leviticus*, p. 96.

103. See Moore, *Judaism*, I, p. 65.

104. See ARN 4, pp. 35-37.

105. See Matt. 21.19; Mark 13.28; John 1.50; James 3.12 (figs). See Matt. 7.16; James 3.12 (grapes).

106. See Mark 6.37-44; 8.4-7 (bread and fish); 1.16-19 (fish); Luke 24.30 (bread).

107. Edersheim, *Jesus*, I, pp. 208f. Cf. Bouquet, *Everyday Life*, pp. 74-79.

108. Tohoroth 4, 10. Cf. Terumoth 10.3.

109. So R. Joshua at Zabim 5.1.

110. Cf. וזה at Lev. 11.19 referring to a following plurality.

111. Neusner, *Traditions*, I, p. 341. Cf. Saldarini, 'Rabbinic Chain', p. 105.

112. *Mishnayoth, ad loc.*

113. At 2.8 it is stated that Johanan b. Zakkai received the law from Shammai and Hillel, but this seems rather an afterthought; Saldarini

(pp. 104-106) thinks that this statement was added later, through Hillelite influence.

114. See Neusner, *Traditions*, I, p. 316; Friedman, *Soncino, ad loc.*

115. See ARN 4, pp. 35-37.

116. Saldarini, pp. 103-104.

117. Neusner, *Traditions*, I, p. 341, writes, 'Forms linking a Gamaliel to Eliezer, Joshua, Aqiba and others of Yavneh must mark traditions of Gamaliel II'.

118. Cf. *Bellum* 4.159.

119. Harper, *Amos and Hosea*, comments at p. 329 that there is nothing in this text to prove the observance at this time of the Levitical cult. At Judges 13.4 the mother-to-be of Samson is told by the angel not to eat anything unclean, but (a) the angel announced the unborn to be a Nazirite and (b) prohibited or non-kosher food is more probably intended than contaminated food. See Moore, *Judges*, p. 317.

120. Kümmel, *Introduction*, p. 175.

121. Lindars, *John*, pp. 124f.

122. Or deliver.

123. But compare Luke 11.38.

Notes to Chapter 5

1. See Heyd, *Supererogation, passim.*

2. Jer. 35.3-11.

3. Num. 6.1-21.

4. *Qumran*, p. 8.

5. Vermes, p. 79.

6. *Halakhah*, p. 102, his translation.

7. Vermes, p. 112.

8. *Essene*, p. 152 n. 6.

9. See Maccoby's caveat at Chapter 3.a.

10. T. Demai 2.2. Indeed, it seems that at a later stage Jews generally handwashed before *hullin*; cf. Numbers R. XX.21.

11. *Pharisees*, II, pp. 74-76, 266.

12. Jeremias, *Jerusalem*, pp. 231-36, notes that before AD 70 many priests, including some leading ones, were scribes, but that they were far outnumbered by scribes from lower classes. In his statement (p. 236) that only ordained teachers transmitted and created the tradition, he appears with Finkelstein to identify the scribes with the Sages.

13. *Jesus and the Pharisees*, pp. 21-23.

14. Gittin 67a; Sotah 20a.

15. *Ant.* 13.297; *Bellum* 2.162-3.

16. See Shab. 14a.

17. Similarly, anonymous lemmas at Toh. 4.12 and Hag. 2.7 refer to

perushim in terms indicating that the standards of purity applicable to them are different from those applicable to other people.

18. Cf. Spiro, 'Haber', p. 215 n. 146.

19. *Ibid.*, pp. 38-39.

20. Spiro, *ibid.*, pp. 187-90, 211-14, insists that the *ne'aman* and the *haber* were separate categories after Hyrcanus's centralized tithing system broke down.

21. *Pharisees*, II, pp. 74-76.

22. *Ibid.*, p. 76.

23. *Judaism*, II, p. 73.

24. *Fellowship in Judaism*, p. 34 n. 1.

25. *Jesus*, p. 35.

26. A similar conclusion in reached by Rivkin, 'Defining the Pharisees', pp. 245-46, and *Revolution*, ch. 3, using different methodology. Because of the confused use of the term *perushim* in the tannaitic texts, he classifies them primarily into those where the *perushim* are opposed to the Sadducees, and those where they are not, and analyses the interests and behaviour attributed in each text to the various kinds of people called *perushim*.

27. Another example is probably at Toh. 4.12.

28. 'Spurious Interpretations', p. 125.

29. *Jesus*, p. 38.

30. Neusner, *ibid.*, writes that 'purities' includes concern for the purity of both the initiate's own food and of consecrated food.

31. *Tosefta Kipshuta*, pp. 215-16.

32. *Soncino*, Bekh. p. 192 n. 7.

33. Although the majority view is that the two Schools persisted from c. AD 20 to 100 (e.g. *Encyclopaedia Judaica*, IV 737), Guttman, *Judaism*. pp. 106-13, argues that the division ceased shortly after AD 70: it seems that most of the recorded disputes between the Houses stem from before AD 70 (*Enc. Jud. ibid.*; Moore, *Judaism*, I, p. 80).

34. See above, n. 30.

35. *Qumran*, p. 19.

36. There is OT evidence that כָּנָף means garment or robe, e.g. Ezek. 5.3; 16.8.

37. See P.T. Naz. 6.10.55c, and the Syriac 'kenpē' meaning arms and chest. Cf. Spiro, 'Haber', pp. 207-208.

38. Maksh. I.1.

39. *Fellowship* p. 37 n. 17.

40. Since *kodashim* and *terumah* were susceptible without water being 'put on'.

41. Parah, 8.7.

42. Parah, 8.5-7.

43. See above, n. 30.

44. 'Bounds', p. 216 and n. 69.

45. See above, n. 33.

46. *Traditions*, I, p. 247.

47. Rabin, *Qumran*, p. 20, also thinks the Hillelite view in the Tosephta is secondary, having been conformed to the B.T. The preservation by the tradition of so uncharacteristically severe a Hillelite view may be evidence of its authenticity (cf. the 'harder' reading in NT textual criticism).

48. At Eduyoth 4.1-5, five cases where the Hillelites ruled more strictly, are specifically enumerated as being exceptional; cf. Shab. 77a.

49. See above, n. 33.

50. Vermes, p. 82.

51. Rabin, *Qumran*, pp. 1-21, compares the procedure for novices at Qumran in the Community Rule with the procedure for *haberim*, and finds it so similar as to demand a 'common organizational origin'. Handwashing, however, was not a requirement at Qumran.

52. 'Corban', *Jewish Quarterly Review* 19 (1907), pp. 616-50 at pp. 626-27.

53. And repeating the appropriate blessing.

54. Westerholm, *Jesus*, thinks this suggestion is made on very slight evidence, but 'the impulse may be correct'.

55. So, Slotki, *Soncino*, Midrash R. Numbers, p. 816 n. 3.

56. *Jesus*, p. 39.

57. 'Defining', p. 246.

58. See above, n. 33.

59. 'Bounds', p. 216.

60. Cf. Westerholm, *ibid.* pp. 66-67, who writes that the requirement of the *haburah* to eat *hullin* in purity is a starting point in the Schools' discussion at T. Demai, and that it can be assumed to have been established by the time of Jesus; he does not, however, examine the texts critically. Cf. also Alon, 'Bounds', p. 216.

61. See e.g. Rabin, *Qumran*, pp. 34-35, and Neusner, p. 278 supra.

62. 'Scripture', p. 190.

63. Thus, Baumgarten, 'Controversies', p. 158. Cf. Rivkin, 'Defining', p. 229.

64. Similarly, some pietists offered supererogatory sacrifices: Baba b. Buta brought a guilt-offering for a doubtful sin daily, except after the Day of Atonement (Kerithoth 6.3). See generally Büchler, *Piety*, pp. 73-74.

65. Spiro, 'Haber', *passim*, argues that in the Hasmonean age the *haberim* collected tithes and *terumah* directly from the farms and villages on behalf of the High-priestly Kings, and maintained constant purity (even eating *hullin* in purity) so as not to defile these taxes. The weakness of this argument lies in the absence of Talmudic authority attesting such direct collection. Even according to Spiro, the collection of these dues had largely reverted to a voluntary basis in the time of John Hyrcanus (135-105 BC).

66. Perhaps the *haberim* regarded produce of the land of Israel as holy; at Kelim 1.6 its holiness is said to lie in the fact that only from that land may the Omer, the First-fruits and the Two Loaves be brought. At Sotah 30b a

minority view which applies the laws of defilement to *hullin* in the land of Israel is acknowledged; but contra, A.Z. 56a.

67. Or, perhaps, pietists who were not *haberim*, for T. Demai 2.10 indicates that some non-*haberim* followed the rules of the *haburoth* in private.

68. Cf. the Pharisees' ingratiating approach at Matt. 22.16.

Notes to Chapter 6

1. We thought that this was the first treatment of the logion as a possible comparison between cultic sources of impurity, but we have found in *The Earliest Gospel* by A. Menzies, 1901, a similar interpretation at pp. 152-53.

2. At Ezek. 44.18 the Levitical priests are enjoined not to wear, when ministering, 'anything that causes sweat'. This may be another example of a bodily excretion deemed impure.

3. Cf. Neusner, *Purities*, XXII, p. 74. Contra Maccoby, 'Authenticating'.

4. Cf. Oholoth 1.1 and Danby's n. 3 thereon.

5. Cf. Oholoth 1.6.

6. *Jesus*, p. 54.

7. Like the priest from Beth Ramah, ARN 12, p. 71. Cf. AZ 11a.

8. See also Matt. 23.16-22.

9. Bowman, *Mark*, p. 168, mentions that the priestly tradition about *shechitah* must have originated before the Samaritan schism (4th Cent.), since the Samaritan priestly halakhah knows it.

10. Sifra is the earliest Midrash on Leviticus, but it is difficult to date its contents. Schürer (*History* I, p. 90) mentions that the tannaitic Midrashim (Mekhilta, Sifra and Sifre) are closely related to the Mishnah in regard to age and contents. At Sanh. 86a it is said that R. Judah is the author of an anonymous dictum in Sifra and, according to the Soncino Rabbinical Index, this is Judah b. Ilai, a tanna of the second century. Strack (*Introduction*, p. 206) considers that the basic element in Sifra is the work of this Judah but that the final compiler was R. Hiyya, a friend of R. Judah, the Prince. This accords with Schürer's general conclusion. However, Albeck (cited by Stemberger, 'La Recherche', p. 560) argues that the two Talmuds did not know or use these halakhic Midrashim, and he places their final redaction at not before the fifth century. Finkelstein (cited by Stemberger, *ibid.*) stresses the many interpolations in the halakhic Midrashim, but claims that the kernel of the material goes back to Ishmael or Akiba (both c. AD 120-140 per Dandy's Appendix). In view of the alleged late redaction and interpolations, we cannot be confident of the date of these halakhoth in Sifra.

11. Per the Hananiah decree. At Toh. 2.2 R. Eliezer assigns, contra R. Joshua, first degree to the eater of first-degree food, but this seems a minority view.

12. *Jesus*, p. 137.

13. *Ibid.*, pp. 137-38. This argument from silence seems weak, since, as argued earlier, the Gospels can only contain a fraction of the total sayings of Jesus during his ministry.

14. At 15.11

15. Vide Staniforth, *Early Christian Writings*, p. 226.

16. John 3.25 is also evidence of Jesus' depreciation of cultic purity, if Richard Bentley's conjecture is accepted. He would alter μετὰ Ἰουδαίου which is impossible Greek (Lindars, *John*, p. 165) to μετ' Ἰησοῦ or μετὰ τῶν ιυ (Ellis, *Bentleii Critica Sacra*, p. 19). This alteration has no textual support, but it harmonizes better than the text with John's disciples' complaint at v. 26 about the success of Jesus' ministry. We prefer the alteration, and suggest that, in addition to the purpose of forgiveness mentioned by Mark 1.4, John's baptism had a cultic content, as indicated by Josephus's ἐφ' ἁγνείᾳ τοῦ σώματος (*Ant.* 18.117), while the purpose of Jesus' baptism was purely spiritual; contra Flemington, *Baptism*, p. 16, who denies that John laid any stress on ritual purification. Cf. also John 13.10; 15.3.

17. See Jeremias, *Unknown Sayings*, p. 9; cf. Hennecke, *NT Apocrypha*, I, p. 92 (4th or 5th Cent.); James, *Apocryphal NT*, p. 29 (3rd Cent.).

18. *Ibid.*, p. 30.

19. *Fragment*, p. 12.

20. *Ibid.* pp. 51-59.

21. 'New Fragment', p. 346.

22. See plan in Edersheim, *Temple*, p. 23.

23. See Mark 11.15-19; John 2.13-17.

24. *Ibid.*, pp. 52, 53, 59.

25. *Ibid.* p. 338.

26. See list in Jeremias, *Jerusalem*, pp. 377-78.

27. *Ibid.*, p. 12.

28. *Ibid.*, p. 343.

29. See Jeremias, *ibid.*, p. 54.

30. *Ibid.*

31. *Ibid.* p. 344.

32. Barr, 'Which Language', p. 17, while admitting that Jesus' language is a more open question now, concludes, 'for the moment it seems likely that his language was Aramaic, or that he spoke more Aramaic than he spoke Hebrew'.

33. At *TDNT*, III, p. 797, F. Hauck states that κοιναῖς in the phrase κοιναῖς χερσίν corresponds to the Hebrew טמא.

34. See, for example the use of the verb at Lev. 18.19-24.

35. See Büchler, *Types*, p. 111.

Notes to Chapter 7

1. See Chapter 5.f.

2. See Chapter 5.d.(c), and f.

3. See Chapter 6.a (conclusion).

4. See Chapter 6.a (conclusion).

5. See Chapter 6.c.

6. See Chapter 2.C.e.

7. See, e.g., the support derived from Jesus' attitude to the law for a relative interpretation of οὐ . . . ἀλλά in Chapter 2.A.g. and C.e.

8. See e.g. Chapter 2.B.b.

9. See e.g. Chapter 5.d.(a).1.

10. See e.g. Branscomb, *Mark*, p. xxxi.

11. See Chapter 2.B.b.

12. Taylor, *Mark*, p. 128, specifically mentions v. 19c as reflecting a Pauline environment.

13. Matthew's emphasis of τὸ στόμα in addition to ἡ καρδία as the origin of evil is reminiscent of LXX Psalm 140.3-4 (where τὰ χείλη are also mentioned).

14. Barth in Bornkamm, *Tradition*, p. 88, argues that Matthew can scarcely base his rejection of handwashing on rejection of the tradition, since elsewhere he adopts the tradition. Barth does not distinguish, however, between the traditional law applying to all, and the practices of the *haberim* which, by Matthew's day (c. 80-100 AD), were incorporated into the traditional law, but, of course, only applied to them.

15. The danger here, as with Mark, is that we attribute to Matthew fine distinctions that were not present to his mind. But the alterations which he almost certainly made (e.g. εἰς τὸ στόμα for εἰς αὐτόν) indicate that he was a sophisticated redactor.

16. See Douglas, *Purity and Danger*, *passim*, and 'Pollution'.

BIBLIOGRAPHY

Ancient Writers

Irenaeus, *Adversus Haereses, Anti-Marcionite Prologue.*
Josephus, *Bellum Judaicum, Vita, Antiquitates.*
Justin Martyr, *Apologia.*
Philo, *De Migratione Abrahami, De Specialibus Legibus, De Legatione ad Gaium, De Praemiis et Poenis, Apologia pro Iudaeis.*
Pseudo-Phocylides, *Sententiae.*

Modern Writers

Abrahams, I. "Am Ha-'Areç', in C.G. Montefiore, *The Synoptic Gospels*, infra at pp. 647-69.
Ackroyd, P.R. and Evans, C.F. *The Cambridge History of the Bible*, 3 vols. (Cambridge, 1963-70).
Albertz, M. *Die synoptischen Streitgespräche* (Berlin, 1921).
Alon, G. 'The Levitical Uncleanness of Gentiles' at pp. 146-89, and 'The Bounds of the Laws of Levitical Cleanness' at pp. 190-234 in *Jews, Judaism and the Classical World* (ET; Jerusalem, 1977).
Bamberger, B.J. 'The Dating of Aggadic materials', *JBL* 68 (1949), pp. 115-23.
Banks, R. *Jesus and the Law in the Synoptic Tradition* (Cambridge, 1975).
Barr, J. 'Which Language Did Jesus Speak?—Some Remarks of a Semitist', *Bulletin of John Rylands Library* 53 (1970-71), pp. 9-29.
Barrett, C.K. *The Pastoral Epistles* (Oxford, 1963).
Baumgarten, J.M. 'The Unwritten Law in the Pre-Rabbinic Period', *JSJ* 3 (1972), pp. 7-29.
—'Form Criticism and the Oral Law', *JSJ* 5 (1974), pp. 34-40.
—'The Pharisaic-Sadducean Controversies about Purity and the Qumran Texts', *JJS* 31 (1980), pp. 157-70.
—*Studies in Qumran Law* (Leiden, 1977).
Beilner, W. *Christus und die Pharisäer* (Vienna, 1959).
Belkin, S. 'Dissolution of Vows and the Problem of Anti-social Oaths in the Gospels and Contemporary Jewish Literature', *JBL* 55 (1936), pp. 227-34.
Bell, H.I. and Skeat, T.C. *Fragments of an Unknown Gospel and Other Early Christian Papyri* (London, 1935).
Berger, K. *Die Gesetzesauslegung Jesu. Ihr historischer Hintergrund im Judentum und im Alten Testament. Teil I: Markus und Parallelen* (Hamburg, 1972).
Betz, H.D. *Galatians* (Philadelphia, 1979).
Black, M. *An Aramaic Approach to the Gospels and Acts* (Oxford, 1946).
Bornkamm, G., Barth, G., and Held, H.J. *Tradition and Interpretation in Matthew* (ET: London, 1963).
Bouquet, A.C. *Everyday Life in NT Times* (London, 1953).

Bowker, J. *The Targums and Rabbinic Literature* (Cambridge, 1969).

—*Jesus and the Pharisees* (Cambridge, 1973).

Bowman, J. *The Gospel of Mark, The New Church Passover Haggadah* (Leiden, 1965).

Branscomb, B.H. *Jesus and the Law of Moses* (New York, 1930).

—*The Gospel of Mark* (London, 1937).

Bruder, C.H. *Concordantiae Omnium Vocum Novi Testamenti Graeci* (Leipzig, 1867).

Buchanan, G.W. 'The Use of Rabbinic Literature for NT Research', *Biblical Theology Bulletin* 7 (1977), pp. 110-22.

Büchler, A. *Der Galiläische 'Am-ha'Areṣ des zweiten Jahrhunderts* (Wien, 1906).

—*Types of Jewish-Palestinian Piety from 70 BCE to 70 CE* (London, 1922).

—'The Law of Purification in Mark vii 1-23', *Expository Times* (1909-10), pp. 34-40.

—'The New "Fragment of an Uncanonical Gospel"', *Jewish Quarterly Review* 20 (1907-8), pp. 330-46.

Bultmann, R. *The History of the Synoptic Tradition* (ET by J. Marsh; 2nd edn; Oxford, 1968).

—'The New Approach to the Synoptic Problem', in *Existence and Faith. Shorter Writings of Rudolf Bultmann* (Selected and Translated by S.M. Ogden, London, 1961), pp. 39-62.

—'Is Exegesis without Presuppositions Possible?', *ibid.*, pp. 342-51.

Burkitt, F.C. *The Gospel History and its Transmission* (Edinburgh, 1911).

Burney, C.F. *The Poetry of our Lord* (Oxford, 1925).

Burton, E. De W. *The Epistle to the Galatians* (Edinburgh, 1921).

Butler, B.C. *The Originality of St. Matthew* (Cambridge, 1951).

Cadbury, H.J. *The Making of Luke—Acts* (London, 1965).

Caird, G.B. *The Gospel of St. Luke* (London, 1963).

Calvert, D.G.A. 'An Examination of the Criteria for Distinguishing the Authentic Words of Jesus', *NTS* 18 (1972), pp. 209-19.

Carlston, C.E. 'The Things that Defile (Mark VII.14) and the Law in Matthew and Mark', *NTS* 15 (1968), pp. 79-95.

Catchpole, D.R. 'Tradition History', Ch. 10 in *New Testament Interpretation*, ed. I.H. Marshall (Exeter, 1977).

—'Paul, James and the Apostolic Decree', *NTS* 23 (1977), pp. 428-44.

Charles, R.H. *The Apocrypha and Pseudepigrapha of the OT*, 2 vols. (Oxford, 1913).

Charlesworth, J.H., 'The Origins and Subsequent History of the Authors of the Dead Sea Scrolls', *Revue de Qumran* 38 (1980), pp. 213-33.

Chilton, B.D. *A Galilean Rabbi and His Bible* (Delaware, 1984).

Cohen, B. *Mishnah and Tosefta: a Comparative Study. I. Shabbat* (New York, 1935).

Cohn, H. 'Prolegomena to the Theory and History of Jewish Law', in *Essays in Jurisprudence in Honor of Roscoe Pound* (Connecticut, 1962), pp. 48-81.

Conzelmann, H. *The Theology of St. Luke* (ET; London, 1960).

—*Die Apostelgeschichte* (Tübingen, 1963).

Cowley, A.E. (ed.) 'The Book of Judith', in Charles, *Apocrypha and Pseudepigrapha*.

Cranfield, C.E.B. *The Gospel according to St. Mark* (Cambridge, 1963).

Creed, J.M. *The Gospel according to St. Luke* (London, 1930).

Crum, J.M.C. *St. Mark's Gospel. Two Stages of its Making* (Cambridge, 1936).

Cullmann, O. *The Christology of the NT* (ET; 2nd edn; London, 1963).

Danby, H. *The Mishnah* (Oxford, 1933).

Daube, D. *The New Testament and Rabbinic Judaism* (London, 1956).

Davies, W.D. *The Setting of the Sermon on the Mount* (Cambridge, 1964).
—*Paul and Rabbinic Judaism* (London, 1948).
Derrett, J.D.M. *Jesus's Audience* (London, 1973).
Dibelius, M. *From Tradition to Gospel* (ET; London, 1934).
—*Studies in the Acts of the Apostles* (ET; London, 1956).
Dodd, C.H. *According to the Scriptures* (London, 1952).
Douglas, M. *Purity and Danger* (London, 1966).
—'Pollution', *International Encyclopaedia of Social Sciences* 12 (1968), pp. 333-43.
Dugmore, C.W. *The Influence of the Synagogue upon the Divine Office* (Oxford, 1944).
Dupont-Sommer, A. *The Essene Writings from Qumran* (Oxford, 1961).
Edersheim, A. *The Life and Times of Jesus the Messiah* (London, 1900).
—*The Temple* (London, 1874).
Ehrlich, E. *Fundamental Principles of the Sociology of Law* (ET; Cambridge, Mass., 1936).
Ellis, A.A., (ed.) *Bentleii Critica Sacra* (Cambridge, 1862).
Ellis, E.E. 'How the New Testament uses the Old', in *New Testament Interpretation*, ed. I.H. Marshall (Exeter, 1977), pp. 199-219.
Encyclopaedia Judaica, 16 vols. (Jerusalem, 1971).
Epstein, I. (ed.) *B. Talmud* (Soncino) 18 vols. (London 1935-52).
Epstein, J.N. *Mevo'ot leSifrut HaTannaim* (Jerusalem, 1957).
Etheridge, J.W. *The Targums on the Pentateuch*, 2 vols. (London, 1862).
Farrand, J.T. *Contract and Conveyance* (London, 1980).
Farrer, A.M. *A Study in St. Mark* (London, 1951).
Filson, F.V. *A New Testament History* (London, 1965).
Finkelstein, L. *The Pharisees*, 2 vols. (Philadelphia, 1966).
Fishman, I. (tr.) *Yadayim, B. Talmud* (Soncino) (London, 1948).
Fitzmyer, J.A. *Essays on the Semitic Background of the New Testament* (London, 1971).
Flemington, W.F. *The New Testament Doctrine of Baptism* (London, 1948).
Frankel, Z. *Darke ha-Mishnah* (Leipzig, 1859).
Freyne, S. *Galilee from Alexander the Great to Hadrian* (Delaware and Indiana, 1980).
Gereboff, J. *Rabbi Tarfon: the Tradition, the Man and early Judaism* (Montana, 1979).
Gerhardsson, B. *Memory and Manuscript. Oral Tradition and Written Transmission in Rabbinic Judaism and Early Christianity* (Lund, 1961).
Gesenius' Hebrew Grammar, edited and enlarged by E. Kautzsch (Oxford, 1910).
Gnilka, J. *Die Verstockung Israels: Jes. 6.9-10 in der Theologie der Synoptiker* (München, 1961).
Goldin, J. *The Fathers according to R. Nathan* (ET: Yale, 1955).
Goulder, M.D. *Type and History in Acts* (London, 1964).
Graetz, H. *Geschichte der Juden*, 3 vols. (Leipzig, 1905).
Grant, R.M. with Freedman, D.N. *The Secret Sayings of Jesus* (London, 1960).
Gray, G.B. *Numbers* (Edinburgh, 1903).
Grenfell, B.P. and Hunt, A.S. *Fragment of an Uncanonical Gospel from Oxyrynchus* (Oxford, 1908).
Grundmann, W. *Das Evangelium nach Marcus* (Berlin, 1971).
Guttmann, A. *Rabbinic Judaism in the Making* (Detroit, 1970).
Haenchen, E. *Der Weg Jesu* (Berlin, 1966).
—'Quellenanalyse und Kompositionsanalyse in Act. 15', in W. Eltester, *Judentum Urchristentum Kirche* (Berlin, 1964), pp. 153-64.

Halivni, D.W. 'Contemporary Methods of the Study of Talmud', *JJS* 30 (1979), pp. 192-201.

Haran, M. 'Behind the Scenes of History: Determining the Date of the Priestly Source', *JBL* 100 (1981), pp. 321-33.

Harper, W.R. *Amos and Hosea* (ICC; Edinburgh, 1910).

Hart, J.H.A. 'Corban', *Jewish Quarterly Review* 19 (1907), pp. 615-50.

Heinemann, J., 'Early Halakha in the Palestinian Targumim', *JJS* 25 (1974), pp. 114-22.

Hengel, M. 'Mc 7 3 πυγμῇ: Die Geschichte einer exegetischen Aporie und der Versuch ihrer Lösung', *Zeitschrift für die neutestamentliche Wissenschaft* 60 (1969), pp. 182-98.

—*Die Zeloten* (2nd edn; Leiden, 1976).

Hertz, J.H. (ed.) *The Pentateuch and Haftorahs. Leviticus* (Oxford, 1932).

Heyd, D. *Supererogation. Its Status in Ethical Theory* (Cambridge, 1982).

Hiers, R.H. 'Eschatology and Methodology', *JBL* 85 (1964), pp. 170-84.

Higgins, A.J.B. *The Lord's Supper in the NT* (London, 1952).

Hill, D. 'On the Evidence for the Creative Role of Christian Prophets', *NTS* 20 (1974), pp. 262-74.

Hirsch, E. *Frühgeschichte des Evangeliums I: Das Werden des Markusevangeliums* (2nd edn; Tübingen, 1951).

Holdsworth, W.S. *An Historical Introduction to the Land Law* (Oxford, 1927).

Holmes, O.W. Jr *The Common Law* (Boston, 1881).

Holtzmann, H.J. *Einleitung in das Neue Testament* (Freiburg, 1885).

—*Die synoptischen Evangelien* (Leipzig, 1863).

Hooker, M.D. 'On Using the Wrong Tool', *Theology* 75 (1972), pp. 570-81.

Hoskyns, E.C. and Davey, F.N. *The Riddle of the New Testament* (3rd edn; London, 1947).

Hübner, H. *Das Gesetz in der synoptischen Tradition* (Witten, 1973).

Hultgren, A.J. *Jesus and His Adversaries. The Form and Function of the Conflict Stories in the Synoptic Tradition* (Minneapolis, 1979).

Jackson, B.S. 'The Fence-Breaker and the actio de pastu pecoris in Early Jewish law', *JJS* 25 (1974), pp. 123-36.

—*Theft in Early Jewish Law* (Oxford, 1972).

Janowski, M., Lichtenberger, H. 'Enderwartung und Reinheitsidee', *JJS* 34 (1983), pp. 31-63.

Jastrow, M.A. *A Dictionary of the Targumim, the Talmud Babli and Yerushalmi, and the Midrashic Literature* (New York, 1975).

Jeremias, J. *Unknown Sayings of Jesus* (ET; 2nd edn; London, 1964).

—*New Testament Theology*, 2 vols. (ET; London, 1971).

—*The Parables of Jesus* (ET; 3rd edn; London, 1972).

James, M.R. *The Apocryphal NT* (Oxford, 1953).

Johnson, S.E. *The Theology of the Gospels* (London, 1966).

Jones, H. *The Act of Baptism* (London, 1876).

Kahle, P.E. *The Cairo Geniza* (Oxford, 1959).

Käsemann, E. 'The Problem of the Historical Jesus', in *Essays on New Testament Themes* (ET; London, 1964).

Klausner, J. *Jesus of Nazareth* (ET; London, 1925).

Klostermann, E. *Das Markus-Evangelium* (Tübingen, 1950).

Knox, W.L. *Some Hellenistic Elements in Primitive Christianity. The Schweich Lectures on Biblical Archaeology 1942* (London, 1944).
—*The Sources of the Synoptic Gospels*, 2 vols. (Cambridge, 1953).
Kohler, L. *Hebrew Man* (London, 1956).
Kümmel, W.G. 'Äussere und innere Reinheit des Menschen bei Jesus', in *Heilsgeschehen und Geschichte* (Marburg, 1965).
—*Introduction to the New Testament* (ET; London, 1966).
Kruse, H. 'Dialektische Negationen als semitisches Idiom', *Vetus Testamentum* 4 (1954), pp. 385-400.
Lagrange, M.-J. *Évangile selon Saint Marc* (5th edn; Paris, 1929).
Lambrecht, J. 'Jesus and the Law, an Investigation of Mk 7.1-23, *Ephemerides Theologicae Lovanienses* 53 (1977), pp. 24-79.
Lanchester, H.C.O. (ed.) The Sybilline Oracles, in Charles, *Apocrypha and Pseudepigrapha*.
Le Moyne, J. *Les Sadducéens* (Paris, 1972).
Liddell, H.G. and Scott, R.A. *A Greek-English Lexicon* (8th edn; Oxford, 1901).
Liebermann, S. *Tosefta Kipshuta* (New York, 1955).
Lightfoot, J. *Horae Hebraicae et Talmudicae* (Leipzig, 1684).
Lindars, B. *New Testament Apologetic* (London, 1961).
—*The Gospel of John* (London, 1972).
Lohmeyer, E. *Das Evangelium des Markus* (Göttingen, 1967).
Ludwich, A. 'Über das Spruchbuch des falschen Phokylides', in *Program Königsberg* (Königsberg, 1904), pp. 1-26.
Maccoby, H. *Revolution in Judaea* (London, 1973).
—'The Washing of Cups', *JSNT* 14 (1982), pp. 3-15.
—'Authenticating Authority', *Times Literary Supplement*, 13th August, 1982, p. 887.
Maier, J. *Jesus von Nazareth in der Talmudischen Überlieferung* (Darmstadt, 1978).
Maimonides *The Code of, Book Ten, The Book of Cleanness* (Yale, 1954).
Maine, H.S. *Ancient Law* (London, 1894).
Margoliouth, G. 'The Tradition of the Elders', *Expository Times* 22 (1910-11), pp. 261-63.
Marshall, I.H. *The Gospel of Luke* (Exeter, 1978).
Marxsen, W. *Mark the Evangelist* (ET; Nashville, 1969).
McArthur, H.K. 'Basic Issues: A Survey of Recent Gospel Research', *Interpretation* 18 (1964), pp. 39-55.
—'The Burden of Proof in Historical Jesus Research', *Expository Times* 82 (1972), pp. 116-79.
McEleney, N.J. 'Authenticating Criteria and Mark 7.1-23', *CBQ* 34 (1972), pp. 431-60.
McNamara, M. *The NT and the Palestinian Targum to the Pentateuch* (Rome, 1966).
Menzies, A. *The Earliest Gospel* (London, 1901).
Merkel, H. 'Markus 7.15—das Jesuswort über die innere Verunreinigung', *Zeitschrift für Religions- und Geistesgeschichte* 20 (1968), pp. 340-63.
Metzger, B.M. *A Textual Commentary on the Greek New Testament* (London and New York, 1971).
—*The Text of the New Testament* (2nd edn; Oxford, 1968).

Mielziner, M. *Introduction to the Talmud* (Cincinatti, 1894).

Miller, L. and Simon, M. (tr.) Bekoroth, B. *Talmud* (Soncino) (London, 1948).

M'Neile, A.H. *The Gospel according to St. Matthew* (London, 1915).

Montefiore, C.G. *The Synoptic Gospels*, 2 vols. (2nd edn; London, 1928).

—and Loewe, H.A. *Rabbinic Anthology* (London, 1938).

Moo, D.J. 'Jesus and the Authority of the Mosaic Law', *JSNT* 20 (1984), pp. 3-49.

Moody Smith, D. 'John and the Synoptics: some Dimensions of the Problem', *NTS* 26 (1980), pp. 425-44.

Moore, G.F. *History of Religions*, 2 vols. (Edinburgh, 1914-20).

—*Judaism in the First Centuries of the Christian Era*, 2 vols. (Boston, 1930).

—*Judges* (ICC; Edinburgh, 1895).

Moulton, J.H. and Geden, A.S. *A Concordance to the Greek Testament* (2nd edn; Edinburgh, 1899).

Muddiman, J. 'Jesus and Fasting, Mark ii.18-22' (Ph.D. Thesis; Oxford, 1976).

Moule, C.F.D. *An Idiom Book of NT Greek* (Cambridge, 1959).

Neill, S. *Christian Faith To-day* (London, 1955).

Neirynck, F. *Duality in Mark, Contributions to the Study of Marcan Redaction* (Leuven, 1972).

Nestle-Aland *Novum Testamentum Graece* (Stuttgart, 1979).

Neusner, J. *Fellowship in Judaism* (London, 1963).

—*Development of a Legend: Studies on the Traditions concerning Yohanan ben Zakkai* (2nd edn; Leiden, 1970).

—*The Rabbinic Traditions about the Pharisees before 70*, 3 vols. (Leiden, 1971).

—*The Idea of Purity in Ancient Judaism, with a Critique by M. Douglas* (Leiden, 1973).

—*A History of the Mishnaic Law of Purities*, 22 vols. (Leiden, 1974-77).

—'Redaction, Formulation, and Form: The Case of Mishnah' with comments by R.S. Sarason, *Jewish Quarterly Review* 70 (1980), pp. 1-22.

—'Scripture and Tradition in Judaism' in *Approaches to Ancient Judaism*, II, ed. W.S. Green (Michigan, 1980), pp. 173-93.

—'The Written Tradition in the Pre-Rabbinic Period', *JSJ* 4 (1973), pp. 56-65.

—'Exegesis and the Written Law', *JSJ* 5 (1974), pp. 176-78.

—'The History of Earlier Rabbinic Judaism: Some New Approaches', *History of Religions* 16 (1977), pp. 216-36.

—'The Use of the Later Rabbinic Evidence for the Study of First-Century Pharisaism', in *Approaches to Ancient Judaism: Theory and Practice*, ed. W.S. Green (Missoula, 1978), pp. 215-28.

—'Judaism after the Destruction of the Temple', in *Israelite and Judaean History*, ed. J.H. Hayes and J.M. Miller (Philadelphia, 1977), pp. 663-77.

—'The Formation of Rabbinic Judaism: Yavneh (Jamnia) from AD 70 to 100' in *Aufstieg und Niedergang der Römischen Welt* (Berlin, 1979), pp. 3-42.

—(transl.) *The Tosefta*, Divs. 2-6 (New York, 1977-81).

Norden, E. *Agnostos Theos* (Leipzig-Berlin, 1913).

Noth, M. *Leviticus* (ET [revised]; London, 1977).

Paschen, W. *Rein und Unrein* (Munich, 1970).

Perrin, N. *Rediscovering the Teaching of Jesus* (London, 1967).
—*What is Redaction Criticism?* (London, 1970).
Pesch, R. *Das Markusevangelium*, I. Teil (2nd edn; Freiburg, 1977).
Pfeiffer, R.H. *Introduction to the Old Testament* (London, 1952).
Podro, J. *The Last Pharisee* (London, 1959).
Pollock, Sir F. *A First Book of Jurisprudence* (London, 1929).
Pryke, E.J. *Redactional Style in the Marcan Gospel* (Cambridge, 1970).
Quesnell, Q. *The Mind of Mark* (Rome, 1969).
Rabin, C. *Qumran Studies* (Oxford, 1957).
Rahlfs, A. *Septuaginta* (Stuttgart, 1935).
Rawlinson, A.E.J. *St. Mark* (London, 1925).
Recasens-Siches, L. 'The Logic of the Reasonable as Differentiated from the Logic of the Rational (Human Reason in the Making and Interpretation of the Law)', in *Essays in Jurisprudence in Honor of Roscoe Pound* (Connecticut, 1962), pp. 192-221.
Rendel Harris, J. *Testimonies* (2 vols.; Cambridge, 1916 and 1920).
Reynolds, S.M., 'ΠΥΓΜΗΙ (Mark 7.3) as "Cupped Hand"', *JBL* 85 (1966), pp. 87-88.
—'A Note on Dr Hengel's Interpretation of πυγμῇ in Mark 7.3', *Zeitschrift für die neutestamentliche Wissenschaft* (1971), pp. 295-96.
Riches, J. *Jesus and the Transformation of Judaism* (London, 1980).
Rivkin, E. 'Defining the Pharisees: the Tannaitic Sources', *Hebrew Union College Annual* 40 (1969-70), pp. 205-49.
—*A Hidden Revolution* (Abingdon, 1978).
Robertson Smith, W. *The Old Testament in the Jewish Church* (London, 1895).
—*The Religion of the Semites* (London, 1901).
Robinson, J.A.T. *Redating the New Testament* (London, 1976).
Rost, L. *Die Damaskusschrift* (Berlin, 1933).
Russell, D.S. *The Jews from Alexander to Herod* (Oxford, 1967).
Rzach, A. *Oracula Sybillina* (Vindobonae, 1891).
Saldarini, A.J. 'The End of the Rabbinic Chain of Tradition', *JBL* 93 (1974), pp. 97-106.
—'"Form Criticism" of Rabbinic Literature', *JBL* 96 (1977), pp. 257-74.
Sanders, E.P. *Paul and Palestinian Judaism* (London, 1977).
Sandmel, S. 'Parallelomania', *JBL* 81 (1962), pp. 1-13.
—*Philo of Alexandria. An Introduction* (Oxford, 1979).
Sarason, R.S. Comments at end of 'Redaction, Formulation and Form: the Case of Mishnah' by J. Neusner, *Jewish Quarterly Review* 70 (1980), pp. 1-22.
Sawer, G. *Law in Society* (Oxford, 1965).
Schiffman, L.H. *The Halakhah at Qumran* (Leiden, 1975).
—'The Temple Scroll in Literary and Philological Perspective', in *Approaches to Ancient Judaism* II, ed. W.S. Green (Chicago, 1980), pp. 143-55.
—'Communal Meals at Qumran', *Revue de Qumran* 37 (1979), pp. 45-56.
Schmidt, K.L. *Der Rahmen der Geschichte Jesu* (Berlin, 1919).
Schürer, E. *The History of the Jewish People in the Age of Jesus Christ*, Revised by G. Vermes, F. Millar and M. Black (Edinburgh, 1973).

Schürmann, H. 'Die Sprache des Christus', *Biblische Zeitschrift* 2 (1958), pp. 54-84.
Schwab, M. *Le Talmud de Jérusalem*, 11 vols. (Paris, 1871-89).
Schweitzer, A. *The Mystery of the Kingdom of God* (ET; London, 1914).
—*The Quest of the Historical Jesus* (ET; 3rd edn; London, 1954).
Segal, M.H. (tr.) Makshirin, *BT* (Soncino) (London, 1948).
Slotki, J.J. (tr.) *Numbers Rabbah* (Soncino) (London, 1977).
Snaith, N.H. (ed.) *Leviticus and Numbers* (London, 1967).
Spiro, S.J. 'Who was the Haber? A New Approach to an Ancient Institution', *JSJ* 11
    (1980), pp. 180-216.
Staniforth, M. *Early Christian Writings* (ET; London, 1968).
Stanton, G.N. 'Presuppositions in NT Criticism', in *NT Interpretation*, ed. I.H.
    Marshall (Exeter, 1977), pp. 60-71.
—'Interpreting the NT Today', Inaugural Lecture at University of London King's
    College on 14th Nov. 1978.
Stein, P. *Legal Evolution* (Cambridge, 1980).
Stein, R.H. 'What is Redaktionsgeschichte?', *JBL* 88 (1969), pp. 45-56.
—'The Proper Methodology for Ascertaining a Marcan Redaction History', *Novum
    Testamentum* 13 (1971), pp. 181-98.
—'The "Criteria" for Authenticity', in *Gospel Perspectives* I (Sheffield, 1980), pp. 225-
    63.
Stemberger, G. 'La recherche rabbinique depuis Strack', *Revue d'Histoire et de
    Philosophie Religieuses* 55 (1975), pp. 543-74.
Stendahl, K. 'The Called and the Chosen. An Essay on Election', in *The Root of the
    Vine*, by A. Fridrichsen and others (London, 1939).
Stenning, J. *The Targum of Isaiah* (Oxford, 1949).
Stone, J. *Human Law and Human Justice* (London, 1965).
Strack, H.A. *Introduction to the Talmud and Midrash* (ET; Philadelphia, 1931)
Streeter, B.H. *The Four Gospels* (London, 1924).
Suhl, A. *Die Funktion der alttestamentlichen Zitate und Anspielung in Markusevangelium*
    (Gütersloh, 1965).
Sundwall, J. 'Die Zusammensetzung des Markusevangeliums' in *Acta Academiae
    Aboensis*, Humaniora IX (Abo, 1934), pp. 1-86.
Taylor, V. *The Gospel according to St Mark* (London, 1952).
—*The Formation of the Gospel Tradition* (2nd edn; London, 1935).
Theological Dictionary of the NT, ed. G. Kittel and G. Friedrich (ET; Michigan, 1964-
    76).
Torrey, C.C. *The Four Gospels: A New Translation* (New York, 1933).
Towner, W.S. *The Rabbinic 'Enumeration of Scriptural Examples'* (Leiden, 1973).
Turner, C.H. 'ὅτι recitative (after λέγειν or similar verbs)', *JTS* 28 (1926-27), pp. 9-
    15, in series of articles on Marcan usage.
—'πυγμῇ', *JTS* 29 (1927-28), pp. 278-79, in the said Marcan series.
—'The Lausiac History of Palladius', *JTS* 6 (1904-5), pp. 321-55.
Van der Horst, P.W. *The Sentences of Pseudo-Phocylides* (Leiden, 1978).
Vermes, G. *The Dead Sea Scrolls in English* (London, 1962).

—*The Dead Sea Scrolls: Qumran in Perspective* (London, 1977).

—*Jesus The Jew* (London, 1973).

—'Jewish Literature and NT Exegesis', *JJS* 33 (1982), pp. 361-76.

Wacholder, B.Z. 'A Reply', *JBL* 91 (1971), pp. 114-15.

—'Review of J. Neusner, *Development of a Legend* etc.', *JBL* 91 (1972), pp. 123-24.

Wächter, T.R. *Reinheitsvorschriften im griechischen Kult* (Giessen, 1910).

Weeden, T.J. *Mark: Traditions in Conflict* (Philadelphia, 1971).

Weiss, I.H. *Dor Dor ve-Doreshav* I (Wilna, 1893).

Weiss, J. *Die Predigt Jesu vom Reiche Gottes* (Göttingen, 1892).

—*Die Schriften des Neuen Testaments*, 2 vols. (3rd edn; Göttingen, 1917).

Weisse, C.H. *Die evangelische Geschichte kritisch und philosophisch bearbeitet*, 2 vols. (Leipzig, 1838).

Wellhausen, J. *Einleitung in die drei ersten Evangelien* (2nd edn; Berlin, 1911).

Westerholm, S. *Jesus and Scribal Authority* (Lund, 1978).

Wenham, G.J. *The Book of Leviticus* (London, 1979).

Wettstein, J. *NT Graecum* 1752 (Graz, 1962).

Wheeler Robinson, H. *Religious Ideas of the Old Testament* (London, 1913).

Winer, G.B. *Grammar of the NT Diction* (6th edn; ET; Edinburgh 1866).

Wolfson, H.A. *Philo*, 2 vols. (Cambridge, 1948).

Wrede, W. *Das Messiasgeheimnis in den Evangelien* (Göttingen, 1901).

Yaron, R. *Gifts in Contemplation of Death in Jewish and Roman Law* (Oxford, 1960).

York, A.D. 'The Dating of Targumic Literature', *JSJ* 5 (1974), pp. 49-62.

Zeitlin, S. 'Spurious Interpretations of Rabbinic Sources in the Studies of the Pharisees and Pharisaism', *Jewish Quarterly Review* 65 (1974), pp. 122-35.

—'Les dix-huit mesures', *Revue des Études Juives* 68 (1914), pp. 22-36.

Zerwick, M. *Untersuchungen zum Markus-Stil* (Rome, 1937).

INDEXES

INDEX OF ANCIENT PASSAGES CITED

Old Testament

New Testament

Matthew
5	102
5.8	211
6.11	122
6.34	134
7.2	134
7.16	244n105
9.20	234n132
10	56
10.5-6	110
10.10	137
10.11-12	137
11.5	111
11.19	110
12.5	110
12.6-7	235n143
15.1-20	23
15.11	98, 227n4
15.12-14	23, 233
21.19	244n105
22.16	248n68
23.16-22	248n8
23.16-19	94
23.23-36	191
23.23	94, 192
23.25-26	192
23.25	24, 94, 99, 211
23.26	227n3
26.1-2	227n17
26.23	184, 244n94
27.24	119

Mark
(Citations of verses in our passage are not included as they occur *passim*.)
1.4	249n16
1.16-20	156
1.16-19	244n106
1.41	111
1.44	63, 102, 109
2.14-17	110
2.15-17	81
2.16	190, 192, 193
2.17	63, 111, 219
2.18-22	31
2.23-28	31, 111
2.26	121
2.27	102, 134
3.1-6	31
3.1-5	77, 111
3.4	102, 219
3.20	121
3.23-30	59
4	56
4.17	63
5.22-43	230n14
5.35-42	112
6.8	121
6.31-8.26	56
6.34f.	28-29
6.37-44	244n106
6.41, 44	121
6.45-56	29
6.45	30, 59
6.51-52	29, 59
6.54-56	31
6.54	30
6.56	110
7.1-30	28
7.24-30	29
7.27	28, 110, 121, 228n23
8.1	30
8.4-7	244n106
8.12	76
8.34	29
9.2	29
9.37	69
10.1-9	225n4
10.2-12	59
10.2-9	192
10.3	76
10.17-19	110
10.19	102
10.40	63
11.15-19	249n23
11.27-33	77
12.14-17	77
12.14	91
12.18	231n48
12.25	63
12.28-31	110
12.29-31	102
13.11b	69
13.14f.	150
13.28	244n105
14.1	227n17
14.51	79

Luke
6.4	111
7.22	111
7.34	110
7.36f.	118
8.44	234n132
10.4	136
10.7	137
11.3	122
11.38-41	23, 99, 200
11.39	192
11.41	227n3
11.42-52	191
11.42	192
13.10-17	111
14.1-6	111
15.1	110
17.11-19	111
19.2-7	110
21.20	150
21.24	150
24.30	244n106

John
1.50	244n105
2.1-10	185
2.13-17	249n23
3.25	249n16
4.22	110
11.43-44	112
13.2f.	118
13.10	249n16
13.26	184
15.3	249n16
18.28	81
21.3-14	156

Acts
2.44	120
4.32	120
6f.	103
6.9	78
7.27, 39, 44-50, 52, 53	81
8.1	81

Rabbinic Literature

Mishnah

INDEX OF AUTHORS

Quesnell, Q. 28-29, 228n25

Rabin, C. 189, 195, 242n41, 247nn47,51
Rabinowitz, L.I. 242n45
Rahlfs, A. 229n40
Rawlinson, A.E.J. 70, 114, 228n32
Recasens-Siches, L. 146
Rendel Harris, J. 40
Riches, J. 210
Rivkin, E. 198, 246n26, 247n63
Robertson Smith, W. 225n2, 239n99
Robinson, J.A.T. 240n106
Rost, L. 236n16
Russell, D.S. 243n64
Rzach, A. 160

Saldarini, A.J. 140-42, 143, 244nn111, 113, 245n116
Sandmel, S. 135, 136, 232n76
Sarason, R.S. 125
Sawer, G. 239n93
Schiffman, L.H. 190, 242n38
Schmidt, K.L. 27, 30
Schneider, J. 228n30
Schürer, E. 248n10
Schürmann, H. 69-70
Schwab, M. 162
Schweitzer, A. 27
Slotki, J.J. 234n120, 247n55
Snaith, N.H. 174, 176, 240n109, 244n97
Spiro, S.J. 246nn18,20,37, 247n65
Staniforth, M. 249n15
Stein, R.H. 26, 98, 101, 107
Stemberger, G. 237nn41,43,46
Stenning, J. 229n39

Strack, H.L. 237n47, 244n92
Streeter, B.H. 98
Suhl, A. 35-36, 39-40
Sumner, W.G. 147
Sundwall, J. 41, 43

Taylor, V. 44-45, 49, 66, 73, 150, 235n136
Torrey, C.C. 159
Towner, W.S. 136
Turner, C.H. 43

Van der Horst, P.W. 80-81
Vermes, G. 151, 160-61, 190, 227n24, 239nn95,104, 242n41, 245nn5,7

Wacholder, B.Z. 132, 237n69
Wächter, T.R. 86
Weeden, T.J. 79
Weiss, B. 231n38
Weiss, I.H. 166-67
Weiss, J. 26
Weisse, C.H. 27
Wellhausen, J. 18
Westerholm, S. 70, 114, 152, 235n12, 247nn54,60
Wheeler Robinson, H. 239n102
Winer, G.B. 69
Wolfson, H.A. 142
Wrede, W. 27

Yaron, R. 237n65
York, A.D. 126-27

Zeitlin, S. 162-67, 193, 237n69, 243n71
Zerwick, M. 43, 49
Zuckermandel, M.S. 132

INDEX OF RABBIS

INDEX OF SUBJECTS

Index of Subjects 273

anti-Gentile, 162-68
chart summarizing traditions of, 164
purpose of, 163, 165
Hands,
anxiety leads to washing of, and then
assumption, 171, 173
assumed impure, 121, 168-69
defiling power of, 123-24, 213, 179-84
development of law on, 170-73, 179-80
diner likely to contact liquid with, 184
fidgety, 171, 195
first degree, if, bodily immersion needed,
129, 222
impurity decreed by Hillel and
Shammai and Houses,
172-73
pouring water over, 185
priests, of, 168-69
rinsing, 185
second degree, 171, 179-80
susceptibility, first, to actual defilement,
then assumed, 171
Handwashing,
Diaspora, in, 159-60
Gentiles, no attempt to impose on,
113-14
haberim, by, in time of Jesus,
199-200
holy food, to avoid defilement of,
155-56
hygiene and cult, on boundary between,
119
impurity, takes away, 185-86
ineffective if body unclean, 185-86
living law, as, 149
LXX translators, and, 160
Matthew's attitude to, 222-23
Pentateuch, in, 156-58
source of, 119, 156-58
symbol of moral cleansing, as, 158-
59
symbol of whole law, as, 70, 198
'wings' and, 194-95
zab, by, 157-58
Hellenism, infiltrated Palestine, 78
Hellenistic,
Gentile Church, 72-73
Judaism, link with purity logion, 83-
88, 90
Hillel/Shammai decree, 169-73

Hillelites,
ruled more strictly in 5 cases, 247n48
Hullin,
defined, 130
predisposed by water, 175-76, 183-84
susceptibility to impurity, 173-78
unclean in 2nd degree, not in 3rd,
176-77
nor, separately, in 1st, 179-80
unclean, renders *terumah* invalid,
172-73, 170
Hypocrisy, charge of, in Isaiah Unit,
90-94
Hyrcanus, John, and centralized tithing
system, 246n20, 247n65

Immersion,
ritual, 23-24, 169
whole body, of, in Lucan parallel, 24,
99, 100, 218
Impurity,
basic rules, of, settled in Priestly Code,
122-23, 128
contribution of anthropologists, 223
duration of, varies according to defiler,
124, 207, 236n14,
degrees of, whether developed pre-70,
123-25, 244n91
external, does not defile, per early
church, 107
father and offspring of, 128
identifiable by duration of, 207
female, 148, 238n90
folkways dictate scope of, 148
Gentiles, land of, 159
kodashim, of, Shammai/Hillel decree,
171
nature and transferability of, 128-29
route to be taken by, 156
sources of, 128
external compared with internal,
206-207
study of, in total thought structure,
223
terumah, of, Houses decreed, 171
Isaiah Unit, 38-40, 61, 65-67, 74, 81-82,
90-94
significant use of LXX in, 39-40, 91

James, Jesus' brother, 82-83, 109

wives of, 238n90

Sages,
 hakhamim of the Mishnah, 190, 193
 mastery of law, their hallmark, 193
 origin of, 190

Samaritans, treated as Gentiles, 167

Scholars, temptation of unduly sophisticated approach, 30, 221,
   250n15

Scribes, 190
 commission of, 34, 73-74
 history of, 190
 justify custom from Scripture, 190

Scroll,
 Fasts, of, 166
 Scripture, of, impurity of, 168-69

Semitisms, indicate Palestinian not
   dominical origin, 47, 97,
   114

Shammai/Hillel decree, 169-73

Shammaites, sympathize with Zealots,
   166-67

Shechitah, 208, 232n73, 248n9

Sociological critics, 228n24

Sopherim, 131, 190

Stephen, 81, 83

Supererogation, 154, 189
 haberim, 192-203
 Nazirites, 189, 202
 pious persons, 189, 202
 Rechabites, 189

Susceptibility,
 early development of rules of, 123-25
 rules of, 128-29

Synopsis,
 Hananiah decrees, of, 164
 Isaiah and Korban Units, of, 42

Table,
 domestic, as locus of purity, 153-54,
   201-203
 Roman manners, possible origin of
   handwashing, 148

Talmud, Palestinian, text corrupt,
   242n45

Targumim, some halakhoth in, conflict
   with Mishnah, 126-27

Tassell, legal significance of, 31, 109-10

Tax collectors, 80-81, 110, 125

Teaching, private, 48

Tebulei yom, 168-69, 186, 201-202

Temple,
 focus of purity, 128, 151-54, 240n2
 gatekeepers of, and entry of unclean,
   151

Terefah, 184, 208-209

Terumah,
 defined, 129-30
 eating of, is divine service, 157
 first fruits and, confusion in OT,
   241n7
 gedolah, terumah most likely to be
   defiled in Galilee, 155-56
 hands, and, 162-73

Tithe,
 second, defined, 130
 terumah of, mis-use of, 172

Tobit, and washing, 240n113

Tosephta,
 anonymous sayings in, 131
 relationship of, to Mishnah, 125,
   131-32

Tractates, of Jesus' teaching, 56-58

Tradents, the memory of, 56-58

Tradition,
 chains of, 176, 181
 common store of, 134, 136-37
 expansive, 152-54, 200-202
 restrictive, 151-54, 155-56, 186-87

Transmissibility,
 early development of rules of, 123-25
 rules of, 128-29

Uncleanness,
 not breach of Mosaic law except in
   Temple, 240n2
 system of, in Mishnah, 128-29

Unfitness, rules affecting, 128-29

Unjust man, is unclean, 84

Vices, list of, 33, 50, 73

War, Jewish, broke transmission of traditions, 140

Wisdom saying, purity logion as, 84-88

Yavneh, formulas imposed on Sages'
   sayings at, 135

INDEX OF SELECTED HEBREW AND GREEK WORDS

JOURNAL FOR THE STUDY OF THE NEW TESTAMENT
Supplement Series